Economic Development Issues: Latin America

Committee for Economic Development
Supplementary Paper No. 21

I

A CED SUPPLEMENTARY PAPER

This Supplementary Paper is issued by the Research and Policy Committee of the Committee for Economic Development in conformity with the CED Bylaws (Art. V, Sec. 6), which authorize the publication of a manuscript as a Supplementary Paper if:

a) It is recommended for publication by the Project Director of a subcommittee because in his opinion, it "constitutes an important contribution to the understanding of a problem on which research has been initiated by the Research and Policy Committee" and,

b) It is approved for publication by a majority of an Editorial Board on the ground that it presents "an analysis which is a significant contribution to the understanding of the problem in question."

This Supplementary Paper relates to the Statement on National Policy, *How Low-Income Countries Can Advance Their Own Growth,* issued by the CED Research and Policy Committee in September 1966.

The members of the Editorial Board authorizing publication of this Supplementary Paper are:

While publication of this Supplementary Paper is authorized by CED's Bylaws, except as noted above its contents have not been approved, disapproved, or acted upon by the Committee for Economic Development, the Board of Trustees, the Research and Policy Committee, the Research Advisory Board, the Research Staff, or any member of any board or committee, or any officer of the Committee for Economic Development.

Included in this volume is a study of Brazilian inflation, published originally in Rio de Janeiro by the Instituto de Pesquisas e Estudos Sociais (IPES), which CED is publishing in this country under reciprocal arrangements with its foreign counterparts.

PRAEGER SPECIAL STUDIES IN
INTERNATIONAL ECONOMICS AND DEVELOPMENT

Economic Development Issues: Latin America

Prepared for the Committee for Economic Development

Roberto Alemann	ARGENTINA
Hernan Echavarria	COLOMBIA
Romulo A. Ferrero	PERU
Gustavo Romero Kolbeck	MEXICO
Sergio Undurraga Saavedra	CHILE
Mario Henrique Simonsen	BRAZIL

FREDERICK A. PRAEGER, Publishers
New York · Washington · London

v

The purpose of the Praeger Special Studies is to make specialized research monographs in U.S. and international economics and politics available to the academic, business, and government communities. For further information, write to the Special Projects Division, Frederick A. Praeger, Publishers, 111 Fourth Avenue, New York, N.Y. 10003.

FREDERICK A. PRAEGER, PUBLISHERS
111 Fourth Avenue, New York, N.Y. 10003, U.S.A.
77-79 Charlotte Street, London W.1, England

Published in the United States of America in 1967
by Frederick A. Praeger, Inc., Publishers

This is the first cloth edition of a report originally
issued by the Committee for Economic Development in 1967

Library of Congress Catalog Card Number: 67-29353

Printed in the United States of America

Foreword

The papers in this volume are the outgrowth of the work of CED's Subcommittee on Development Policy, which was set up three and a half years ago to study the key factors influencing the rate of growth in low income countries. Whereas previous CED policy statements relating to development had dealt largely with the roles of foreign aid, trade, and investment, the subcommittee concentrated its attention on the conditions that must be present within the low income countries themselves if they are to achieve high rates of growth in per capita income. The subcommittee's findings were presented in the policy statement entitled *How Low Income Countries Can Advance Their Own Growth: The Lessons of Experience,* issued in September 1966 by CED's Research and Policy Committee.

In attempting to find answers to the question why some low income countries have been successful in achieving a healthy economic growth while others have not, CED drew heavily on the advice of knowledgeable people within these countries themselves. It commissioned economists from Latin America, Southeast Asia, and the Mediterranean region to prepare studies analyzing for fifteen selected countries the successes and failures of their efforts to achieve economic development. In choosing countries for study, CED sought examples both of rapid growth and of lagging growth.

Having found these papers to be of substantial value in its work, the subcommittee decided to make available to a wider audience those that seemed of general significance. In accordance with procedures established by CED by-laws, the papers were submitted to an editorial board comprised of Trustees and academic advisors to the CED, whose names appear on page 341. This volume contains the Latin American country studies that were approved for publication by a majority of the editorial board.

A brief description of the authors' backgrounds will help the reader in understanding the nature of the papers in this volume. In almost every case, the author has had an active role in helping to shape the economic policy of his country, either as a policy-maker at cabinet level or as an advisor to government.

Hence there is a quite understandable tendency for the writers to state rather forcibly their feelings about national economic policy — to express gratification where the policies they espouse have been followed and frustration where these have been rejected. Each writer chose the manner of his presentation, for example with respect to the scope of his treatment and the use of statistics. Moreover, the special conditions in each country have naturally influenced the authors in singling out for emphasis those issues of economic development policy that seem of paramount importance to them.

Among the Latin American countries, Peru and Mexico over recent years have had outstanding records in terms of economic growth, and also of monetary stability. Rómulo A. Ferrero, a former Minister of Finance and Commerce, attributes Peru's attainments mainly to its encouragement of export industries, foreign investment, and a generally high level of economic freedom. The paper on Mexico concentrates on a different aspect of growth. Gustavo Romero Kolbeck, who is professor of economics and director of the Investment Commission of the President of the Republic, stresses the role of the government in facilitating the growth of the private sector through public financing of the basic infrastructure.

Argentina, Chile, and Colombia have had in this period less satisfactory rates of economic growth, and in the first two cases there has also been a high degree of monetary instability. Roberto T. Alemann, a former Argentine Minster of Economy, analyzes his country's inadequate performance in terms of the heritage of erroneous economics and social doctrine from the Perón era. Sergio Undurraga Saavedra, a young Chilean economist, finds the key to his country's erratic and sluggish growth in its long history of inflation. Hernan Echavarría, a businessman and former cabinet minister, now Colombia's Ambassador to the United States, finds that two factors in particular — the "proyectista" school of economic thought and excessive government spending including that financed by foreign aid — have had a distorting and unhealthy effect on the economy of his country.

With these five papers of supplementary research is included a special study on Brazilian inflation, by Mário Henrique Simonsen, director of the Graduate School of Economics of the

Getúlio Vargas Foundation. The Brazilian case is particularly interesting because of the co-existence, until recently, of a rapid inflation and a lively rate of economic growth. The author's very thorough analysis challenges some traditional thinking about the causes and effects of inflation; it shows that inflation and growth can proceed together but does not at all support the theory that inflation promotes growth. Mr. Simonsen's paper was published by the Instituto de Pesquisas e Estudos Sociais (IPES) in Brazil, which has an affiliation with CED. The paper is being published in this country under a special arrangement between CED and IPES.

On behalf of CED, I would like to acknowledge the invaluable assistance of various organizations and individuals in bringing this volume into being. Both IPES in Brazil and the Consejo Interamericano de Comercio y Producción (CICYP) were very helpful in obtaining the services of the authors. Frank Brandenburg, formerly of the CED staff, conducted the background research of the Subcommittee on Development Policy and supervised the translations. Carl Rieser, CED Editorial Supervisor, helped prepare the volume for publication. To the authors is owed a special debt of gratitude for their contributions and cooperation. The editors are particularly grateful to Messrs. Ferrero, Simonsen, and Undurraga, who at CED's request have revised and updated the material and statistics in their papers.

Roy Blough, *Project Director,*
Subcommittee on Development Policy

Contents

Economic Development of Argentina / *Roberto Alemann*

Key Factors in
Chilean Economic Development / *Sergio Undurraga Saavedra*

Tables

Appendix Tables

Economic Development of Colombia / *Hernan Echavarría*

Economic Development of Mexico / *Gustavo Romero Kolbeck*

Economic Development of Peru / *Rómulo A. Ferrero*

SPECIAL STUDY **Brazilian Inflation**
Postwar Experience and Outcome
of the 1964 Reforms */ Mário Henrique Simonsen*

*By arrangement with IPES of Brazil.

Tables

Economic Development Issues: Latin America

Committee for Economic Development
Supplementary Paper No. 21

ECONOMIC

DEVELOPMENT

OF

ARGENTINA

Roberto Alemann

The Author

ROBERTO T. ALEMANN, an economist trained at the National University of Buenos Aires and the University of Berne, has filled high governmental posts in three Argentine adminstrations. Under the Provisional Government of General Aramburu, he served from 1956 to 1959 as Financial Counselor in London, Treasury Director, Advisor to the Ministry of Economy, Under-Secretary of Economy, and Financial Counselor in Washington. In 1961, Mr. Alemann was appointed Minister of Economy by President Frondizi. He was Ambassador to the United States in 1962 and 1963 under the Guido administration. Since 1962 he has been Professor of Economic Policy at the Law School of the University of Buenos Aires.

Contents

Economic Development of Argentina / *Roberto Alemann*

4.

Introduction

The present study is a brief description and a critical analysis of the economic development of Argentina in the two decades from 1945 to 1964. This was a highly contradictory period involving many opposing forces, divergent streams of economic thought, and conflicting courses of action. The rapid succession of measures, the doctrines offered to support them, and the results, often different from those desired, were so numerous and complex that it is not easy to explain coherently what happened.

So that events may be more readily understood, this paper describes the economic measures that were employed and the doctrines that inspired or served to justify them. Economic processes are a product of human action, and the prevailing economic thought of the moment usually leaves its impress on events. Argentina is not an exception to this rule, but rather an eloquent example.

Past events have been greatly influenced by the traditional centralization of political decisions in the executive power functioning in the metropolitan area of Buenos Aires, which has more than one-third of the population of the country. The Argentine economy depends, to a large degree, on the actions or omissions of the national authorities, despite the great variety and diversity of its production and its reasonably well-organized national markets. Thus the economic measures that were used and their supporting doctrines deserve a considerable degree of attention.

But there is more. The period with which we are dealing was marked by inflation, which had an average rate of about 25 per cent annually, with fluctuations of from 5 to 110 per cent, as measured by the cost-of-living index. The result was that the economy was shaken by recurrent jolts and that great distortions occurred in its functioning. In each instance, the inflationary waves were set off by political actions, accompanied by justifying doctrines. Involved in the process also were attempts to correct the inflationary surges. It is not possible to grasp what happened during the period without a clear understanding of the cause of the recurring inflation, which was the large deficits of the National Treasury financed by money issued by the banking system.

Inflation within a country spawns an astonishing excess of doctrine, among other effects. Solutions based on partial explanations of what is taking place are offered repeatedly while the real cause of the evil persists. Meanwhile, an attack on the basic evil is avoided, apparently for social and political reasons. Such remedies as are tried are directed at the problems generated by inflation. The effect of all this is to make things worse. It is all part of the paradoxical process of inflation. New obscure explanations bob up, and mysticism becomes a false science widely approved.

The centralization of decision-making power that characterizes the Argentine body politic makes it necessary to keep in mind the successive regimes that ruled the country during the period under review. While it is true that economic policy is never entirely autonomous, in the case of Argentina the economic actions of the authorities are incomprehensible unless one knows the nature of the political system as well as the peculiar orientation of the principal actors.

For this reason, it should be recalled that Argentina, up until 1943, had a civil government with authorities elected by the people. In June of that year, the established government was overthrown by a military coup d'etat and a dictatorship was set up under Juan Domingo Perón, who installed himself as President in 1946. Perón ruled the country until September, 1955, when he was overthrown by a civilian-military movement, which was succeeded by a de facto government. The first President under this government was General Eduardo Lonardi; he was succeeded in November, 1956, by General Pedro Eugenio Aramburu, who was in office until May, 1958. A new constitutional regime, elected by the people, was headed by Arturo Frondizi, who governed until March, 1962. He was overthrown by the three chiefs of staff of the armed forces and was succeeded by his Vice President, José Maria Guido, who after a call for elections in October, 1963, turned over the power to Arturo Humberto Illia. Frondizi, Guido, and Illia came from the Radical

Party, which was divided in 1956 into two major movements. Frondizi and Guido belonged to the movement that reached power in 1958; Illia to the one that took over in 1963. Illia's party, La Unión Cívica Radical del Pueblo (Civic Radical Union of the People), has since governed the country.[1]

To make it easier to understand what has happened during these regimes, this study begins with a description of the Argentine economy, emphasizing its demography and the degree of utilization of resources. An attempt has been made to avoid the over-use of figures, which are available in abundance. The evaluation of the actions taken and of the doctrines advanced is, of course, the responsibility of the author.

---

[1] This paper was written prior to the overthrow of the Illia government by a military junta on June 28, 1966, and the installation of Lieutenant General Juan Carlos Ongania as Provisional President.

1. The Argentine Society and Economy

The Republic of Argentina is not an underdeveloped country. On the contrary, its population and natural resources place it among the developed countries of the world, although a marked difference exists between it and the nations more technologically advanced.

This statement may seem questionable because of the serious economic difficulties experienced by Argentina in the last two decades. Looking from the outside at the balance-of-payments deficit, the short-term foreign debt, the meager monetary reserves, and the pressing need for foreign capital and credits, the economic difficulties of Argentina seem to parallel those typical of numerous underdeveloped countries during the same period. This analogy should not mislead the reader with regard to the chief causes of Argentina's economic problems, which are essentially different from those of underdeveloped countries seeking economic improvement.

Regardless of how underdevelopment may be defined, it seems reasonable that the stage of a nation's development may be adequately described by the characteristics and composition of its population and by the degree of development of its economic resources. In giving priority to these simple standards, however, others must not be overlooked; e.g., per capita income, technological progress, extent of internal capitalization.

Social Characteristics

The population of Argentina, around 22 million at the end of 1964, is singularly homogeneous for a nation formed of migratory movements in the last century. Only in the mountain fringes of the north and in the Patagonian territory are Indian ethnic groups still to be found, though Indian blood runs in the veins of many of the rural inhabitants. The population of the nation comes from Europe, especially from Spain and Italy. More than 70 per cent of the population is of Spanish or Italian ancestry. There is also a high degree of religious homogenity; according to the 1947 census, 93 per cent of the population is Roman Catholic.

Large-scale immigration from Europe began in the 1880's reaching a record total of 1,120,000 persons in the first decade of the twentieth century and dropping to 72,700 in the decade of the 1930's. Immigration climbed after World War II, but again dropped substantially in the 1950's, dramatizing the transformation that has occurred in the country in the last two decades. A country of immigrants, Argentina has also become a country of emigrants. Many Europeans return to their native lands, and Argentines also leave, especially scholars and students. Meanwhile, immigration from neighboring countries persists. The motivations of long ago that induced millions of Europeans to try their fortunes overseas have disappeared. Instead, Western Europe now attracts labor from Latin America.

Because of the massive immigration of Europeans before 1930, the percentage of foreign-born in the population increased from 12.1 per cent in the first national census of 1869, to 25.5 per cent in 1895, and then to a maximum of 30.3 per cent in 1914. The last two censuses showed a drop in the foreign-born population to 15.3 per cent in 1947 and to 12.8 per cent in 1960. One hundred years after the first census, the percentage of foreign-born will be comparable to that in 1869, even though the population will have increased over the period from 1,737,076 to an estimated 24 million in 1969.

The rate of population growth, which was 2 per cent and sometimes 3 per cent annually in the period of large immigration, has declined in the last few years to 1.7 per cent. The present rate is considerably smaller than that in many underdeveloped countries. Birth and mortality rates also show marked declines. The birth rate dropped from 38.3 per thousand in 1910 to 22.7 per thousand in 1958, the mortality rate from 18.9 per thousand to 8.1 per thousand in the same period. No matter what yardstick is applied, the present vital statistics of Argentina are not characteristic of the so-called underdeveloped countries. Likewise, the age composition of the Argentine population reveals a pyramid more nearly like that of the highly industrialized nations than of the underdeveloped countries. The pyramid base, consisting of the younger age groups, is narrower than in the underdeveloped countries with high birth rates.

Although the Argentine economy is basically agricultural, the composition of the urban and rural population is not substantially different from that of highly industrialized countries. The rate of urbanization has shown persistent increase, as elsewhere in the world. By 1914 the urban population has risen to more than half the total; it was 62.5 per cent in 1947 and 68 per cent in 1960. As has been pointed out, more than a third of the population now lives in the federal capital proper and in the surrounding areas that expand into Greater Buenos Aires. On the basis of the last estimates, there are 7 million people in this metropolitan complex. Outside of this highly urbanized zone, there are a dozen cities in Argentina with a population of from 100,000 to 600,000.

In its educational and cultural aspects, Argentina more nearly resembles the industrialized countries.

The cultural life of Buenos Aires can be compared with that of other world cultural centers. Higher education, even though disorganized after two decades of confusion in public finances, is being diversified through private institutions and the recent creation of research centers and cultural foundations. More and more people have become interested in art and music. There are many interested readers of large newspapers, magazines, and books, as in most advanced communities. Television has experienced an explosive growth since it was introduced a little more than a decade ago, and in the next decade it will cover the greater part of the continental territory, thereby influencing the formation of taste, opinions, and ways of living.

The Argentine people, particularly the intellectual groups and a good portion of the middle class, maintain traditional ties of interest and affinity with their European homelands, and more recently they have established ties with other countries of Latin America and the United States. Influenced by public education, which is universal in character, the Argentine people have a cosmopolitan outlook and a lively interest in current events the world over.

Illiteracy in Argentina, even allowing for a reasonable margin of error, dropped sharply from 13.6 per cent in 1947 to 8.6 per cent in 1960. The constantly lowering percentage of illiteracy reveals the educational effort to which generations of Argentines have devoted thought, time, and energy. This does not mean, of course, that Argentina can relax in its dedication to education and reduce its educational services. On the contrary, experience shows that when education becomes more advanced, and there is a need to satisfy superior technological and cultural needs, a greater and more expensive effort is required than when the primary purpose was to abolish illiteracy.

In its medical and public health services, Argentina also is closer to highly developed rather than underdeveloped nations. It has eight physicians and 63 hospital beds for each 10,000 persons. The progress and diversity of the pharmaceutical industry and the abundance of drug stores are indications of a relatively advanced degree of development in this field. Deficiencies, however, persist in the general public health services, due not to a low educational level but to the disorganization and lack of capital characteristic of long periods of inflation.

Distribution of income and property in Argentina does not reveal the marked division between the wealthy few and the impoverished masses characteristic of many underdeveloped countries. On the contrary, the great fortunes, originally from rural sources, have been divided through the generations. Only in a few family groups engaged in traditional enterprises, and in some other isolated cases, have these fortunes been maintained reasonably unimpaired, but these instances are the exception. Actually, Argentina today has a distinctive middle class with more than modest resources. The middle class constitutes the majority of the population. It includes the professional, the entrepreneur, the business executive, the rural landlord, the public employee, the skilled worker, etc.

The Argentine community is a reasonably open society. No insurmountable obstacles exist to social ascent. The increasing homogeneity of the population has not created different classes or prevented fast ups and downs on the social ladder. Access to public office or to positions of social prestige is not generally denied to anyone because of his origin, religion, or social position. Likewise, there is relatively open access to education, and the opportunities for talent are increasing.

Finally, Argentina has had one advantage that is often over-looked. Since 1880, when the intermittent and bloody struggles between the settling population and the Indian nomad tribes ended in the submission of the latter, the country has not experienced any military action comparable to the wars or civil conflicts that have devastated so large a portion of the world during this century. Thus Argentina has enjoyed more than eight decades of relatively peaceful coexistence, and this without doubt has been a great asset.

Physical Resources

Argentina is one of the most extensive areas of productive territory in the temperate zone of the Southern Hemisphere. Continental Argentina has 2,776,655 square kilometers, and its total area is 4,024,458 square kilometers if the Antarctic region, the Falkland Islands, and other nearby islands are included. There is a wide variety of climates — tropical and subtropical areas on the northern boundary; the semi-arid zone in the northeast, west, and south; the humid and fertile pampas in the center and the east; the huge mountainous and forest regions of the Andes; the barren plains of Patagonia; and the polar cold of the southern tip. Except for the heat in some continental regions and the cold in the Antarctic portion, the various climates offer marked seasonal variations whose stimulating effect on human activity is well known.

A favorable climate combines with an exceptionally fertile soil in the pampas, which need only rain at the right times and frequent sunshine to bless any agricultural effort. However, the lack of snow in this region removes the advantage of winter moisture, making it more sensitive to the rainfall variations.

Close to 30 million hectares of the continental territory are given over to agriculture, of which almost 20 million are under continuous cultivation. More than 100 million hectares have natural pasturage suitable for raising livestock. Sixty million hectares are covered by scrub or forest. Only 30 per cent of the continental territory — slightly over 80 million hectares — cannot be used for crops or livestock production.

Fertile soil and a mild climate made possible the development of agriculture on a mass-production basis a century ago. Farming and cattle breeding are so completely diversified that Argentina is one of the six or seven leading world exporters of temperate-zone agricultural products. It is the only nation that commercializes the complete range of the crops and livestock that it raises.

Wheat, linseed, rice, oats, barley, rye, millet, peanuts, alfalfa, sunflower, and sorghum are the most important field crops; these are cultivated in the pampas and surrounding regions. There are also extensive areas in the semi-arid temperate and sub-tropical zones where olives, cotton, sugar cane, manioc, tobacco, tea, tung nuts, yerba maté, grapes, and other products are cultivated as raw materials for many processing industries.

The climate and soil conditions are such that cattle can be raised cheaply over a wide area. Cattle raising can be carried on in the open, without the need for protection against the weather. At the same time, wages are low. This explains why Argentine red meat is among the cheapest in the world. Because of its low cost, meat naturally comprises a very important part of the Argentine diet. Per capita meat consumption has exceeded 100 kilograms a year, and though it dropped to 60 kilograms in 1964, it is still one of the highest in the world. Cattle, sheep, and their by-products account for nearly half the nation's income from exports, and they are also the source of many industrial and commercial activities. Wool no longer has the importance it had during long periods of the nineteenth century, when it was Argentina's chief export. But even though wool production in Argentina has dropped in comparison with that of competing countries, it is still a source of income from abroad.

Until very recently, the relatively high productivity of cattle raising hindered the intensive development of the poultry industry, hog breeding, and similar competitive activities. However, there has been recent growth in these industries because of the change in the relationship in the prices of red and white meat that took place in 1962 and 1963 because of drought conditions. The increase in the raising of poultry and hogs has also been aided by introduction of new techniques, which in turn has been spurred by incentives to investors and by the expectation of larger markets.

Argentina has a continental shelf of nearly a million square kilometers that is a potentially rich fishing ground. These resources have not been exploited to any considerable degree, though it is to be hoped that the factors that have been mentioned above will also benefit the fishing industry.

There have been some efforts recently at reforestation, though the area involved — only 200,000 hectares — is negligible compared with 70 million hectares of forest land in Argentina. About 58 million hectares are accessible, of which 28 million hectares are heavily forested and 30 million are covered by scrub forest. More than 3 million hectares have been set aside in national parks as a tourist attraction for the time when car ownership is comparable with that in industrialized countries and when the highway system has been sufficiently improved. Numerous industries have been developed from the forest resources. The exploitation of "quebracho," although a declining industry, still maintains an important position among the productive activities of the heavily forested regions in the northern part of the country.

Besides its food resources and the production of raw materials, Argentina has sufficient energy sources to satisfy its needs. More than 80 per cent of the national consumption of energy is provided by petroleum and gas resources. The oil fields under development are in the extreme north (Salta) and the south (Tierra del Fuego), along the Andes (Mendoza and Neúquer), and in Atlantic Patagonia (Chubut and Santa Cruz). The country ranks thirteenth in the world in annual production. Total crude oil production in 1964 was 96 million barrels.

Gas is being developed in a number of fields. It has undergone a substantial increase in the last few years because of the construction of three central pipelines and several local ones. These pipelines carry the gas from Salta in the north and Comodoro Rivadavia in Patagonia to consumption centers along the coast. Gas production already has exceeded the equivalent of 3 million cubic meters of petroleum, and will increase in coming years with the recent opening of the third central pipeline.

Even though mining resources are varied, they do not reach significant quantities. The country is relatively poor in high grade coal, a condition which it shares with all of Latin America. Yet it maintains, for reasons of prestige and inertia, production from a high-cost mine. Only in recent years has the country begun to export iron ore, although thus far it has extracted no significant quantities.

The reason for the relatively high degree of development of Argentine natural resources is the ready access of many parts of the country to each other and to overseas points. There are a number of ports along the Atlantic coast, while the Plate, Paraná, and Uruguay river systems make overseas navigation possible for long stretches. Besides water transportation, the country is covered by a vast network of roads and railroads. There are more than 40,000 kilometers of railroads, extending from the north of Patagonia to the western, northern, and eastern boundaries, with a heavy concentration in Buenos Aires province, which has great agricultural wealth. With respect to highways, the network of main and secondary roads is practically completed. However, paved roads for year-round use by vehicles cannot be compared with those in industrialized countries. The construction of paved roads, previously suspended, was begun again a few years ago. The telephone service, which has declined since it was nationalized two decades ago, still has around 1,400,000 units and is the most dense in all Latin America.

Argentina has a large and complex banking and financing system. The institutional picture comprises a central bank, several official agricultural and industrial promotion banks, mortgage banks, numerous commercial banks, a national savings bank, insurance companies, a national reinsurance institute, investment companies, savings and loan associations, and several securities exchanges revolving around the Buenos Aires Stock Exchange (Bolsa de Comercio de Buenos Aires). The exchange and money markets are perfectly capable of functioning well as long as they are allowed to do so by official policies.

As this survey of the natural resources, the characteristics of the people, and the communication links of the country would suggest, industrialization has a certain degree of development.

This has been particularly true in the last three decades. In a disorganized way, and in spite of official government planning, the manufacturing and processing industries have expanded during this period and have acquired a high degree of diversification with the use of modern techniques.

Argentine industry manufactures virtually all the products that are produced in highly industrialized countries, though its output of heavy and specialized machinery and electronic products is very limited. However, the quality of some of the products made in the country, the quantity and variety of other products, and the prices of most cannot be compared with what the highly industrialized countries are able to do.

If the industrial progress of the last few years maintains its pace, Argentine industry will be able to advance as long as it maintains commercial ties with the centers of technological development and improves its efficiency by the adoption of new techniques and modern machinery. The participation in expanded markets through exports should promote industrial growth in a more rational way than in the past, when it occurred under the shadow of excessive protection and inflationary financing.

2. "New Doctrines" and the Perón Era

Argentina experienced its most remarkable growth in the 70 years that began with the so-called "national organization" in the decade of the 1860's and ended with the first military revolution of 1930. The forces behind this growth were the heroic efforts of many generations of native-born and immigrants; the introduction of foreign capital and techniques; the construction of railroads and highways; and the expansion of markets for the export of cereals, grains, wools, meats, and other products.

The economic doctrine prevailing during this period was based on the philosophy of the liberal constitution of 1853; liberty for the individual, respect for private property, belief in unlimited progress, national and international competition, and legal order assured by authorities elected according to established rules that limited the President to two consecutive terms.

After World War I, new economic doctrines appeared and spread slowly among the political leaders and the intellectual groups. These doctrines fostered a political organization different from the traditional one, an organization frankly tinged with authoritarian tones and inclined toward corporate-state concepts. The interruption of the constitutional process that came with the 1930 revolution gave impetus to these doctrines.

The new theories encouraged greater intervention in the economic sector by the state. The commercial organization of the world was collapsing with the abandonment of the gold standard, the spread of restrictive and discriminatory practices, and the trend toward economic self-sufficiency. Economic nationalism gained adherents among the political leaders of all countries.

During the decade of the 1930's, the introduction of new doctrines was tempered by a sensible and efficient financial administration. The government, however, intervened in economic processes that theretofore had been in private hands. It fixed minimum prices for cereals, created the Central Bank, introduced exchange controls, established several rates of exchange, nationalized the existing petroleum companies and denied new concessions, and took over some public services.

The export of grains and meats was severely hurt by the world economic crisis and the restrictive measures adopted by purchasing countries. This situation was responsible to a large degree for the measures that were then adopted as safeguards. The system functioned quite efficiently, especially after the introduction of the monetary stabilization program of 1934, which gave Argentina access once again to credit and investment sources that had practically dried up with the crisis of 1930. During those years, numerous new industries were established, with only moderate tariff protection, and public services operated efficiently. The National Treasury had its finances in balance and the external debt was reduced.

The beginning of the World War II brought about a profound change in Argentina's economic policy. The country isolated itself from the rest of the world. Imports were restricted. Industrialization expanded because the country was unable to supply itself from abroad. This expanding economic activity was accelerated by a change in fiscal policies. Public works were initiated and the national budget ran a deficit, the excess in spending being covered by an increase in the public debt.

The Dictatorship under Perón

The new political and economic doctrines, in the meantime, were gaining adherents in the political and military groups. All facets of the new doctrines were successively tried by the de facto government of 1943 that led to the dictatorship of Perón. These new doctrines were deeply rooted in the Spanish and Italian corporate-state concepts, and the fascist, national socialistic, and British labor ideologies. In economic theory, it is quite likely that the most influential author of government policy was Lord Keynes. His clear and penetrating words, his worldwide prestige as a theoretician in countries with few economists, and his excessive ideas concerning the effect of fiscal deficits spread quite easily among those who needed a doctrinal justification for unbalancing public finances in order to reach certain political objectives.

These "new doctrines," though actually as old as social organization itself, had their political expression in the installation of a one-man dictatorship that subjected all institutions to its will. Argentina's economic activities were subordinated to the conveniences of the charismatic and Caeser-like regime, which derived support from the masses through the vertical organization of the labor unions. Accepted ideas about sound administration, balanced budgets, access to capital markets, private investment, risk and competition, were replaced by economic concepts of political origin, supported by demagoguery.

In order to achieve political objectives, the regime — as soon as it was truly in power and backed by the masses that were receiving the benefits of demagogic social measures — moved rapidly to take over the financial tools. It threw out the men who had been working them, transformed the institutions, and eliminated the legal limitations on the abuse of financial power.

The Central Bank, created in 1935 as a mixed, autonomous entity, was nationalized and subordinated to the government. Bank deposits were turned over to the Central Bank through a measure called "nationalization of deposits," which in the last analysis represented an effective reserve of 100 per cent. Commercial banks, deprived of the traditional resources, had to adopt the so-called rediscount process, which was a simple authorization to lend, granted discretionally under certain conditions by the Central Bank.

An Industrial Credit Bank (Banco de Crédito Industrial), was created to supply the working capital for the new light industries that sprang up under the protection of the system of exchange controls. The Instituto Nacional de Reaseguros (National Institute of Reinsurance) was created with monopoly powers on reinsurance activities. With official banks granting more than 80 per cent of all credits in the country and the deposits of private banks in the hands of the Central Bank, the financial dictatorship was quite complete.

With a system of this nature, all the problems inherent in the financing of a fiscal deficit disappeared. The budget was reasonably in balance until 1940, and subsequent deficits had been covered without too much difficulty by long-term public credits. Later on, the demogogic regime of the dictatorship increased expenditures excessively through various measures. These are worth listing since they are the root causes of Argentine inflation, which still persists after two decades:

- Massive increases in wages and salaries by government decree;
- Increases in social welfare benefits;
- Constant increases in government employment, particularly in state enterprises;
- Take-over of public services;
- Construction of luxury buildings for governmental offices;
- Acquisition or confiscation of commercial and industrial enterprises;
- Loans to provinces, municipalities, and state enterprises, which are not capable of financing themselves through their own means;
- Subsidies for certain goods and services, with prices and rates held down to assure mass consumption;
- Multiplication of controls over the economy, which are costly to administer.

The fiscal deficit resulting from these policies was covered by the official banks through credits that the Central Bank could not legally grant to the government itself, or through the multiple exchange-rate system, which made available foreign exchange at preferential rates for government-sponsored activities. The latter was an outright subsidy that did not have to be accounted for, being merely a transfer of resources within the economy.

The real magnitude of the fiscal deficits during these years probably never will be known. When the principle of an over-all budget was abandoned, and expenditures were spread out among special accounts, autonomous institutions, state enterprises, and other organizations with the authority to borrow money, any effective way of calculating the true fiscal deficit disappeared. The uncertain deficit thus created was accentuated by the subsidies granted by use of the multiple exchange-rate system.

During these years, economic and social theories supported measures for so-called income redistribution, selective credit, special rediscounts, and other formulas for allocating non-existing resources through the mere creation of means of payment by the omnipotent financial power.

The deficit spending policy was initiated with extremely high international reserves, thanks to the prudent financial and exchange administration of earlier years, the excellent public credit Argentina once enjoyed in world financial centers, and the effects of World War II, which increased exports at high prices while imports were restricted. At their peak, these reserves reached almost $1.7 billion.

The monetary reserves, however, were soon depleted. This occurred as a result of the heavy purchases of obsolete war material for the armed forces supporting the dictatorial regime, the acquisition of public services from foreign owners (e.g., railroads and telephone lines), and the repatriation of foreign loans that had been obtained at low interest rates and with extended repayment terms.

Simultaneously, imports increased as an unavoidable effect of the internal monetary expansion, the accelerated creation of light industries, and the massive salary increases. Exports were hurt by the oppressive impact of a policy aimed broadly at transferring resources from agriculture to the manufacturing industries, while emphasizing industrial raw material crops at the expense of agricultural activity on the Pampas. Resources were also shifted into the services of the public sector, whose costs increased and whose inefficiency declined.

Meanwhile, as the market for fiscal obligations and mortgages was destroyed through the well-known effect of inflation on securities of constant yield, the exchanges started dealing more and more in stocks of numerous corporations that were looking for capital to finance manufacturing expansion. The first impact felt by the stock exchanges was the massive reimbursement to mortgage holders of funds that were being transferred to corporate stocks.

Taxation and Social Welfare

Tax administration in Argentina, which used to compare favorably with Europe, deteriorated in a very few years. As tax rates increased and became practically confiscatory, at the same time new taxes were levied, quite an ingenious variety of techniques for tax evasion gradually came into being.

The very system of exchange and price controls favored evasion. Multiple exchange rates were an invitation to the under-invoicing of exports and the over-invoicing of imports, so that a great majority of the profits remained outside of the country and were not subject to Argentine taxes. In a similar manner, industrialists, businessmen, and agricultural producers carried on transactions in goods subject to price controls outside the official markets and did not record them in their financial statements.

Thus, in a country with a relatively good distribution of income, income and other direct taxes declined gradually in their relative importance as sources of fiscal revenues, despite the high rates. Inflation contributed to this tendency. In such a redistribution of income and taxes, it is well known that inflation hits hardest those who are least able to protect themselves: wage-earners, employees, people receiving pensions, and other similar groups. The doctrine of income redistribution, which provided comforting explanations to justify inflation, paradoxically worked against the less privileged persons, the very ones who were to have received protection from the mighty by these measures.

The deterioration in tax administration engendered a vicious circle. As tax evasion increased, the authorities, in need of ever-increasing amounts of money to counteract inflation, increased tax rates, tightened controls, and multiplied taxes — all of which did nothing except intensify tax evasion.

Tax ethics in Argentina, before inflation set in, were no better or worse than in the majority of the southern European countries, and perhaps they were better than in some of them. But as a result of the actions of the authorities, a feeling quickly spread that tax evasion was justified. The Argentine taxpayers became convinced that their only protection against a cheating government, which was debasing through inflation the value of their incomes and properties, was to use any method compatible with personal security to lower their contribution to the government.

A similar thing happened with the compulsory contributions to the welfare funds which proliferated during the dictatorship as still another demonstration of the social conscience of the government. These funds were based originally on an actuarial computation involving contributions, savings, investments in securities of constant yield, and financing of pensions. Naturally, under the actions taken by the government[2], the funds became bankrupt, though this was never admitted. The government forced the welfare funds to buy securities that could not be placed with the public, and the low interest rates paid by these securities were insufficient to finance the various benefits. In order to solve this problem, contributions by employers and workers were increased to 26 per cent of all compensation.

For the employers, such contributions represented an outright tax. As for the beneficiaries, there is no doubt that their contributions to the funds were nothing but a hidden tax, since they did not receive, when the time came, an amount equivalent to what they had contributed in good currency.

Social welfare contributions, furthermore, added a great deal of rigidity to production costs and opened a door for unfair competition from those enterprisers who made no contribution. In spite of rigid controls and the threats of punishment, many employers, particularly the small and medium-sized ones, simply failed to participate in the social welfare system. Other enterprisers, of greater financial size, did not contribute or fell behind in their contributions, heavily pressed as they were by the effects of inflation and the deterioration of working capital so typical of an inflationary process. In effect, evasion both of taxes and of contributions to the welfare funds represented a form of financing for employers.

Not only was such evasion general, but the government itself contributed to it by granting repeated postponements and consolidations to debtors in arrears. Each one of these actions created an incentive for employers to procrastinate even further, since credit was granted at low interest rates and the many years allowed for reimbursement permitted payment in a currency of smaller purchasing power. Hence the vicious circle kept growing bigger.

Economic Self-Sufficiency

This financial and economic system had, of course, a purely political inspiration and served the objectives of the one-man regime in power.

Nationalization of public services and basic industries, such as oil and steel, was supported by marxist and the socialist thinking, as well as by the nationalist doctrines of corporative, fascist, or national-socialist extraction. The influence of Catholic-Hispanic thought, attributed to St. Thomas Aquinas, prevailed in intellectual and political circles. Centralized control of public finance also had similar inspiration, and the nationalization of the Central Bank reflected the same kind of measures adopted a short time before by the Labor government of England and by the post-war government of France.

The notion of economic self-sufficiency, so prevalent at the time, was imported from Germany and Italy, which had been moving toward this objective during the previous decade. Exchange controls, bilateral trade, multiple exchange rates, and control of capital movements were common in all European and many other countries, so that no intellectual effort was required to support the implementation of similar measures in Argentina.

The unlimited protection of industry initiated at the time, with restrictions on imports of articles produced in the country — as long as they did not belong in the so-called indispensible category — was the counterpart of the policy of exchange controls. Such a system still prevailed in the European countries, where a policy of trade liberalization was just being started on a regional scale. This policy was easily justified from the standpoint of doctrine, by simply mentioning the arguments: e.g., the protection of national labor — a variation of the full employment theme — or the need to save scarce foreign exchange by invoking the economic self-sufficiency dogma.

Absolute protection, added to an inflated demand, represented quite an incentive for the installation of facilities to process imported raw materials.

There were many cases of enterprises put together with little equity capital and with extensive credit from the official sector, in part through arrearages in taxes and social benefit payments. These enterprises were allowed to import raw materials at preferential exchange rates. They sold their products at three or four times the international level, made large profits, and were able to amortize their investments quickly.

Quite a few manufacturers diverted funds to other activities or fields of investment, such as deposits abroad, urban real estate, summer residences, farms and luxury items, or to commercial activities connected with the enterprise itself, such as insurance and financing.

It should come as no surprise, therefore, that under these conditions a new social group of lucky entrepreneurs sprang up to enjoy a most luxurious standard of living, although they had little experience in their enterprises. They had vested interests, however, against the reinstatement of external competition as a factor in regulating prices and allocating resources, and they acquired great political and social power. They fed the political parties without distinction of flag or color, and they were present in social and entrepreneurial organizations of every tendency and in every area. The nationalist theories about import substitution, protection of the work force, full employment, need for home industry, deterioration of free market trade terms, and so forth were used by them to justify their position of convenience. Organized labor, in its own way, defended similar objectives, and as a result the alliance of both pressure groups became unbeatable.

State Enterprises

Inflation is a way of distributing privileges. There are probably few clearer demonstrations of this assertion than the administration of the state enterprises.

The persistent campaign of nationalist, marxist, and socialist theories undoubtedly helped in creating a favorable political climate for the transfer of certain economic activities to the state. The state interventionist measures of the British Labor Party and of the French Socialists, who came to power after World War II, served as encouraging examples.

The nationalization of banks, public services, and important industries which took place in those countries, had a tremendous impact on the political conscience of Argentina. Furthermore, prevailing political nationalism and economic xenophobia added strictly emotional elements in support of those measures.

A political doctrine of "national recuperation" was propagated by the dictatorship. It defended transfer to the state of principal public services — particularly those in foreign hands — and demanded direct control of public finances, money, credit, and insurance. The railroads were purchased from British and French interests precisely at the moment when, after many years without any reinvestment, their operations were in the decline.

All kinds of imaginable errors were perpetrated during the administration by the state. The state enterprises, in the hands of civilian backers of the regime or of military personnel, had a decisive impact on the policy of absolute protection and served as factors toward "cartelization" of the respective markets. The jobs that were handed out, with their possibilities for personal enrichment, gave tremendous political influence and prestige to the state enterprises.

The triumph of the new doctrine gave the state oil enterprise, Yacimientos Petrolíferos Fiscales (YPF), a monopoly of exploration and exploitation. Originally, this entity was created in 1922 to supplement exploratory activities and exploit those fields which private capital was unable to develop. Nationalist sentiment was in the wind, and the 1930's brought about a prohibition against new concessions and the establishment of a distribution "cartel" for gasoline in the country made up of the state enterprise and the two existing private concerns (Esso and Shell). With private capital ousted, all the vices of an overloaded official administration followed — lack of authority and continuity of management, bribes and corruption, and the inevitable investment difficulties.

This evolution of YPF would have been only another episode in state enterprise and scarcely would have been worth mentioning, had it not affected the supply of the principal source of energy in the country. Light industries, expanding because of the massive concentration of population in urban centers, escalated the demand for fuel. Local production, concentrated in

YPF, could not satisfy the demand. YPF then converted itself gradually into the main importer of petroleum, as it was much easier to import at a preferential rate of exchange than to continue exploration and exploitation activities.

The result was that YPF neglected its true objective of carrying on exploratory operations. In order to meet a growing demand for oil, it transformed itself progressively into an enterprise engaged primarily in the refining, transportation, and sale of petroleum products. The result of this change was a noticeable increase of oil imports while internal oil production remained practically at a standstill, even though some new productive fields had been discovered. The point was reached finally where domestic oil production supplied only 40 per cent of total demand, while fuel imports reached 25 per cent of total purchases abroad. These figures illustrate eloquently the paradoxical results of a policy of self-sufficiency and of control over a fundamental resource. Argentina had never been as unprotected from a national defense standpoint as it was at this time. The country became so dependent on foreign fuel supplies that its balance-of-payments situation was greatly affected when oil freight rates jumped suddenly as a consequence of the Suez conflict in 1957.

Though less dramatic than the nationalization of the railroads and petroleum, the other state take-overs had the same kind of consequences. Telephones and transportation — urban, maritime, air, and highway — were also taken over by state enterprises, in a monopoly position in some cases and in competition with private enterprise in others. Many enterprises in the industrial, commercial, and construction fields were confiscated from German owners at the end of World War II and became part of the patrimony of the state. Ports and grain elevators were transferred to the public sector with a noticeable decrease in the efficiency of this very important export service.

In every case the same thing happened. As the personnel increased, particularly the administrative personnel in Buenos Aires, efficiency diminished. The enterprise began losing money, did not pay taxes, and asked the National Treasury for help. Services were neglected. Authority declined and discipline was relaxed. Prices and rates were fixed on a political basis, and private capital was discouraged from entering the field.

The combined effects of all these factors increased the Treasury deficit as expenditures went up and revenues dropped below expectations. The general efficiency of the economy deteriorated, a result intensified by inadequate service and the exclusion of private individuals from activities that they could have handled more responsibly.

The upshot was that the so-called "national recuperation" of basic activities left the Argentine economy more defenseless than ever before against international events — the Suez crisis being an example. Thus, the actual results were precisely the reverse of what was intended. Instead of acquiring a stronger bargaining position through administrative centralization of the main economic activities, the country suffered from a lack of monetary reserves, a rigidity of imports, an inability to obtain financing, and a deterioration in efficiency. State enterprises played a fundamental role in achieving these results.

Planning the Economy

Also derived from marxist and corporative theory was the fashionable view regarding the effectiveness of planning the national economy. The dictatorship successively started two five-year plans (1947-1951 and 1953-1958). In both cases, a great collection of statistics was assembled, and many public works projects were launched without much coherence. In the case of the second five-year plan, the planners undertook to program the main sectors of the economy through the use of all manner of seemingly scientific methods — including input-output techniques and mathematical formulas — that impressed the layman.

Though this policy failed to produce results, it served quite adequately the political objectives of the regime. In an inflationary economy, subject to the three-year cycles of adjustment and expansion that are discussed in the next chapter, any planning measure undertaken would have been risky. And even if that had not been so, it happened that the political needs of the moment had priority over economic goals. Whenever a conflict between a political objective and a long-term economic goal arose, politics got the upper hand.

It should also be pointed out that the promoters of the doctrines that inspired the planners were alike in their aversion to competition and the price mechanism as regulatory forces of the market. They preferred the direct action of the state to the interplay of market forces.

3. Foreign Trade and Exchange Problems

In general, as results turned out to be quite different from those predicted, new doctrinal explanations had to be found so that somebody or something could be blamed for all the failures.

Naturally enough, the external sector posed the most problems as it failed to respond to the objectives of the regime. In spite of renewed controls and ever-more detailed regulations, the country's monetary reserves, which had been practically exhausted during the first three years of the period under examination, were never replenished sufficiently to form a true reserve to protect against setbacks due to climate or to foreign events. Thus, periodic crises took place in foreign exchange.

The Three-Year Cycle

In 1948, monetary reserves had fallen to an extremely low level and the peso had to be devaluated. In 1949, the first crisis took place without any factors other than artificial inflation and erroneous economic policy to account for it. Three years later, following the recovery of monetary equilibrium thanks to good international prices during the Korean conflict, there was a severe drought that practically eliminated all export surplus. The serious recession that followed therefore had some plausible explanation.

Lacking monetary reserves, the country asked for external credits, which were granted by different governments through overdraft authorizations under existing bilateral payment agreements. The crisis of 1949 had also been followed by a refinancing — the first of a long series of such refinancings — granted by the United States Export-Import Bank in the amount of $95 million to pay for obligations incurred by the Central Bank with suppliers in the United States. In 1955, after the dictatorship had fallen, a new devaluation permitted a return to a cost and price reality, and another refinancing for about $500 million by European countries and Japan alleviated somewhat the balance-of-payments problem. The recession, however, was light.

Still another devaluation, combined with a profound reform

of the exchange system, again readjusted inflationary pressures in 1958, and this time there was a pronounced recession. Once again, external debts were refinanced. In 1962, a combination of several circumstances, including another severe drought, made necessary a new adjustment in the relation of the peso to other currencies in order to compensate for the increases in costs and prices which had taken place in the previous three years. A very serious recession followed, and the refinancing of external indebtedness again alleviated the balance-of-payments difficulty.

At the end of 1964, there were again clear signs that the three-year cycle was repeating itself and that another refinancing would be necessary in 1965. The increases in costs and prices, plus the excessive monetary expansion to finance the National Treasury deficit, had created distortions requiring devaluation as a corrective. The usual symptoms had reappeared — the discouragement of exports and encouragement of imports, the flight of capital, and a decrease in international reserves.

With monotonous repetition, the Argentine inflation has generated every three years a crisis in the balance of payments, even though for dissimilar reasons. Only twice — in 1952 and 1962 — were the crises caused by droughts, whose effects could have been counteracted by adequate monetary reserves. On the other occasions, the crises reflected monetary and cost expansions during the previous years, which were factors likewise present in the two crises of agricultural origin.

The short-term external indebtedness, the rigidity of imports as a consequence of a disorganized industrialization, and the lack of confidence for institutional reasons, such as the overthrow of the President in 1962, were concurrent factors in the three-year crises.

Terms of Trade

The cyclical crises inspired diverse doctrinal explanations, among which the theory of the deterioration of the terms of trade must be underlined because of its wide acceptance in political circles. The theory was ennunciated in 1949 by Raúl Prebisch, Secretary of the Economic Commission for Latin America (ECLA), and developed with great detail in the works of this Commission. In a fatalistic manner, the theory explained that the prices of export products of countries producing primary articles had a downward trend, whereas the prices of the goods these countries imported, such as manufactures and capital goods, tended to go up.

Both tendencies were attributed to the different degree of elasticity of the two types of products. Their dissimilar behavior was said to result from the strong negotiating position of the market factors in the industrialized countries, particularly the labor unions whose demands for higher wages affected prices. The exporters of raw materials thus lost their participation in the fruits of technical progress.

According to the theory, the effect of these tendencies led to the so-called external exchange bottlenecks, which could be overcome only through adequate planning to administer meager exchange resources. By the planning process, substitutes for imports could be provided through industrialization, which in turn would absorb the underemployed labor in primary activities.

The theory was certainly ingenious, and it appealed to a common political feeling in Latin America. Monetary reserves accumulated during the war had been lost as a consequence of the massive purchases of products from the industrialized countries as soon as they became available after the war. The scientific value of the theory is disapproved by analyses of the elasticities of the two types of products and by the supply and demand behavior of the different products in international markets, which is not basically different from the behavior of the same products internally within the economy.

The apparently objective quality of the theory, which shifts the responsibility for exchange difficulties, and the fatalistic conclusion that this is a process impossible to correct, served as a convenient explanation of Argentine problems, which in fact were affected only occasionally by the tendencies of prices in international markets. The three-year Argentine crises took place with absolute independence of the tendencies of world prices. But in any event, if there was a conviction that such deterioration in the terms of trade actually exists, greater emphasis should have been given to the rebuilding of monetary reserves. All other economic activities should have been subordinated to this main objective, whereas just the reverse happened.

Economic Structuralism

The method of macro-economic analysis, implicit in the theory of the deterioration of terms of trade, diverts attention away from the most important problems of the economy. The same is true when macro-economic analysis is employed to study the monetary and fiscal problems, using data from the national accounts. The controversy between the so-called "structuralists" and the "monetarists"—a nickname given to those who do not think as the "structuralists" do — has been going on in Argentina for more than a decade. It dramatizes how misleading macro-economic analysis of social accounts can be when applied to practical economic policy and, particularly, to monetary and fisal problems.

The controversy was started by the so-called structuralists, who attempt to solve economic and social problems through changes in structure. There is a noticeable lack of semantic precision, as no clear explanation is given of what is meant by "structure" or of how changes in the structures take place. Such imprecisions usually happen when terms are borrowed from other disciplines, as in the case of "structures," which is an engineering expression.

In fact, the structuralists use very simple monetary tools in formulating or preparing the changes in structure; e.g., exchange controls, multiple exchange rates, monetary expansion to finance the deficit of the National Treasury, and rediscount facilities to take care of the demands of certain sectors or groups.

On the opposite side, the monetarists mainly rely on monetary measures in establishing economic policy, and they usually handle these tools with great care. They are able to introduce basic reforms by limiting monetary expansion, financing public expenditures with real resources, eliminating political tariffs, unifying the exchange market, and eliminating subsidies and similar measures.

A paradox thus has resulted in which the structuralists abuse monetary tools and the monetarists implement structural reforms. This shows that the argument between the two groups is a sterile one, that it has not been posed in its real terms. If things were called by their real names, a controversy of this nature never would have arisen.

Monetarism

Examples of the two policies in action are afforded by the events that began in 1955 and by those that have occurred since October, 1963.

Beginning in 1955, monetarist policies were tried out and produced some very serious reforms in the functioning of the economy. Beginning late in 1955 and continuing through 1959, the exchange market was freed in several stages. As a consequence, economic activities that previously had been isolated behind the bureaucratic curtain of exchange controls gained access to international credit, investment, and know-how.

Moreover, the reasons for the fiscal deficit were attacked at their very roots. In the three years between 1959 and 1962, a total of 200,000 employees were transferred from the public to the private sector. The assistance of the National Treasury to the state enterprises was suspended, and these concerns resorted once more to self-financing with the help of private capital. Political pricing was abandoned. Reforms were initiated involving simplification or elimination of certain taxes and some reducton in tax rates. Thus, through increased revenues, transfer of expenditures to the private sector, private investment and contraction of public expenditures, the national deficit was shrunk to a manageable size between 1959 and 1961.

All the reforms introduced at this time could be called structural ones. However, inasmuch as these reforms were accompanied by a simple restrictive monetary policy, they were blamed for the inevitably painful effects of a transfer of resources between sectors of the economy. The so-called monetary restriction was not a strict one. Nevertheless, when it was relaxed, cost increases and a rising fiscal deficit brought on a new adjustment through devaluation and an unavoidable recession.

A restoration of structuralist theories, as will be described later, has occurred since the shifting tides of politics ushered a new group into power in October, 1963.

Trade Bilateralism

The resurrection of old-type mercantilism reflected in strong self-sufficient tendencies, which had predominated in Europe and the United States since the decade of the 1930's, has had a strong effect on Argentine trade policy in the two decades under review.

The three-year exchange crises starting in 1949 confronted the Argentine authorities with the necessity of adopting corrective measures. Guided by the principle of self-sufficiency, they established exchange controls based on the prohibition of imports and therefore absolute protection for domestic production of prohibited items. This oriented the trade policy of the country towards bilateralism. In support of these commercial practices, new theoretical explanations were advanced that disregarded the principles of comparative costs and of international division of labor.[2]

The practical result of these doctrines, and of the centralized handlings of exchange controls, was the creation of a complex system of bilateral payments agreements with some 25 countries in Europe, South America, and Asia, which also had exchange controls and nonconvertible currencies. In effect, the weak international reserve position of Argentina and the application of self-sufficiency doctrines induced the monetary authorities to associate the country with others that had weak and nonconvertible currencies, instead of attempting to join with nations whose currencies were strong and convertible. The country thus denied itself the benefits of bettering prices for its export products, lowering prices for imported items, strengthening its reserves, and attracting international investment and credit on better terms and conditions. There is no doubt that the country paid a high price, in terms of real resources, for following a bilateral trade policy.

Complicated bilateral payments agreements shaped the machinery of exchange controls. Payments in a unit of account,

---

[2] Advocates of these traditonal principles were charged with sinister international plotting to prevent countries such as Argentina from establishing heavy industry, thereby forcing these countries to devote themselves forever exclusively to agriculture — for which, it just so happened, they were particularly adapted by fertile soils.

almost always in United States dollars, were stipulated, and re- ciprocal credits were granted to cover transactions in import and export products with amounts and prices previously agreed upon.

Placing international trade in such rigid patterns distorted completely the functioning of the market. Argentine importers were forced to buy merchandise where it was not advantageous for them to do so. They had to pay more in foreign currency, but their losses were offset in local currency by taking advantage of preferential exchange rates. Meanwhile, exports continued to flow to the multilateral market through reshipment of products or redirection of cargoes, with negotiations carried out at a loss under the counter. Some particular exporters profited, but the country as a whole lost foreign exchange and producers of export items received less local currency for their exports. The country, in short, was selling cheap and buying dear—transforming into reality the baseless theory of the deterioration of trade terms.

Return to Multilateralism

When the dictatorship fell in September, 1955, the country reverted to multilateralism. Though its weak reserve position hampered Argentina in its attempts to fix a steady course, it was able to re-establish limited multilateralism. This was thanks to the countries of the European Payments Union, which had agreed on a restrictive convertibility of their currencies for payments among themselves and had freed regional trade from exchange obstacles. Argentina became a participant in 1956 in this limited multilateralism of the "Paris Club" through trade and payment agreements and debt consolidation. And when the western European countries returned to full external convertibility of their currencies in December, 1958, Argentina did likewise, re-establishing multilateralism of payments in its trade, without discriminaton against countries of prior convertible currencies. Bilateral payment agreements that were still in existence with countries of eastern Europe and South America were gradually eliminated. Thus, inspired by the sound theory of multilateral trade, with payments in convertible currency, the country was able once again to sell to the highest bidder and buy from the best supplier.

During this period, Argentina gained access to international credit, which had been limited during the era of bilateral trade agreements to medium-term supplier credits, guaranteed by the governments of the exporting countries. Lines of credit from commercial banks, which had been suspended in 1949, were re-established. The country also joined the International Monetary Fund and the International Bank for Reconstruction and Development. In successive stand-by agreements starting in 1957, Argentina drew up to $377.5 million. It also strengthened its monetary reserves by similar agreements with the United States Treasury and other financial entities of the United States government (Development Loan Fund, Export-Import Bank, Agency for International Development) as well as with North American and European commercial banks. The return to multilateralism also permitted the country to have access to credits for investment from international financial entities, such as the Kreditanstalt für Wiederaufbau and the export insurance schemes of European countries and Japan. Private foreign capital likewise began to flow to Argentina once more.

The price paid was high, short-term indebtedness. However, the almost indiscriminate guarantee of private financing by official banks and the granting of medium-term supplier credits generated a massive inflow of foreign funds. This, in turn, brought about the widespread plant re-equipment, as well as the access to more advanced technology, that has increased Argentina's capitalization and productivity in recent years.

4. Distortions in the Domestic Economy

One of the most harmful effects of Peronism resulted from the encouragement that was given to the spread of corporative principles within the labor movement. Where the original aim of unions was to bargain collectively with employers in pursuit of strictly social objectives, the primary goal of the organizations that succeeded them was to uphold the dictatorial regime that had created them and was lending them support. Each economic sector was organized in a labor union. The unions formed federations and at the top of the pyramid was the Confederación General de Trabajadores or CGT (General Confederation of Labor), which obeyed the political objectives of the dictator.

This system took root in two legal principles: the mandatory contribution of each employer to the union and the universal application of the results of collective bargaining on an industry-wide basis. The Labor Ministry granted to one union alone the status of representative of the workers in an industry. A legal system of this nature conveys extraordinary powers to labor unions.

The power of the unions was closely interwoven with the fiscal deficit and the inefficiency of state enterprises, which were overloaded with unnecessary personnel who worked fewer hours on restricted tasks as a result of union regulations. The unions were particularly tough in their dealings with state enterprises, in the knowledge that the employer could ill-afford to split his dual personality and that he was particularly sensitive to political pressure. In contrast with private employers, the state had at its disposal almost unlimited resources to finance fiscal deficits. Paradoxically, then, the unions were more aggressive toward the employer in state enterprises, even though the state itself had given them political power and was the main ruler of the system. Under these conditions, it was only natural for the state enterprises to be particularly vulnerable whenever the Argentine economy was recuperating from one of its three-year crises and reaching an unstable equilibrium.

State enterprises exercised great influence on the national economy, having been the pace-setters in raising salaries and in generating large Treasury deficits. They were constantly seeking subsidies to cover operational losses, additional capital subscriptions, guarantees for external financing, tariff protection to stop the importation of competitive products from abroad, and authority to install a legal price cartel in order to cover up their competitive inefficiency.

Today, Argentine unionism is statist in its concepts, realizing that its political power rests largely on state enterprises. It is also as protectionist as the most marginal producer, for positions and favors are assured in public concerns. It supports easy and selective credits, as a gurantee for the payment of salaries, wages, and bonuses. And finally, it favors multiple exchange rates so as to insure consumer goods and raw materials at cheap prices. As an established political organization, Argentine unionism is quite conservative with respect to past gains, which in war-like terms are called "conquests." It opposes any attempts to improve productivity, change economic activities, substitute machines for labor, or close certain factories in order to open others.

The combination of convenient doctrine and successful political action has worked so effectively that Argentine economic development, both during the dictatorship and in succeeding political regimes, cannot be understood if this factor is not taken into account. Indeed, unionism has been a major factor in the postwar inflation because of its influence on the constant cost and price increases, the fiscal deficit and the way it was financed, and the excessive tariff protection for domestic enterprises.

Urbanization and Its Effects

The growth in the political power of unionism was coincident with other far-reaching social shifts in Argentina. The most significant of these was the massive migration of population to the large urban complexes.

It is estimated that between 4 and 5 million people came from rural to urban areas, from the villages to the cities, from the middle-sized cities to the large cities, and from all over the national territory to the metropolitan concentration of Buenos Aires and its environs. This internal migration occurred between 1945 and 1955, while the total population of the country went up from 15 to 19 million people.

The impact of such a population shift was truly extraordinary. The rural population, settling in the outskirts of the large cities, revealed clear cut symptoms of instability. The change in activity and the new way of life caused unsuspected psychological reactions. At the same time, the long-time residents of the cities, particularly the leading social groups, resented the invasion by strangers of what they considered their own private domain. The social and political tensions of this period were skillfully exploited by the dictatorship, acting with charismatic paternalism and receiving unconditional loyalty in return.

From a strictly economic viewpoint, the massive transfer of so many people in such a short time created complex dislocation. As rural areas became underpopulated, crop production lost ground as contrasted with cattle raising. In the cities, a new demand for light industrial consumer goods and accessory services was generated that could not be met rapidly with articles of simple technology and little capital investment. In the meantime, public services (urban transportation, electricity, telephones, mail and telegraph service, sanitation, streets) deteriorated under the double impact of an explosively growing demand and inadequate supply due to poor administration, excess personnel, short working hours, politically set rates, insufficient capital, and over-all relaxation of work discipline. There was also a serious shortage of housing.

During these years, light industrialization, particularly in the textile and metalurgical fields, achieved an outstanding growth. With easy credit available, created by the Central Bank through rediscounts of the Industrial Credit Bank, the installation and expansion of factories absorbed a good part of the labor force that was job-hunting in the outskirts of the cities. The greatest part of this labor force, however, was employed in the state services that were centrally controlled by the national administration. The number of persons employed by the railroads, social security institutes, aviation and steamship companies, and other state-enterprises grew disproportionately because of the ease with which these could be expanded through deficit financing.

The massive transfer of labor had a deep impact on the Argentine economy. The general productivity of the system declined markedly, and the gains registered by industrial enterprises through the incorporation of modern techniques and adequate management could not offset the lack of productivity resulting from the deterioration of public services and the poor administration by the state. The bottlenecks typical of economies under an acute inflationary pressure appeared. Capital did not go where it was most needed but where it could obtain the greatest yield. Long-term investments in the public service sector and particularly in housing could not be financed adequately. The financial system previously assuring fluid financing for these activities had been destroyed, and the authoritarian measures instituted in its place could not remedy the situation.

As long as the system had a reserve of idle capacity, it could expand. But in a short time the demand for products and services exceeded the supply and the installed capacity. Much the same thing happened in industry, mining, and agriculture. On the other hand, industries that could be amortized rapidly, including luxury services and commercial and professional activities, flourished under an administrative system characterized by tremendous complications and many administrative favors.

Electricity and Transportation

All the factors that have just been discussed came into play with particularly baneful results in two vitally important public sectors—electrical power and transportation.

The supply of energy to metropolitan Buenos Aires and its surroundings was insufficient to satisfy the demand resulting from the explosive growth. The authorities did not permit the re-equipment of obsolete electrical plants or the installation of new facilities for the generation of electricity. Instead, an attempt was made to apply the prescription of an "electrical diet" to Buenos Aires, with the purpose of constraining its growth and promoting expansion in the interior of the country. Moreover, in accordance with the philosophy of not recognizing the profit motive, the authorities fostered the creation of electrical cooperatives of relatively small size instead of granting concessions to companies with abundant capital, as should have been done in large urban centers.

Furthermore, this very doctrine supported the construction of grandiose hydroelectrical stations in places distant from the consuming centers. These plants, because of yields and multiple purposes (energy, irrigation, and water regulation) could only be financed by the state.

The practical result was quite paradoxical. Instead of stimulating the establishment of industries in the interior of the country, more industries were attracted to the metropolitan centers. The new enterprises installed their own generating power, diverting capital to this purpose, which could have been put to better use, and decreasing the over-all productivity of the electrical system on account of the greater efficiency of large plants. The hydroelectrical works took many years to finish—when they were not left in the project stage—as a consequence of the constant lack of public funds for investment, characteristic of the three-year inflationary cycles and the successive changes in the management of the state enterprise charged with implementing the projects.

Next to the electrical power industry, the sector contributing most to the decline of productivity was public transportation. The Argentine economy had depended on railroads as its main means of transportation. The change in administration from private hands to the state had disastrous results for the railroad services. As personnel increased, freight volume came tumbling down, and the attention to the shipper grew progressively worse. Users of the service started losing confidence in the railroads and began transferring freight to highway transportation.

When an automotive industry capable of producing trucks and automobiles was established, the process of shifting traffic from railroads to highway transportation gained additional impetus, and railroad efficiency declined even further. This transfer may have solved some practical problems, but it represented a general lowering of productivity. Railroads are more economical than trucks in a country such as Argentina. But this was disregarded in the political and administrative decisions behind the change.

The resumption in the construction of paved roads in 1960 gave a further advantage to over-the-road hauling. Truckers, who were acutely competitive, were able to render more efficient service than the railroad network. Freight forwarders, consequently, preferred private truckers even though unit rates may have been higher than in the case of the railroads. Security, speed, the ease of door-to-door service compensated for the lower long-distance rail freight rates.

The Pressure on Imports

We have noted the proliferation of new industries that occurred, and it should be noted that these brought about a further distortion not only of the domestic economy but also of imports. The raw materials demanded in ever-increasing quantities and varieties by these newly established industries were usually of foreign origin. In order to import them, preferential exchange rates were obtainable, at a price which was between 20 per cent and 50 per cent of the true value of the foreign exchange.

The unavoidable happened. The pressure for imports brought about a change in the total composition of imports, and raw materials represented close to 60 per cent of the total, rising in relative importance at the expense of consumption goods and machinery imports. Only fuel imports grew at a more rapid pace than raw materials in the composition of imports.

An element of rigidity then appeared in the system. A reduction in imports of consumer goods was no longer possible because these had practically disappeared as a result of import prohibitions. On the other hand, imports of raw materials could only be reduced at the expense of the industrial activity that depended so much on them.

The exchange crisis brought about a rationing of exchange and the granting of quotas for raw material imports. Argentine industrialists, always fearful that their source of supply would dry up, tended to maintain excessive inventories, and the effects of this were intensified by the preferential or overvalued exchange rate used for raw material imports.

The so-called substitution of imports—the ideological justification for the artificial shortages—was not achieved. On the contrary, as an important item disappeared from the list of imports because somebody began producing it in the country, new items demanded by domestic industry appeared on the list.

This explains how Argentina, during those years, was the greatest importer of "palanquilla" in the world. The production of steel remained in the project stage, even though there was sufficient demand to justify it. Besides oil and a very few raw materials, the substitution of imports as a policy does nothing but generate more imports, always under more rigid and costly circumstances.

The New Entrepreneurs

This brings us to the role of private enterprise during the years of the dictatorship. The stifling of initiative had the further unhappy effect of delaying the emergence of a truly skilled and energetic class in Argentina.

There had rarely appeared in Argentina those figures so familiar in nineteenth-century European industrial society — the artisan-turned-entrepeneur or the heir to the manufacturing enterprise. During the period of accelerated industrial development in Argentina, an entrepeneurial class did arise, but it was of commercial or professional origin. Many importers, knowing the product and the market, started to manufacture what they had formerly imported from abroad. The same thing was true of wholesale merchants.

In his approach, the merchant-industrialist differed from the manufacturer, whose basic motivation was to achieve, through continuity of the process, a large volume with relatively small profit margins. The merchant-industrialist, however, was motivated by simple purchase and sale transactions, with no element of continuity or technical innovation. Moreover, the complex and varied state intervention, with all its exchange and supply regulations, prices, quotas, credits, taxes, social burdens, and others, diverted the entrepreneur's attention to bureaucratic and political activities affecting the efficiency of his truly entrepreneurial functions. And the market demand, fed by inflation and protectionism, encouraged him to attend those extra tasks and to postpone his dedication to the truly entrepreneurial ones.

The gradual decline of direct state intervention, starting in 1945, and particularly between 1959 and 1963, as well as the management training courses that were instituted, resulted in a noticeable increase in industrial productivity. Entrepreneurs were finally able to dedicate their efforts, imagination, and talent to technical and administrative innovations, to the incorporation of new methods and production equipment. Thus, they were able to recapture part of the lost time that had been spent in handling paper work, obtaining exchange permits, negotiating credits, or evading the intervention of the state.

5. Readjustments Since Perón

The doctrines that distorted the Argentine economy in the 1945-1955 period still influenced events in the following decade. It is only fair to point out, however, that during the application of the doctrines, there were efforts to counteract their excessively distortionary effects and, above all, to curb monetary deterioration. Particularly between 1952 and 1955, restraints on monetary expansion and cost increases were applied, although they had only a negligible effect. However, in 1954, obliged to choose between political and labor pressure for massive salary increases and monetary stability in a framework of controls, the dictatorship elected to go for salary increases, unchaining a new wave of inflationary pressures which eventually brought about the 1955 devaluation.

Once the dictatorship was overthrown in September, 1955, and there was a free exchange of ideas, the obvious failures of previous measures and the ever-growing needs caused the emergence of several doctrines, that reversed previous courses of action. Inflation had left behind a general frustration, and the country was mentally isolated behind a decade of forced self-sufficiency. While doctrines such as the unavoidable deterioration of terms of trade, and those relating to bilateral trade and planning, still had many adherents, new ideas started to appear. These ideas endorsed a vigorous policy of economic development to promote investment in the basic sectors and in the new industries. They entered forcefully in the political sphere, and the government began to apply them in 1958.

With the introduction of the new ideas, access to short-medium- and long-term credits was re-established, and genuine investments were encouraged through exchange freedom and the return to a single free-rate of exchange. Thus, hidden subsidies on raw materials and fuel disappeared. Moreover, machinery and equipment not manufactured in the country could be imported free of duty.

Fiscal and protectionist duties were imposed on the importation of raw materials and manufactured goods. The impact of this shift in the treatment of capital goods and consumption goods was soon evident in the composition of the imports of the country. In the five years between 1959 and 1963, Argentina imported over $1.6 billion worth of machinery and industrial equipment, whereas the importation of fuel and some raw materials declined.

Insofar as the tax system was concerned, allowances were provided for investments in physical assets over and above normal amortization allowances, for the re-evaluation of assets, and for tax exemption on interest for equipment credits. The strengthening of the financial mechanisms to mobilize savings through the stock exchange, mutual funds, "financieras," savings and loan associations, and underwriting also facilitated the channeling of funds toward productive investments.

Expansion and Modernization

The basic sectors of the economy, formerly neglected or retarded in their development, received direct support from public investment and from private capital and foreign credits.

Oil production, the main bottleneck of the Argentine economy, went up threefold in three years, from about 5 million cubic meters a year to 15 million cubic meters, as a result of new capital and modern methods implicit in the exploitation contracts that were granted. Two gas pipelines, from the north and the south to the coast, increased the transportation capacity from about 1 million to 7½ million cubic meters a day by the end of 1964.

Gas consumption spread rapidly along the coast and in many other regions of the country, benefiting industrial and domestic users generally as well as the petrochemical and fertilizer industries specifically. In a very few years, Argentina occupied the first place in Latin America and the third in the world in gas consumption, with a gas pipeline network surpassed only by the United States and the Soviet Union.

The electric generating capacity in the metropolitan area of Buenos Aires, which had been retarded by application of the "electrical diet" doctrine, was doubled in a few years through the administrative reorganization of the public service enterprises and the abundance of external credit obtained with a sound policy of real rates.

A program of deep administrative reforms in the railroads—after successive re-equipment procured with external credits—reduced drastically the railroad personnel from a maximum of 220 thousand people in 1960 to about 150 thousand in 1962. When the railroads were nationalized in 1947, they employed around 140 thousand persons but carried three times as much freight. Working regulations were modified, ancillary services such as restaurants, printing shops, and others, were turned over to private operators, and obsolete repair shops were shut down. Urban transportation in the city of Buenos Aires and in other cities was transferred to private automotive companies. The last tram cars were eliminated and private transportation contractors were encouraged to establish new fleets of buses and taxi cabs. Only the subway remained in the hands of the state. Nevertheless, the subway deficit was reduced from 8 billion pesos in 1961 to slightly over 550 million in 1963.

Overseas and river shipping were also re-equipped, as well as the fishing fleets, the aviation companies, and the public services, such as sanitation. Other services, however, lagged behind public demand (e.g., post office, telegraph, telephone).

The manufacturing industries took advantage of this opportunity to modernize massively, both from domestic and foreign sources. Numerous new factories were established for the production of automobiles and parts, chemicals and paper, and feed, farm equipment, and insecticides, as well as other items.

The steel industry, which for over three years had been the subject of plans and projects out of which grew only a small steel complex in the northern part of the country, started an expansionary march. With external credits, a complete steel plant was installed on the seaboard. Several private projects for building other integrated steel plants were also initiated. By 1964 the country produced, for the first time in its history, more than 1 million tons of steel, though at a high price because of the excessive protection granted to the industry.

Agricultural Gains

Investment began to flow back to agriculture and cattle raising, hurt by many years of discriminatory exchange treatment and the massive emigration of rural labor. Mechanization made it possible for cultivation to take place at the most opportune moment—right after the rains—and over vast areas. Technological innovations were introduced. For the first time, the hoof-and-mouth disease and other diseases were attacked in a broad and determined fashion, and in a few years most of them were brought under control. The Instituto Nacional de Tecnología Agropecuaria (National Institute of Agricultural Technology), created in 1956 to spread technical knowledge and to assist farmers, gained a prominent role in a few years, and some private groups supported this process of technological innovation.

Forestry, fishing, and poultry farming responded in an extraordinary manner to fiscal and credit incentives, expanding their activities in a way not known before. Fishing and poultry farming in particular increased their total production as a result of the combined affects of investment, technological innovation, and market potential. As the relation between the prices of red and of white meat was reversed, white meats gained in acceptance, for red meats were in short supply and costly, and it was also necessary to fix a quota for exports.

Stagnation in Construction

Until the beginning of inflation in 1944-45, Argentina had always been able to finance its housing needs. The freezing of rents, introduced in 1943 and maintained ever since, has discouraged capital from going into investment for housing. The activities of the Banco Hipotecario Nacional (National Mortgage Bank) replaced private investment and achieved an impact in 1950 and 1951, but were less successful in subsequent years, despite the fact that mortgage loans — financed with special rediscounts from the Central Bank — were granted for 50 years and at reduced interest rates. The social security financed a limited amount of housing for its affiliates with resources derived from contributions. The purely inflationary sources of mortgage credits disappeared in 1959, and the several attempts to revive financing for housing through savings and loan associations, commercial banks, and some external credits, have been unable to offset the negative effects of inflation and frozen rentals.

While the cement industry has doubled its production capacity in the last three years with the expectation of participating in an expanded program of public works, particularly road construction and housing, it has failed to achieve dynamic growth because of the lag in housing. Moreover, an excessive concentration on productive activities, and financing of agriculture and industry, further deprived housing of the necessary resources to expand in accordance with the country's needs, which are estimated to be around a million or more housing units. Construction of luxury housing in the cities and of summer places expanded during the more prosperous periods of the three-year cycles. But the limited number of such dwellings could not make up quantitatively for the lack of construction of popular housing. Moreover, working regulations, declining respect for contractual obligations, and similar factors, lowered substantially the productivity of the construction industry. Technical progress in recent years, through more modern machinery and more rational methods, have been unable to counteract the deterioration in general productivity or the cost-push resulting from the rapid and insecure financing prevailing during inflationary periods.

External Debt

The financing of such an intense investment effort in the short period from 1958 to 1964 forced Argentina into taking on foreign debt at sometimes excessive cost. A succession of poor and normal crops slowed down the country's exports, while international prices for Argentine exports remained at a relatively depressed level. In addition, artificial overvaluation of the peso in the expansive phases of the three-year cycles discouraged possible export activities.

In 1955, when the country reopened its access to international credit and shifted toward an expansionary investment policy, it tapped practically every financing source. Long-term credits flowed in only gradually, as the projects themselves matured and as the international financial agencies (World Bank, Inter-American Development Bank, Export-Import Bank, and others) took care of them with the usual delays and complex negotiations. The country, in the meantime, was obtaining medium-term credit, which was offered by machinery exporters from Europe, the United States, Japan, and Canada. Through the governmental export insurance schemes in these countries, suppliers' credits represented an easy solution to the problem. Both public or private importers were not subjected to the lengthy and tough process of previous feasibility studies, to the preparation of studies of financial sources and flow of funds, or to detailed market analysis. Nor were they required to provide corresponding amounts of counterpart funds or to accept the requirements of international bidding. Such a requisite was frequently omitted so that a direct contract could be handed over to the supplier who was providing the financing.

The country, with no previous experience, went through all kinds of excesses in the financing of its investment needs. Between 1957 and 1961, most of the financing obtained (even for such large works as oil or gas pipelines, power stations, etc.) was for a period of five years or slightly more, with heavy repayments before the project was completed and with most, if not all, of the debt payable at the moment that operations began. Grave errors of programing and decision were thus made. With very few exceptions, it was not until 1961 that long-term credits with reasonable interest rates and lengthy grace periods were obtained.

If the public sector acted with such financial irresponsibility, the private sector did not behave with much greater care. Many industrialists ignored the normal financial channels and ordered equipment and machinery abroad, as long there was financing over a period of years, without taking into account the need of local counterpart money to complement the investments and the expenditures. Furthermore, they also obtained working capital from abroad on a short-term basis, at high interest rates and through bank guarantees. The erroneous financing, combined with overly optimistic calculations and market expectations, had its effect in 1962 and 1963. The resulting recession was severe for the enterprises that had overcommitted themselves, particularly over the short term, in foreign currencies, and they had to face the impact of a devaluation of from 83 pesos to 130 pesos to the United States dollar in just about six months. Meanwhile, the market was narrowing, bank financing as well as external resources for direct financing were disappearing. How painful this process was for many enterprises was clearly indicated by the many bankruptcies and the unemployment that appeared for the first time in the industrial sector.

The deterioration of working capital, characteristic of inflation, combined with a financing situation, which in itself was tense because of excessive investment, created a demand for foreign financing on a short-term basis with bank guarantees, preferably from the Banco Industrial de la República Argentina (Industrial Bank of the Argentine Republic) and the Banco de la Nación Argentina (National Bank of Argentina); i.e., basically from the National Treasury. The recuperation of the country's external credit made easier the procurement of funds from Europe and New York, at extremely high interest rates (sometimes even 12 and 14 per cent in dollars) with bank guarantees. The cost of this "hot" money was prohibitive. When devaluation occurred, the official banks had to meet the heavy credit obligations that they had guaranteed, and which they could not renew as lack of confidence spread through the international financial world following the removal of President Frondizi in March, 1962, the subsequent devaluation, and the uncertain political and financial picture of the country during that year. The Central Bank then prohibited further bank guarantees for direct financing as a measure of monetary prudence, so that the excesses which were committed would not be repeated during the next expansionary phase of the business cycle.

These investment excesses on the part of the public and the private sectors, and the financing through suppliers' credits and guaranteed loans, were the subject of a great deal of criticism. The constitutional authorities, who took over the government on October, 1963, prudently blocked the easy contracting of external debts, although the lack of confidence prevailing in the financial markets of the world also helped to prevent a repetition of the process.

Excessive short-term debt has been one of the accompanying characteristics of the inflationary process during the last twenty years. Ever since the country lost its large monetary reserves and repatriated the long-term debt, short-term, high-interest debt has provided the only answer. Successive refinancing schemes and debt consolidations followed each expansionary phase of the three-year cycles in 1949, 1952, 1956, 1959, and 1962, as well as the cycle that began developing in 1965. However, these have been only temporary breathing spells.

Effects of Wage Pressures

During the last decade under examination, union pressure for wage increases was just about as strong as during the dictatorship. Only in the corrective phases of the cycles were massive salary increases avoided. But the labor organizations retained all their power and were always able to overcome the efforts to prevent wage increases of an inflationary nature.

Added to the obvious need for investments, wage pressures increased the demand for credit, which was satisfied in part through monetary expansion during the upward phases of the cycles and, marginally, with direct financing from abroad.

It must be noted also that wage pressures induced the employers to accelerate the process of substitution of labor, by importing new equipment and machinery whenever permitted. When the recession in 1962-63 ended, labor that had been dismissed was not re-employed as after previous cycles.

Another effect of wage pressures, as well as of the readjustments brought about by massive investments and recurrent devaluations, was the reduction of certain marginal activities and the shutting down of factories that could not withstand competition during the declining phases of the cycles. Two such cases are sugar in Tucuman and the "quebracho" industry.

The Return of Planning and Controls

The demand for orderly planning, with fixed goals for future investments, was intensified by certain negative aspects of the expansion that occurred between 1958 and 1963, particularly by the excessive external debt, by the abuses that occurred in certain public and private investment, and by the violent fluctuations in the business cycle.

Arrears in the payments to public employees and suppliers, accumulated by the National Treasury and state enterprises during the recessive phase of the last cycle of 1962-63, prompted the new authorities to resort to purely inflationary financing from the Central Bank, which had been avoided during the previous period. Moreover, the sentiment for nationalization of public services and basic industries—particularly the extractive ones—arose once more. This change in climate provided the basis for canceling the contracts with the private oil companies that had made oil self-sufficiency possible for the country since 1961. Likewise, the country again turned to controls over supply, prices, and foreign exchange rates, as well as to artificially low rates for public services. The exchange rate was soon overvalued, as had happened in previous expansionary phases of the three-year cycles, and exchange controls created a free market called the "parallel" (or black) market.

At the end of 1964, with the official rate of exchange fixed at 150 pesos to the dollar, the free rate exceeded 200 pesos and in a few months reached 240 pesos. Exports of industrial goods, which had been initiated and had grown vigorously during the 1962-63 period, were suspended and countless traditional exports could only be made at cost or even at a loss. The familiar over-invoicing of imports and under-invoicing of exports reappeared, as well as false declarations of quantity and quality of shipments. Transactions in the black market became common. External credit was not employed to its full availability and foreign investments were discouraged. The policy of investment incentives was abandoned when tax advantages for certain investments were canceled and there was no longer access to international sources of financing. Public services were once again behind in their needs for investment capital, and agriculture suffered an unfavorable tax impact as well as the depressing effect of the dual exchange system. A bumper crop and high export prices hardly offset the real impact of this discrimination against agriculture. Only cattle raising was able to expand, as high prices and direct measures to reduce meat consumption slowed down domestic demand.

Economic structuralism reappeared in its purest expression in the financial area. Complex investment programs for a new five-year program (1965-1969) were formulated by the Consejo

Nacional de Desarrollo (National Development Council) on the basis of structural changes to be attained in the different sectors. Official explanation of the economic policy which was being applied was inspired by the concepts of structuralism and used its terminology.

Just as in the decade of 1945-55, in which similar doctrines prevailed, the fiscal deficit grew once again to hideous proportions. In 1964, the Treasury deficit not covered with genuine resources was the equivalent of one year of imports at the official rate of exchange; it was one of the highest in the world in relation to the population, to gross national product, and to public expenditures. The deficit, which amounted to 188 billion pesos, was financed mainly through the banking system. In consequence, a spectacular monetary expansion took place — from 175 billion pesos in October, 1963, to 271 billion pesos in December, 1964.

This process did not tackle the real causes of the fiscal deficit or monetary expansion. New personnel was hired and fiscal resources were used once again to finance the capital needs of state enterprises and public services. The paradox of structuralism was demonstrated all over again. Instead of bringing about structural reforms, the government policies strengthened existing distortions, and they abused monetary tools through monetary expansion and exchange controls.

The evolutionary cycle of this policy was not completed at the time this paper was written, at the end of 1964. Nevertheless, it could easily be observed that a new exchange crisis at the end of a three-year period again lay ahead, without a real reason for such a development.

Monetary reserves, which had increased in 1963 as a consequence of higher exports and the refinancing of a large part of the external commitments, declined to previous levels and showed a downward trend in spite of an exceptional wheat crop and good international prices for meat. The overvalued peso discouraged exports and encouraged imports. Capital flight and short-term commitments were once again weighing heavily on the exchange picture. A new devaluation appeared unavoidable on account of the forthcoming depletion of monetary reserves, and a new refinancing operation seemed inevitable.

The three-year process was reaching its maturity after the expansionary period, which started at the middle of 1963 and advanced spectacularly during 1964, with an increase of 8.2 per cent in the GNP. There were no bad crops, as in 1952 and 1962, that would explain the end of the cycle. The cause, as in 1949, 1955, and 1958, would appear to be internal monetary expansion and its repercussions on the economic process. Once again, it would seem that a policy of inflationary expansion and fiscal deficits solves no problems and simply makes existing ones worse.

6. Conclusions

1. In twenty years, the Argentine economy assimilated very profound changes in population, technology, and production.

2. Inflation, unchained in 1944-46, could not be controlled during this period in spite of various attempts to curb inflationary pressures and to correct the distortions which were feeding them.

3. The fiscal deficit is the principal cause of inflation.

4. These factors in Argentina's inflation should be given particular attention:

> Excessive protection against competitive imports.
> Intensive intervention by the state in the economy.
> Excessive short-term external debt with official bank guarantees.
> Deficient public administration, particularly in state enterprises.

5. In spite of these factors, the Argentine economy has made noticeable progress in various sectors in terms of productive capacity, production increases, and higher productivity.

6. This progress has not been even for all sectors, and it has occurred during successive three-year crises; it has also been inferior to what has been attained during the same period by countries in a similar stage of development.

7. In order to correct these deficiencies and to redirect the Argentine economy toward orderly growth and a more equitable distribution of income, the following is required:

> Sustained monetary stability.
> Elimination of legal privileges for labor unions.
> Complete elimination of the fiscal deficit.
> Substantial increase of monetary reserves in the Central Bank.

Marked reduction of protection against competitive imports at all levels.

Significant improvement of public administration, particularly of state enterprises and public services.

A reform of the tax system and of the social security system, lower rates, and improved tax-collection procedures.

Encouragement of exports.

Prudent administration of basic investment through moderate incentives and through internal and external financing under appropriate terms and conditions.

KEY FACTORS

IN

CHILEAN

ECONOMIC DEVELOPMENT

Sergio Undurraga Saavedra

The Author

SERGIO UNDURRAGA SAAVEDRA, at the age of 27, has established himself in the fields of both commercial and academic research. He is director of the Research Department of Banco de A. Edwards y Cía, one of the oldest and best-known Chilean banking houses. In his academic role, he is assistant professor of political science at the School of Economics and Administration of the Catholic University in Santiago, where he earned his degree in commercial engineering. He is also a member of the board of directors of the Center for Social and Economic Studies (CESEC).

Key Factors in
Chilean Economic Development / *Sergio Undurraga Saavedra*

Key Factors in Chilean Economic Development

Tables

Appendix Tables

Introduction

The purpose of this study is to analyze some key aspects of Chile's economic development. The sections that follow are concerned with *economic stability* and problems of inflation and governmental intervention; *copper* and its prospects for development, under the new policies; *agriculture* and the main problems it faces; and the effect of *education* upon both economic development and equalization of incomes.

In order to place these subjects within the general context of the country's economic development it is necessary to give a brief review of the basic characteristics of the Chilean economy.

The population of the country is approximately 8.5 million, of which 67 per cent is urban and 33 per cent rural. The labor force has been calculated at 2.6 million. Of this, 78 per cent are men and 22 per cent women. The population distribution by age groups shows a very high percentage of young people—40 per cent are 14 years or younger, 51 per cent are between 15 and 54 years, and only 9 per cent are over 55. A high rate of population growth, a demographic structure in which more than half the people are under 20 years of age, and a labor force that represents only 30 per cent of the total—all these impose a heavy burden on the country's economy.

Political parties are not particularly preoccupied with the population problem, and there is even a widespread view that it is advantageous for the country to support a population considerably larger than the current one. This belief is supported by the limited size of the domestic markets and by the argument that this situation will remedy itself as the population increases. Only in the past few years has there been a recognition of the importance of foreign markets, particularly of the future possibilities offered by the Latin American Free Trade Area (LAFTA).

During 1954-1963, the growth rate of real gross national product (GNP) averaged 3.3 per cent a year and that of real per capita averaged 0.5 per cent (Table 2). These figures show that GNP grows slowly, but nevertheless it does grow, and in recent years the rate of growth has tended to increase. From 1960 to

1963, the growth of real GNP averaged 4.9 per cent, that of real per capita income 2.3 per cent a year, not too far off the annual targets — 5.5 per cent and 3.0 per cent respectively — established in the ten-year Development Plan for 1961 to 1970.

It should be pointed out that growth rates have varied sharply from year to year. In 1964, the increase in real GNP was 3.1 per cent, and real per capita income was 0.3, while in 1965 the figures were 7.1 per cent and 4.1 per cent respectively. The most recent estimates available indicate that these growth rates in GNP and national income were maintained during 1966.

Table 1   **GROSS NATIONAL PRODUCT**
(In 1961 escudos)

	TOTAL IN MILLIONS OF 1961 ESCUDOS	INDEX	PER CAPITA IN 1961 ESCUDOS	INDEX
1940	2,566.0	47.0	507	73.8
1941	2,532.0	46.4	492	71.6
1942	2,662.0	48.8	510	74.2
1943	2,764.0	50.7	522	76.0
1944	2,804.1	51.4	521	75.8
1945	3,067.5	56.2	561	81.7
1946	3,250.8	59.6	584	85.0
1947	3,032.1	55.6	534	77.7
1948	3,415.6	62.6	589	85.7
1949	3,442.2	63.1	583	84.9
1950	3,620.5	66.3	600	87.3
1951	3,813.8	69.9	619	90.1
1952	4,080.7	74.8	647	94.2
1953	4,354.6	79.8	674	98.1
1954	4,325.9	79.3	655	95.3
1955	4,363.1	80.0	645	93.9
1956	4,407.0	80.8	634	92.3
1957	4,785.4	87.7	670	97.5
1958	4,923.6	90.2	671	97.7
1959	4,920.1	90.2	653	95.1
1960	5,286.6	96.9	684	99.6
1961	5,457.0	100.0	687	100.0
1962	5,821.0	106.7	713	103.8
1963	5,948.0	109.0	708	103.1
1964	6,131.0	112.4	710	103.3
1965	6,568.0	120.4	739	107.6

Note: In 1961, one U.S. dollar equalled 1.05 escudos.
Source: 1940-1963 Corfo; 1964-1965 Odeplan.

This increase is corroborated by the figures for domestic income, which according to the National Planning Office rose 7.3 per cent in 1965 and 7.0 per cent in 1966. The changes in the activity of various sectors of the economy can be analyzed by examining the figures for domestic income. These can be seen in Table 3, though only for the years 1958, 1963, and 1965 because of incomplete data.

For the three years under consideration, the components of income have not changed much. Agriculture and construction are the two sectors showing the highest relative changes. Agriculture dropped from 12.6 per cent in 1958 to 9.4 per cent in 1963, recovering slightly in 1965 to 10.4 per cent. Construction rose from 2.8 per cent to 3.8 per cent and declined to 3.4 per cent

Table 2   **ANNUAL VARIATION IN**
GROSS NATIONAL PRODUCT
(In 1961 escudos)

YEAR	TOTAL IN MILLIONS OF 1961 ESCUDOS	INDEX	ANNUAL VARIATION (PER CENT)	PER CAPITA IN 1961 ESCUDOS	INDEX	ANNUAL VARIATION (PER CENT)
1954	4,325.9	79.3	0.6	655	95.3	— 3.1
1955	4,363.1	80.0	0.9	645	93.9	— 1.5
1956	4,407.0	80.8	1.0	634	92.3	— 1.7
1957	4,785.4	87.7	8.5	670	97.5	5.7
1958	4,923.6	90.2	2.9	671	97.7	0.1
1959	4,920.1	90.2	— 0.1	653	95.1	— 2.7
1960	5,286.6	96.9	7.4	684	99.6	4.7
1961	5,457.0	100.0	3.2	687	100.0	0.4
1962	5,821.0	106.7	6.7	713	103.8	3.8
1963	5,948.0	109.0	2.2	708	103.1	— 0.7
1954-63 Average annual rate of change			3.3%			0.5%
1964	6,131.0	112.4	3.1	710	103.3	0.3
1965	6,568.0	120.4	7.1	739	107.6	4.1

in 1965. Among the main components of income, commerce comprised 21.1 per cent of the total in 1958 and 20.3 per cent in 1965. Next in importance are manufacturing industries, with 18.8 per cent in 1958 and 17.6 per cent in 1965.

From the rates of growth of the main sectors, it can be seen the construction has had the highest rate of growth, followed by mining and commerce. The growth of income during the 1958-63 period had an average annual rate of 4.2 per cent for the same period, with only agriculture and manufacturing industries having a lower rate.

Between 1958-1960 the net investment related to total income was slightly over 1 per cent. The year 1960 showed a deficit, and between 1961 and 1963 the rate of investment fluctuated between 5 per cent and 6 per cent. In 1965 it declined to about 5 per cent and almost all net investments were public

Table 3   **INCOME BY SECTORS OF ECONOMIC ACTIVITY**
(In millions of 1961 escudos)

SECTORS	1958	COMPO-SITION PER CENT	1963	COMPO-SITION PER CENT	1965	COMPO-SITION PER CENT
Agriculture	531.9	12.6	475.0	9.4	578.0	10.4
Mining	210.2	5.0	299.0	5.9	391.0	7.0
Manufacturing industries	797.0	18.8	869.0	17.2	975.0	17.6
Construction	119.3	2.8	192.0	3.8	186.0	3.4
Electricity and other services	35.3	0.8	39.0	0.8	66.0	1.2
Transport and communications	305.6	7.2	398.0	7.9	490.0	8.8
Commerce	892.9	21.1	1,123.0	22.3	1,127.0	20.3
Banking and insurance	178.3	4.2	201.0	4.0	186.0	3.4
House rents	351.4	8.3	413.0	8.2	392.0	7.1
Public administration	373.2	8.8	483.0	9.6	572.0	10.3
Services	441.8	10.4	548.0	10.9	585.0	10.5
Total	4,236.9	100.0	5,040.0	100.0	5,548.0	100.0
Adjustments due to changes in terms of trade	− 64.9		+77.0		+ 108.0	
Domestic income	4,172.0		5,117.0		5,656.0	
Adjustments for net income received from abroad	− 49.7		− 113.0		− 123.0	
National income	4,122.3		5,004.0		5,533.0	

ones. We can state without any doubt whatsoever that the low
rate of net investment is one of the main causes of the slow
growth of the Chilean economy.

From 1954 to 1965 the trend in foreign trade was upward.
The increases were not regular or continuous, showing great
differences between one year and another. The peak figure was
26.8 per cent in 1964; the lowest was −8.6 per cent in 1958, as
seen in Table 4.

Table 4   **CHILEAN FOREIGN TRADE**

YEAR	TOTAL FOREIGN TRADE (MILLIONS OF U.S. DOLLARS)	GROWTH RATE (PER CENT)
1954	547.3	......
1955	649.0	18.6
1956	657.8	1.4
1957	687.2	4.5
1958	628.1	− 8.6
1959	730.0	16.2
1960	840.4	15.1
1961	1,003.4	19.4
1962	1,082.0	7.8
1963	991.2	− 8.4
1964	1,257.7	26.8
1965	1,318.8	4.8

For the 1954-62 period, the average rate of cumulative
growth was 7.3 per cent. This figure is much higher than the
average rate of growth for the gross national product during those
years, which was 3.2 per cent.

In these same years, the average figure for exports was
$448,000,000, this level being a rather stationary one. On the
other hand, imports averaged $473,500,000, showing an upward
trend. Thus, the commercial balance tended to the deficit side,
as seen in Table 5. This deficit was covered mainly by transfers
of capital and other compensatory accounts.

The total volume of Chilean foreign exchange has increased
during the last ten years in spite of government policy to try to
maintain the escudo at too high a value in relation to other currencies. This policy has clearly been harmful to exports and

Table 5

BALANCE OF PAYMENTS
(In millions of U.S. dollars)

	1954		1955		1956		1957		1958		1959	
	CREDIT	DEBIT	CREDIT	DEBIT	CREDIT	DEBIT	CREDIT	DEBIT	CREDIT	DEBIT	CREDIT	DEBIT
VISIBLE FOREIGN TRADE	383.4	348.7	489.4	394.7	497.9	390.2	403.8	473.4	358.0	427.1	457.8	426.2
Exports	383.4	.....	489.4	.....	497.9	.....	403.8	.....	358.0	.....	457.8	.....
Imports	.....	348.7	.....	394.7	.....	390.2	.....	473.4	.....	427.1	.....	426.2
INVISIBLE FOREIGN TRADE	37.6	45.8	46.0	50.6	46.9	60.9	54.6	48.4	77.0	41.5	69.7	48.0
Servicing of goods	24.5	23.4	29.1	29.1	24.9	22.9	23.0	18.7	20.0	16.5	18.1	18.5
Others	13.1	22.4	16.9	21.5	22.0	38.0	31.6	29.7	57.0	25.0	51.6	29.5
CAPITAL FLOW AND SERVICING	84.6	127.8	94.7	167.4	78.7	169.7	115.4	127.3	136.0	128.6	121.7	175.2
Flow of capital	84.6	83.5	92.5	86.6	78.7	71.4	115.4	72.2	136.0	81.6	121.7	97.2
Servicing of capital	.....	44.3	2.2	80.8	.....	98.3	.....	55.1	.....	47.0	.....	78.0
COMPENSATORY ACCOUNTS	26.6	25.0	10.0	36.3	34.3	24.5	113.4	23.4	38.8	30.9	63.2	80.6
Commercial banks	9.5	.....	.....	2.9	5.0	.....	8.0	.....	0.2	6.6	28.9	1.4
Central Bank	0.5	8.2	2.7	.....	14.3	0.8	17.3	0.5	2.6	10.7	33.5	79.2
Others	16.6	16.8	7.3	33.4	15.0	23.7	88.1	22.9	36.0	13.3	0.8	.....
TOTAL	532.2	547.3	640.1	649.0	657.8	645.3	687.2	672.5	609.8	628.1	712.4	730.0
UNITEMIZED BALANCE	15.1	.....	8.9	.....	.....	12.5	.....	14.7	18.3	.....	17.6	.....
GRAND TOTAL	547.3	547.3	649.0	649.0	657.8	657.8	687.2	687.2	628.1	628.1	730.0	730.0

	1960		1961		1962		1963		1964		1965	
	CREDIT	DEBIT	CREDIT	DEBIT	CREDIT	DEBIT	CREDIT	DEBIT	CREDIT	DEBIT	CREDIT	DEBIT
VISIBLE FOREIGN TRADE	464.2	553.0	447.2	614.4	488.8	549.2	489.9	558.1	590.4	623.5	688.9	626.9
Exports	464.2		447.2		488.8		489.9		589.0		678.9	
Imports		553.0		614.4		549.2		558.1		623.5		626.9
INVISIBLE FOREIGN TRADE	129.5	106.2	114.2	115.3	106.8	98.6	97.2	107.9	104.5	100.6	105.5	98.6
Servicing of goods	23.9	19.5	30.4	37.4	33.1	28.6	43.9	44.1	41.5	34.9	44.2	36.2
Others	105.6	86.7	83.8	77.9	73.6	70.0	53.3	63.8	63.0	65.7	61.3	62.4
CAPITAL FLOW AND SERVICING	131.9	146.6	284.8	200.8	379.6	358.5	287.3	270.8	387.7	339.9	371.5	419.1
Flow of capital	131.9	71.3	284.8	123.5	379.6	268.3	287.3	180.8	387.7	236.5	371.5	292.9
Servicing of capital		75.3		77.3		90.2		90.0		103.4		126.2
COMPENSATORY ACCOUNTS	78.7	34.6	157.2	22.3	106.8	35.9	83.9	54.4	166.0	188.7	114.7	174.2
Commercial banks	6.2	6.9	17.8	3.4	51.9	2.7	11.5	11.5	0.1	4.9	1.3	16.9
Central Bank	72.5	27.4	136.6	18.9	53.0	33.2	72.4	42.8	163.3	183.8	113.4	153.4
Others		0.3	2.8		1.9			0.1	2.6			3.9
TOTAL	804.3	840.4	1,003.4	952.8	1,082.0	1,042.2	958.3	991.2	1,248.6	1,252.7	1,280.6	1,318.8
UNITEMIZED BALANCE	36.1			50.6		39.8	32.9		4.1		38.2	
GRAND TOTAL	840.4	840.4	1,003.4	1,003.4	1,082.0	1,082.0	991.2	991.2	1,252.7	1,252.7	1,318.8	1,138.8

beneficial to imports. This higher exchange activity has been possible mainly because of foreign loans obtained by Chile, the most important of which have been loans through the Agency for International Development.

Minerals comprise 85 per cent of Chilean exports. Copper occupies first place, followed by iron and nitrates. Mineral exports have been preponderant in spite of efforts toward diversification, though cellulose, paper, copper products, and fisheries give hope of offering considerable possibilities in the near future.

Table 6   **NATIONAL INCOME**
(In 1961 escudos)

	TOTAL IN MILLIONS OF 1961 ESCUDOS	INDEX	PER CAPITA IN 1961 ESCUDOS	INDEX
1940	2,179.9	48.7	431	76.4
1941	2,169.1	48.4	421	74.6
1942	2,298.5	51.3	440	78.0
1943	2,423.1	54.1	457	81.0
1944	2,426.0	54.2	451	79.9
1945	2,694.9	60.2	493	87.4
1946	2,829.8	63.2	508	90.1
1947	2,672.7	59.7	471	83.5
1948	2,881.9	64.3	497	88.1
1949	2,950.0	65.8	500	88.7
1950	3,135.6	70.0	520	92.2
1951	3,255.5	72.7	529	93.8
1952	3,509.6	78.3	557	98.8
1953	3,789.2	84.6	587	104.1
1954	3,741.7	83.5	566	100.4
1955	3,603.3	80.4	532	94.3
1956	3,813.6	85.1	549	97.3
1957	4,140.4	92.4	580	102.8
1958	4,122.3	92.0	562	99.6
1959	4,254.2	95.0	565	100.2
1960	4,195.1	93.6	543	96.3
1961	4,480.0	100.0	564	100.0
1962	4,837.0	108.0	592	105.0
1963	5,004.0	111.7	596	105.7
1964	5,203.0	116.1	602	104.8
1965	5,533.0	123.5	623	110.5

Note: In 1961, one U.S. dollar equalled 1.05 escudos.
Source: 1940-1963 Corfo; 1964-1965 Odeplan.

1. Elements of Economic Stability

Chile's long democratic tradition, which is very nearly unique in South America, has also given the country a considerable institutional stability. Nevertheless, this has not been translated into economic stability. On the contrary, the internal conditions of the economy are influenced by a high degree of governmental intervention, by an erratic economic policy, and by a continuous inflation. These three factors have had a negative influence on economic development. Their consequence has been economic instability, creating an atmosphere of uncertainty in business and impeding long-range planning.

The key factor to this situation is the country's long inflation, which began in the second half of the nineteenth century, but which had no serious effects until the nitrate crisis. This crisis started during the 1920's with the commercial development of synthetic nitrates, which took the market away from natural nitrate. Chile experienced a decline in international trade and unemployment that extended to every sector of the economy. This situation was made worse by the international crisis of the 1930's, and as the situation became desperate, the country abandoned the gold standard, sought to use inflation as a means of overcoming unemployment, and imposed tariffs to protect national industrialization. From 1932 to 1939 the country succeeded in recovering monetary stability and in making a strong comeback. Nevertheless, during the 1940's inflation returned and, with varying rates, it has continued until the present day.

Table 7 shows the permanent character of the inflationary process during the last quarter century. The years 1953 to 1955 stand out as those of greatest inflation and the years 1960 to 1961 as those of relative stability.

For the last 25 years, inflation has fluctuated between a minimum rate of 5.4 per cent and a maximum rate of 83.8 per cent a year. The average annual rate of inflation since 1940 has been 29 per cent.

As elsewhere in the world, inflation in Chile is associated with internal monetary expansion. The supply of money in 1940 was 3.2 million escudos; in 1964 it amounted to 1,476.1 million

Table 7 **ANNUAL VARIATION IN THE CONSUMER PRICE INDEX**

YEAR	ANNUAL VARIATION	YEAR	ANNUAL VARIATION
1941	22.7%	1954	71.2%
1942	25.6	1955	83.8
1943	7.9	1956	37.7
1944	15.2	1957	17.3
1945	7.8	1958	32.5
1946	29.9	1959	33.3
1947	14.9	1960	5.4
1948	16.9	1961	9.7
1949	20.5	1962	27.7
1950	16.8	1963	45.3
1951	23.2	1964	38.4
1952	12.1	1965	25.9
1953	56.1	1966	17.0

— more than 400 times the original quantity.[1] In this same period money devaluated by approximately 300 times. Between 1950 and 1960 the supply of money increased by an average of 35.9 per cent, and for this same period the consumer price index increased by an average of 35 per cent per year.

The Christian Democratic government of President Eduardo Frei, who was elected to office in 1964, introduced a policy of gradual containment of inflationary forces based on a firm hand with foreign exchange and a strict price control. In 1964 inflation reached 38.4 per cent yearly, but with the new policy it has declined to 25.9 per cent in 1965 and 17.0 per cent in 1966. For 1967 the program contemplates a further reduction to about 12.0 per cent.

Since this inflation and supply-of-money phenomenon is well known, it is important to analyze the factors that have made such an extraordinary monetary expansion possible in Chile's case.

Pressure for an increased supply of money has come from:

• Fiscal budgetary deficits;

---

[1] See Appendix Table A.

- Demands from the private sector for a greater quantity of bank credits;
- Demands from the labor force for general wage increases, thereby making an increase in the money supply necessary to prevent unemployment.

Furthermore, as a result of faulty international trade policies (mainly regarding exchange rates), there have been at times shortages of imported raw materials affecting supply in many industries. Additionally, because of excess tariffs, monopoly exists in several productive sectors. Internal production therefore does not respond to increased demand, the adjustment instead being obtained through a rise in prices.

It must be noted that during the period under consideration, the Chilean economy has permanently been in a full-employment situation or near this level. What unemployment there is has been of a local type, the effect of which has not extended to the rest of the economy. For this reason, the result of the monetary expansion has been permanent rises in the price level.

In foreign trade a certain rigidity prevails. If such a condition is eliminated and resources, particularly labor, are mobilized, problems of unemployment and under-utilization of industrial capacity should find a solution.

Fiscal Deficits

Fiscal deficits are one of the main causes of the inflationary process. The growth of population, the involvement of more people in the political process, the development of education, the increase in the middle class, etc., all have brought strong pressures for a higher standard of living. The voters have been partial to those political parties favoring effective governmental participation in economic activity, not only by means of indirect policies, but preferably through direct measures such as price fixing and the creation of industries. Along with this, the more liberal parties have also backed health and education programs and the construction of roads and irrigation systems. As a consequence, the pressure for public expenditure has been extraordinary. But without the necessary resources, the state has had to resort to external credits and to the internal creation of money. On the other hand, the efforts of some governments to maintain a balanced budget have been frustrated by Parliament, which having initiative in public expenditures, has independently proposed wage readjustments, and subsidies, thus helping to create or increase the fiscal deficit.

It is worth while noting that during the 1940's, the right-wing parties, defending private enterprise and a free economy, had a representation in Parliament of approximately 40 per cent. Little by little they have been losing their strength until in the recently held elections they obtained less than 10 per cent of the elected seats. This means that the center of gravity of Chilean politics is moving to the left, promoting a greater intervention of government and even its direct participation as owner or partner of the country's principal industries.

In this way, the weight of the public sector in the national economy is becoming increasingly great. In 1940 the fiscal budget represented 14.3 per cent of the gross national product. In 1961 this figure was 19.3 per cent, and in 1965 it was estimated to be 23 per cent. To this direct participation must be added the state enterprises, which are not classified in the fiscal budget, forming a decentralized sector that at the present moment represents 40 per cent of public expenditure. In 1940 this decentralized sector was very small but grew rapidly with the creation of enterprises and special services by the state. At the present moment, a reasonable estimate would put state participation at about 35 per cent of GNP. This already high share will be increased by the nationalization of copper mines, telephone systems, and electricity, sectors in which the government has bought enterprises or has associated with established private capital in making new investments.

On the other hand, social security expenditures represent approximately 10 per cent of the national product, and though these expenditures represent income transfers among individuals, they are controlled by the government and they represent an important part of wages. All of this indicates the extraordinarily high degree of direct control of the country's resources exerted by the government — now approximately 50 per cent, probably double the 1940 figure.

The most important element in monetary imbalances during the past few years has undoubtedly been the fiscal deficit. For the period 1940-1950, the fiscal deficit represented 10 per cent of the national budget. In the 1950-1960 decade the figure rose to approximately 20 per cent. To counteract such a situation, the government had to resort to foreign credit on top of its traditional indebtedness to the Central Bank, its permanent source of money.

The following table shows some basic budget figures covering the last seven years:

Table 8   **GOVERNMENT OUTLAYS, REVENUE AND DEBT**
(In 1960 escudos[a])

MILLIONS OF ESCUDOS	1960	1961	1962	1963	1964	1965	1966
Government Outlays							
Current expenditures	636	662	735	666	679	778	873
Investments	267	281	303	332	313	415	443
TOTAL	903	943	1.038	998	992	1.193	1.316
Government Income							
Revenue	708	739	781	765	789	971	1.061
Indebtedness	195	204	257	233	203	222	255
TOTAL	903	943	1.038	998	992	1.193	1.316

INDEX

	1960	1961	1962	1963	1964	1965	1966
Government Outlays							
Current expenditures	100	104.1	115.6	105.0	106.8	122.3	137.3
Investments	100	105.2	113.4	124.3	117.2	155.4	165.9
TOTAL	100	104.4	115.0	110.5	109.9	132.1	145.7
Government Income							
Revenue	100	104.3	110.3	108.1	111.4	137.1	149.9
Indebtedness	100	104.6	131.8	119.4	104.1	113.8	130.8
TOTAL	100	104.4	115.0	110.5	109.9	132.1	145.7

[a] In 1960 the U. S. dollar was worth 1.05 escudos, so figures are roughly equivalent to millions of dollars.
Source: *Exposiciones de la Hacienda Pública, 1960-65.*

It is interesting to note that the level of total annual government outlays increased 10 per cent between 1960 and 1964, then jumped by more than 30 per cent between 1964 and 1966. This big increase was due to the rise in fiscal revenues resulting from higher taxes and better copper prices. In spite of higher revenues, however, the level of annual indebtedness also grew substantially between 1964 and 1966. As foreign sources of credit could not cover the total deficit, the Central Bank was obliged to buy an additional quantity of bonds which in turn increased the supply of money.

Such a process is an obstacle to a truly anti-inflationary policy. Nevertheless, it is gratifying to note that at least investments have grown faster than current expenses.

Credit Policy

The private sector has also caused pressures toward increases in the supply of money, especially during the last decade, by trying to obtain more credits.

To the extent that the inflationary process became permanent, money lost one of its main roles, i.e., as a standard measure of value. As typically happens during an inflationary process, keeping liquid assets in banks becomes unattractive. Thus, the only approximate way of measuring liquid holdings is through the increase in the money velocity of circulation. In 1932 the estimated velocity of circulation in commercial banks was approximately 1.24; in 1940 it had increased to 1.58; in the second half of 1957 to 3.96 and in the second half of 1966 it was estimated to be 2.64. This acceleration in the circulation of money, doubling or even tripling during some periods the velocity that existed during a stable period such as 1932-1938, clearly indicates how people and institutions try to keep their monetary balances down to a minimum. This does not even take into account the increase of income in the last 30 years.[2]

For these reasons, enterprises reduced to a minimum their circulating capital and their money assets, while increasing their stocks of goods and raw materials or transforming them into some other type of assets that will save them from devaluation.

_____
[2] See Appendix Table B.

At the same time, it became much easier to resort to bank loans, which, because of inflation over long periods, have had negative real rates of interest. In fact, while the average rate of inflation has been around 30 per cent, the average rates of interest have fluctuated between 10.4 per cent and 17 per cent. Thus, one can easily imagine the great pressure exerted on banks by the private sector.[3]

However, notwithstanding the great increments in the supply of money, credit in real terms increased very little between 1940 and 1960.[4] Furthermore, in some periods — notably during the very steep inflation of 1954 to 1959 — credit diminished in real terms. It must be noted that in this same period national product was doubled. In 1940, the total credit loaned by the banking system amounted to 1 billion escudos, and in 1960 the quantity was 1.2 billion escudos (in both instances measured by the value of the escudo in 1964); that is, in 20 years there was no change in the amount of credit. Indeed, between 1954 and 1958, the amount of credit actually went down, reaching 700 thousand escudos in 1955 and 1956, or a decrease of 30 per cent as compared with the 1940's.

Since 1960 there has been an expansion in the amount of credit in real terms, though this expansion has not been great. Total credit was 1.2 billion escudos in 1960, 1.4 billion in 1964, and 1.6 in 1965, with no increase in 1966 (these figures are given in 1964 escudos). Such increases are extremely small if measured against the increases in national product of 7.3 per cent in 1965 and 7.0 per cent in 1966.

It should be pointed out that money in circulation increased 52.5 per cent in 1965 and 47.6 per cent in 1966. These inflationary increases were compensated, in part, by a restrictive credit policy. The Central Bank obliged other banks to increase their legal reserves up to 75 per cent of current deposits and 30 per cent on term deposits.

This type of monetary policy is aimed at balancing the national budget by trying to constrain as much as possible the

---

[3] See Appendix Table C.
[4] See Appendix Table D.

elasticity of the means of payment available to the banking system. Furthermore, the Central Bank deemed it necessary to take steps to regulate banking activities, first, in order to exert greater control over credit and, second, to reduce bank liquidity to force the private sector to increase its currency demands. Thus, the inflationary effects of issuing new bank notes were partially absorbed.

However, though the inflationary process was kept in check, the private sector found itself in a difficult situation due to lack of liquidity and credit facilities: banking transactions were much more difficult and long-term absorption of large amounts of new money constituted a very serious problem.

Businessmen's constant complaints about lack of credit can easily be understood. But unfortunately, they have never thoroughly comprehended that credit expansion obtained through money creation will not result in the end in a greater amount of credit in real terms. Rather, it directly contributes to an acceleration of the existent inflation. In fact, the nominal expansion of credit has been great, inflation keeping it down in real terms.

As a result of businessmen's pressures on banks for more credit, commercial banks asked for resources from the Central Bank. Up to 1960, the Central Bank authorized ample rediscounts at lower rates of interest than those exacted by commercial banks. Since then it has become standard practice for the Central Bank to make special loans to cover the private banks' chronic reserve deficits. In 1965, the rediscount will be restored according to the standards in monetary policy established by the new government. The Central Bank also loans money directly to the private sector, this being another source of money creation.

Labor Policy

In Chile, together with the inflationary process, there have been a rising cultural level, a rapid process of urbanization, and other social changes that have created strong aspirations for higher standards of living. This creates pressures from laborers, who try to obtain substantial increases, or where their demands are reasonable, try to maintain their wages in real terms.

As a consequence of this, an automatic wage readjustment system has been established. Since wage increases push up costs, they create a liquidity problem for firms, which have to ask for credit from banks. In addition, it is obvious that cost increments tend to translate into higher prices. Automatic readjustments were abolished in 1956, but they were re-established in 1961.

However, despite these automatic readjustments, there has been a considerable fluctuation in the real value of wages, as shown by the following Table:

Table 9   **"SUELDO VITAL" (MINIMUM MONTHLY LEGAL SALARY) IN SANTIAGO**

YEAR	CURRENT ESCUDOS	IN 1964 ESCUDOS	YEAR	CURRENT ESCUDOS	IN 1964 ESCUDOS
1940	0.460	143.5	1953	7.550	201.1
1941	0.600	152.4	1954	11.600	170.5
1942	0.815	164.6	1955	18.400	155.8
1943	1.050	196.5	1956	26.956	165.8
1944	1.185	192.8	1957	35.086	184.0
1945	1.320	199.2	1958	42.103	166.6
1946	1.470	170.8	1959	57.550	172.1
1947	1.995	188.5	1960[a]	......	......
1948	2.400	194.1	1961	77.170	198.2
1949	3.040	203.8	1962	80.910	162.8
1950	3.800	218.3	1963	103.320	143.0
1951	4.670	217.7	1964	150.230	150.2
1952	6.070	252.4	1965	207.920	161.4
......	......	......	1966	261.720	165.4

[a] None established for 1960.

Editor's Note: In December of 1959, Chile replaced the peso with the escudo, with a fixed rate at that time of 1.049 escudos (1,049 pesos) to the U. S. dollar.

Table 9 represents the minimum earnings for all employees; once established, the *sueldo vital* is used as a basic unit in all labor contracts. In Chile it is very common to refer to "x number of *sueldos vitales.*" Even income taxes are calculated on the number of *sueldos vitales* earned during the year. The table indicates real and nominal values and shows the fluctuations in real terms. These happen partly through delaying or advancing adjustments of the *sueldo vital* to the cost of living index.

Unfortunately there is no adequate wage index, but previous studies seem to indicate that real increments in wages were due to sectoral productivity increments and not to periodic wage readjustments.

It must nevertheless be emphasized that, in real terms, there is no concrete data to show that through the years inflation has contributed to a decrease in workers' wages, or that certain sectors have suffered particularly because government control was stronger in such sectors. Labor's losses occur when the increment in salaries is lower than price increases, due to a time lag between the salary adjustment and the increase in prices. On the other hand, this has been compensated for by adjustments higher than the cost of living.

The Market for Stocks and Bonds

Inflation's principal effects act in such a way that they tend to make this a permanent phenomenon, creating negative influences on economic development and increasing economic instability. This produces a vicious circle in which it is difficult to distinguish between the factors whch are a consequence of inflation and those which contribute to giving permanence to this phenomenon.

We have already mentioned how inflation has reduced individual incentive for holding money. This implies the destruction of one of the most common ways of saving; namely, holding savings in the form of money, which has particular importance in countries such as Chile where other financial mechanisms are very little developed.

It is well known that an economy's quick development needs a growing supply of savings. Permanent inflation keeps saving down, for it increases the tendency to consume. It also destroys an easy way of saving (especially for the middle class) which at once preserves the real value of savings, yields an adequate return, and guarantees liquidity. Bank deposits and bonds are the most common form of saving for the general public where such conditions are found; but as we said above, inflation practically eliminates these savings methods from a capital market's development.

An example of this phenomenon is the one produced in the transaction of bonds in Santiago's Stock Exchange, as seen in Appendix Table E. These figures show that between 1940-1945 there existed a relatively good market for government or industrial bonds. From 1945 onwards there was a constant decrease in the demand for this type of assets. In 1960, due to expectations of stability there was an increase of demand for bonds, though real demand was only 10 per cent of what it was 15 years before. In 1964, it was only 2 per cent of what it was 20 years before. The bond market has continued to decline, reaching extraordinarily low levels.

These two factors — the tendency not to maintain monetary balances, causing a stagnation of bank credits in real terms, and the disappearance of the bond market — have caused the elimination of medium- or long-term loans. This has hindered the development of efficient industries and, consequently the rapid expansion of supply in some sectors.

The distortions caused by inflation permanently alter the stock market, feeding speculative tendencies and creating a lack of confidence in investors. Furthermore, due to the constant currency devaluation, balance sheets do not reflect businesses' true situation, sometimes overestimating profits and concealing real capital losses. Such being the situation, the stock exchange has lost attractiveness as a center of investment. In addition, the constant increase in taxes has diminished capital's net profits. All of these have brought about decreasing stock exchange activity during the past quarter of a century.

Table 10 **TOTAL VALUE OF TRANSACTIONS ON THE SANTIAGO STOCK EXCHANGE**
(In thousands of 1964 escudos)

HIGHEST YEARS		LOWEST YEARS	
1940	220,781	1960	66,867
1941	519,815	1961	56,092
1943	315,305	1962	71,015
1952	278,693	1965	91,344
1955	377,560	1966	46,204

Table 10 shows the years of greatest and least activity, as measured by the value of transaction on the Santiago exchange since 1940[5] The years of greatest activity were 1940 to 1943, followed by a decline. From 1951 to 1955, a period of great inflation, the value of stock traded recovered considerably, but in 1960 there was a sharp decline. There has been another sharp decline in the past two years. Transactions on the exchange fell from 99.8 million escudos in 1964 to 91.3 million in 1965 and then slumped to 46.2 million in 1966. The index for nominal value of shares went from 129 in November 1964 to 100 in November 1966. For the same period, the price index rose from 436 to 664.

In 1961, mutual funds began to develop as a means of stimulating savings in stocks. These funds have had a rapid development, attracting approximately 40 million escudos by 1964. This represented in 1964 approximately 30 per cent of stock exchange transactions, and helped to prevent a greater decline in the stock exchange. But with stock exchange operations reduced by half in real terms over the past couple of years, mutual fund transactions have been virtually paralyzed.

Adjustable Savings

With the object of creating institutions able to attract popular savings by freeing them from inflation's evils, there have been attempts to establish institutions which would offer adjustable savings accounts and medium- and long-term loans that are also adjustable.

Table 11   **NET BALANCES ACCUMULATED BY CORVI AND SAVINGS ASSOCIATIONS**
(In thousands of 1964 escudos)

YEAR	CORVI	SAVING ASSOC.	TOTAL
1961	44,880	7,319	52,199
1962	41,649	43,387	85,036
1963	33,887	103,150	137,037
1964	69,706	155,667	225,373
1965	65,728	231,272	297,000
1966	42,324[a]	326,542	368,866

[a] CORVI data for the first eight months only.
[5] See Appendix Table F.

Credit and savings associations began their activities in 1961. Like CORVI (Dwelling House Corporation), these associations loan money for house construction, and they have attracted a considerable amount of deposits.

This many-fold increase shows that by creating an adequate means of protecting savings from money devaluation, it is possible to obtain considerable resources for investment. Adjustable savings have become the focus for mass-saving. They increased from 225 million escudos in 1964 to more than 368 million in 1966. Furthermore, the Banco del Estado (State Bank) was especially authorized in 1965 to accept adjustable savings deposits. This was a great incentive to small depositors. Such authorization has not yet been given to private banks.

Chilean industry lacks adequate sources of medium- and long-term credits. The existing sources are governmental — the most important being the Corporación de Fomento and the Banco del Estado — and the funds available are insufficient.

The success obtained with savings associations showed that the country had a potential capacity for capital creation that had not been noticed before due to the lack of the adequate means of savings. This caused businessmen and government to bring about creation of development banks to offer medium- and long-term credit for industrial development through the issuance of adjustable bonds. A law authorizing development banks to do this was passed in 1965. But in spite of great interest shown by a large number of foreign as well as Chilean bankers and investors, development banks have not prospered due to political difficulties; the Christian Democrats insist that these institutions be public ones.

As a consequence of the financial problems of the country, the private sector has been going more and more to foreign capital markets. The figures for 1962 through 1964 are $333.2 million, $394.6 million and $480.3 million respectively.

Other Aspects of Inflation

Among the evils of inflation are some well known phenomena that are difficult to evaluate quantitatively but which strike at the very heart of a market economy. Inflation sets up irrational patterns of consumption. Constant price increases spur people to buy before prices rise again without comparing current prices of different goods. Consumption increases without discrimination while competition — especially among retailers of consumer goods — tends to flag.

Inflation also distorts the utilization of resources. There is an expansion of speculative activity. This can be seen particularly in the great quantity of land bought not to be worked but to keep capital from devaluating.

As inflation brought many social problems and great discontent to laborers, adherents of state intervention proposed halting the inflationary process by means of direct measures such as price-fixing, discriminatory tariffs on imports, subsidies, selective credit, etc. This type of policy prevailed for a large part of the period under discussion. The efforts made to hold down public expenditures, to finance the fiscal budget, or to improve the monetary system were sporadic, and political and social pressures prevented their continuance for a period long enough to demonstrate their effectiveness. To advance direct systems of control, legal mechanisms were established to permit total governmental intervention in the economy.

The most important areas of governmental intervention thus have been in price controls and foreign trade controls. Price controls were intensified in 1965-1966 as a means to reduce inflation.

In 1965, to keep the inflationary rate down to 25 per cent annually, the Frei Administration decided that nonagricultural prices should increase 19 per cent at maximum. This meant — in accordance with the Finance Ministry's estimates — during a period when inflation was 25 per cent, urban entrepreneurs' profits (nonagricultural) could not exceed 10 per cent for the year. This amounted to a reduction of the purchasing power and income levels of those sectors with capital. In effect, the government was demanding this sacrifice of them to curb inflation.

In 1966 the administration's stabilization goal was a 15 per cent price increase. To this end, prices of manufactures could rise 13 per cent or 14 per cent maximum, and agricultural prices 17 per cent to 18 per cent. Given the conditions mentioned, the government concluded that there would be no real profit increases in relation to the previous year if production and productivity did not increase.

We have indicated that labor had pressed for higher standards of living and fought for salary adjustments. Such constant demands have given a permanent character to the inflationary spiral. In 1965 and 1966 the government was in favor of higher wages and salaries as a means of quick redistribution of income. In 1965 the wages and salaries index increased 45.8 per cent, while inflation for that period was 25.9 per cent. In 1966 salaries increased 36.2 per cent and inflation 17.0 per cent.

Salary increases in real terms and strict price control were possible partly because of greater production and partly because of smaller returns for private enterprise. It is true that the financial situation of business concerns did not suffer greatly, but they had to face serious cash problems, for when salaries were increased, prices and credit were also strictly controlled.

Greater expenditures resulting from redistribution of income and greater public expenditures contributed to a remarkable expansion of demand, particularly of manufactures, with the result that the pace of economic activity was accelerated. Nevertheless, the impact of all these measures on private investment cannot be clearly ascertained. Investers received small profits and had to face uncertainties due to drastic changes in various sectors of the economy. During the same period, greater public investment had balanced reductions in the private sector. In general, the inflationary process has been slowed, but some of its ill effects persist or pose even more serious threats.

As far as the impact of this policy on employment is concerned, the result is relatively unfavorable. In June 1964 unemployment was approximately 3.8 per cent of the labor force. This figure went up to 5.9 per cent by September of that year, and by September 1966 it had receded slightly to 5.3 per cent.

Foreign Trade Policy

Regarding foreign trade, there has been a favorable turn, as a result partly of higher copper prices and also of a more orderly handling of all copper activities. But the main element in the improved foreign trade picture has been the introduction of a fluctuating rate of exchange, which since 1963 has been adjusted monthly according to the rate of inflation. Given below are dollar values for December of each year:

	ESCUDOS PER U.S. DOLLAR
1962	1,142
1963	1,875
1964	2,750
1965	3,450
1966	4,370

This policy of maintaining a fluctuating exchange rate, which has benefitted export trade and checked increases in imports, represents a sharp break with the past.

Following the crises in nitrate and in international affairs in 1929 and 1930, the country began a process of industrialization, supported mainly by a tariff increase. After World War II this industrialization gained momentum. Customs duties have continued to rise for all industrial goods, but not for needed raw materials. There is a tendency to increase tariffs to a maximum to protect domestic industry, which only in exceptional cases can complete with foreign products.

To curb inflation, high tariffs were accompanied by an exchange policy of undervaluation. In fact, the rate of exchange determines prices of a series of commodities important for official cost-of-living indices. For example, sugar, coffee, tea, and vegetable oils are imported and have a high consumption, but other products like cotton, petroleum (until recently imported), pharmaceuticals, rubber products, etc., also have an important impact on the cost-of-living index. Once the inflationary process was under way, the government tried to check it through direct control of the rate of exchange to avoid further price increases.

According to a study made by the University of Chile, the differences between the official rates of exchange and those of parity are shown in Table 12.

The official exchange rate is the one fixed by the government. For the whole period, it was markedly lower than the parity exchange rate, which is the rate that would equalize internal with international prices, given existing tariffs.

Table 12   **RATE OF EXCHANGE:**
                       OFFICIAL VS. PARITY RATE

	OFFICIAL AVERAGE RATE OF EXCHANGE	PARITY RATE OF EXCHANGE
	ESCUDOS PER DOLLAR	ESCUDOS PER DOLLAR
1950	0.050	0.085
1951	0.059	0.096
1952	0.066	0.115
1953	0.075	0.144
1954	0.098	0.223
1955	0.175	0.388
1956	0.351	0.623
1957	0.623	0.774
1958	0.863	0.953
1959	1.049	1.299
1960	1.049	1.429
1961	1.049	1.516

Source: University of Chile.

Exports were adversely affected, for it was traditional policy to keep exchange rates at a lower level than the one corresponding to the supply and demand for dollars. In addition, the exchange rate was set for political reasons, and it was customary to freeze the rate for relatively long periods, in spite of inflation, as a way of keeping down the prices of imported goods or of the ones usually exported. This made the demand for imported goods expand extraordinarily and forced the government to establish quantity restrictions and very high tariffs, thus encouraging national monopolies. In addition, as is easy to understand, this policy impeded the development of export industries.

This type of exchange policy led to sudden devaluations of considerable magnitude, and these have had a profound impact on prices, considering that imports represent 15 per cent of national product. In addition there were important indirect effects, as well as others of a psychological nature.

Furthermore, the domestic price of exportable goods — in particular the price of farm products — tended to rise as a result of the higher rate of exchange.

From 1940 to 1960 the criteria applied to foreign trade were inconsistent. The objectives of such policies were fundamentally incompatible — to equalize the balance of payments and to get a cheaper rate of exchange. Numerous devices were tried, such as subsidies for certain exports, a multiple exchange, a single fixed-rate, a fluctuating rate, etc. This policy was beneficial in certain aspects and harmful in others.

For one thing, high tariffs on foreign manufactures, even absolute embargoes on importing certain products such as textiles, shoes, luxury items, and the like have been imposed. Such high industrial protection is very difficult to evaluate in social costs, but in any case, it can be considered a large one, since the price of the domestic product is considerably higher than its equivalent on the world market. As another incentive, raw materials could be imported using a below-parity currency. Thus the situation is very hard to evaluate, especially over the last ten years.

Also, it has been difficult for industry to obtain raw materials. Therefore certain manufacturing sectors have been unable to raise short-term output. When strict currency restrictions have been in force, the importing of machinery and spare parts has been a serious problem. This, added to high tariffs, has reduced the system's flexibility for increasing production.

All of these exchange problems tend to aggravate the inflationary process, since they bring about great economic instability and act as psychological accelerators for the velocity of money circulation.

A study made by Kurt Ullrich tries to establish for a period of ten years the effect of government intervention on agricultural prices. By way of comparison, international prices for a group of products, representing more than 60 per cent of production, were used to study the effects of price-fixing and of restrictions on exports. According to the study, these policies kept agricultural internal real prices from 10 per cent to 20 per cent lower than they would have been had there been free commerce and no internal price restrictions. (On the other hand, it must be said that there has never been a minimum price policy.) These policies seriously damaged agricultural income.

This system of controls, regulations, and restrictions not only affects agriculture and international trade. It also affects the industrial sector, for industries have to ask for a decree from the government to raise their prices.

The Central Bank regulates domestic interest rates; it has established selective credit arrangements, which entail strict control of bank activities. Private investors have been discouraged since price controls on basic services are very rigid. House rents are fixed by law.

But even with its enormous power of control, the government must accept price increases so as to prevent the paralyzing of industries or the stagnation of some sectors.

It is easily seen that with such a complex system of controls and regulations, business activity largely depends on governmental decisions, and the private enterprise system loses its fundamental dynamism. Furthermore, governmental economic policies are subject to abrupt change, which adds to natural market risks.

The Problem of Savings

Savings and investment are fundamental elements of the economic development of a country. The volume of private savings is closely related to national income level. To save, a special attitude is required: part of current income must be sacrificed for a larger future income, a desire for security, and the real possibility of an eventual return which will compensate for present sacrifices in consumption. Also certain other factors must exist, such as orderly ways to reap the benefits of savings, respect for private property, and a favorable climate in which business can flourish.

Unfortunately, in the case of Chile, many of the prerequisites are absent or exist only in limited form. The general income level is low and there is little interest in providing for the future. Investment returns tend to diminish because of tax increases, capital markets do not develop for fear of inflation, new laws tend to restrict property rights, business conditions are ruled by political considerations.

From Table 13 it can be seen that gross investment has fluctuated between 9.1 per cent and 13.0 per cent of the total income. There is a trend to a moderate growth except for the last two years. Such figures are misleading, however, if no attention is paid to depreciation. Table 14 shows low rates and even negative ones, with maximum net savings at 5.8 per cent of income. If these figures are compared with those of more advanced countries, the conclusion can be drawn that such a low savings rate is the cause of slow Chilean economic growth.

Table 13   **GROSS INVESTMENT AND TOTAL INCOME**
(In millions of 1961 escudos)

YEAR	TOTAL INCOME	GROSS INVESTMENT	% INCOME INVESTED
1958	5,023	485	9.7
1959	4,957	452	9.1
1960	5,471	578	10.6
1961	5,735	743	13.0
1962	5,989	766	12.8
1963	6,108	758	12.4

Source: Corfo, National Accounts.

Table 14   **NET INVESTMENT AND TOTAL INCOME**
(In millions of 1961 escudos)

ITEM	1958	1959	1960	1961	1962	1963
Gross investment	485.0	451.5	578.2	743.0	766.0	758.0
Depreciation	426.7	375.4	732.3	411.0	431.0	448.0
Net investment	58.3	76.1	−154.1	332.0	335.0	310.0
Ratio of net investment to total income	1.2%	1.5%	−2.8%	5.8%	5.6%	5.1%

One of the most important contributing factors to creating and maintaining this condition is inflation, with its unfortunate consequences that permeate all the economic and social processes.

The inflationary process has induced the government to increase tax rates, but these increments have not been equal for every sector. The consequence is distortion in resource allocation. The high taxes have been alleviated somewhat by exemptions established for some sectors, such as fishing and homebuilding. These exemptions in turn bring pressure for the same treatment from the sectors that have not benefited. This ends in revisions in the tax system and creates new confusion.

In this way, the fundamental stability necessary to make a private enterprise system attractive and efficient has not been achieved. Thus, not only has the economy's growth based on the private sector been delayed but the enemies of private enterprise have also been given the weapons necessary for promoting the growth of the already powerful state enterprises (petroleum, sugar, transport, electricity, etc.). The situation has also served to create a tendency in businessmen to expect everything from the government, thereby weakening the market economy.

2. Copper and Its Impact on Chilean Development

Mining has been, and still is, a basic factor of the Chilean economy. During the last century, silver and copper — and later nitrates — gave impetus to the economy and made an important contribution to domestic savings and to development of foreign trade. During the twentieth century, copper has replaced nitrates as the main source of export revenue.

At present, most Chilean exports come from mineral exploitation: copper, iron, nitrates, iodine, molybdenum. Table 15 shows the dominant place minerals occupy in this field.

Table 15   **COMPOSITION OF CHILEAN EXPORTS**
(Per cent)

TYPE OF EXPORTS	1960	1961	1962	1963
Mineral products[a]	86.5%	84.4%	87.1%	87.1%
Agricultural products	6.5	8.3	8.3	8.2
Industrial products	6.9	7.1	4.3	4.6
Other	0.1	0.2	0.3	0.2
TOTAL	100.0%	100.0%	100.0%	100.0%

[a] Copper constitutes 49 per cent of mineral exports.

For many years, copper has been a source of long and passionate discussion among economists, politicians, and other opinion-molding groups in Chile. This situation is due to the importance of copper in the national economy. No other product affects so sharply the balance of payments or the fiscal deficit, and for the next decade copper will continue to be a fundamental pillar of Chilean economic development. Another reason why copper has been a topic of heated debate stems from the fact that its production has been developed in large part by foreign companies of North American origin. These two factors explain copper's political importance and the nationalistic pressures that have arisen.

Large-scale copper mining[6] has a great impact on national economic activity for these three main reasons:

1. Copper mining is the country's principal source of foreign exchange. In 1963 the total value of Chilean exports was $590 million, of which copper accounted for $290 million.

2. It is a major source of fiscal receipts, its contribution in 1963, for example, amounting to $87 million, or 12 per cent of total fiscal receipts.

3. It is a source of work for a great number of Chileans, and requires from the country a considerable amount of inputs. In this way, a multiplier effect is produced on the national economy. The total number of laborers employed amounts to 12,000, and expenditures within the country amount to $100,000,000.

The powerful influence that copper production has on the national economy forces government and Parliament to a constant preoccupation with this industry's fluctuations.

There are some political groups, such as marxists, who absolutely oppose foreign investments in the country. They deny that these investments produce any benefit at all, or that they contribute in any way to economic development. Foreign investment appears to them as an example of capitalist imperialism, and they are constantly pointing to foreign profits obtained from Chilean copper companies, while never considering the benefits for Chile.

Other center and left-wing parties support nationalization of basic industries, although they do not object to foreign investments in other activities. They argue that copper, being a vital element for growth, must be controlled by the national government, since foreign interests do not coincide with those of the country.

Usually, arguments against foreign investments are not based on economic reasoning; they are generally political and are highly subjective. They have their origin mainly in nation-

[6] In Chile, copper mining is traditionally divided in "Gran Minería del Cobre" (large-scale copper mining) and "Pequeña Minería del Cobre" (medium- and small-scale mining) according to the size of the mines.

alist sentiments that find ample echo in public opinion, sentiments which are constantly exploited by politicians.

Taxation is based on three main categories of copper mining:

1. Large-scale mining, including companies producing over 75,000 metric tons per year. These are foreign-owned and account for 85 per cent of the total copper production.

2. Small-scale mining, with a capital of less than 20,000 in 1963 escudos. They represent investors with small capital; primitive means of production are used.

3. Medium-scale mining, comprising all other companies.

As the political groups opposing foreign investment in copper production increased their influence and power, discussions of policies pertaining to copper became more and more heated. Though not directly leading to nationalization, they resulted in greater taxation on the great copper companies. This reduction of profits led to a decrease in investment. In addition, the unfavorable climate for foreign investment and the constant risk of nationalization were decisive factors in discouraging foreign capital from increasing copper production.

Copper Production in Chile and Abroad

In spite of the importance of copper mining to the national economy, Chile has not been able to implement a policy likely to develop and strengthen this sector. For an objective evaluation it is necessary to compare national indexes of production with those of other countries.[7]

As can be observed in the Appendix, while Chile produced 19 per cent of the world's total production in 1948, it produced only 13 per cent in 1963. The expansion of Chilean production from 1943 to 1963 was 35 per cent versus a world increase of 92 per cent. The contrast is greater when it is considered that Peru increased production nine-fold, Asia and the Soviet groups three-fold, Australia eight-fold, and Canada nearly two-fold.

[7] See Appendix Table I.

The constantly diminishing relative copper production of Chile is not due to the exhaustion of mines, for the country has abundant reserves of copper.[8] Explanation for this poor showing can be found mainly in a lack of interest in investment: in other words, economic and political conditions have not made investment in copper attractive. According to the staffs of Anaconda and Braden Copper (the largest copper companies operating in Chile), the suitable conditions would be:

- Reasonable taxation;
- Revenue security;
- Stability of governmental policies toward the industry;
- Absence of exchange rate or other discriminations.

Reasonable Taxation

Large-scale copper mining pays considerably higher taxes than important producers in other countries.

Braden is the company paying highest taxes: 84.74 per cent of profits in 1963. As can be seen in the Appendix,[9] this compares with a range of from 29 per cent to 57 per cent for taxes on similar companies in other countries.

With respect to the taxation of copper in different countries, it must be remembered that there exist different metal qualities, natural facilities for exploitation, etc. Consequently, tax figures do not reflect exactly equal conditions. Even so, it is hard to believe that Chile would have natural facilities so great as to compensate for tax differences of such magnitude.

With the coming of extensive reform legislation, additional taxes of 5 per cent and 8 per cent were imposed on copper companies. In addition, exchange policy has been unfavorable to the big copper companies, especially during a period when multiple exchange rates existed. In general, the traditional policy of fixing an excessive value to our currency has implied an additional tax on export activities. It must also be noted that with the existing favorable atmosphere for expropriation and nationalization of

---

[8] See Appendix Table J.
[9] See Appendix Table K.

foreign capital and companies, these, of course, show a certain reticence toward running the risk of investing in the country.

If Chilean policy for large-scale copper mining is evaluated realistically, it must be recognized that the pre-1964 programs did not result in an expansion of production. This policy emphasized maximizing the tax percentage on profits of foreign companies, while ignoring the possibility of increased tax revenues obtainable from increased mining activities.

Table 16 **FOREIGN CURRENCY GAINS ATTRIBUTABLE TO LARGE-SCALE COPPER MINING**
(U. S. dollars)

	1961	1962	1963
Taxation	$73,973,660	$88,997,016	$84,148,980
Domestic Expenditure	99,066,506	107,529,889	99,394,903
Investment	6,705,645	3,773,000	6,428,344
	$179,745,811	$200,299,905	$189,972,227

As the table above indicates, Chile gained more than $80 million in foreign currency in 1963 through the taxation of the copper companies and approximately $100 million through their expenditures on wages, raw materials, and so forth. This represents for the country clear and tangible benefits that could have been greatly increased with an adequate policy encouraging greater investment.

The New Policy for Copper

In September, 1964, Chile's new, left-of-center Christian Democratic government announced a far-reaching new policy for copper with these main elements:[10]

1. OBJECTIVES

    a. Increase copper production from 617,000 tons per year to 1,200,000.

---

[10] For details, see Appendix Table L.

b. Refine Chilean copper to the greatest extent possible inside the country. Refining will rise from 275,000 to 700,000 tons.

c. Increase the mining companies' consumption of national products. In order to attain this objective, there will be a greater specialized industrial production for the mining consumer group. It is also expected to raise domestic industry's technological capacity so that it can be reasonably competitive with foreign industry. Details of this plan for increased consumption have not been specified, as the relevant studies have not as yet been developed.

d. There will be active participation by government in the administrative and commercial management. Possible trade with the Soviet group is also included. These forms of participation are made through associations.

e. There are to be diverse social improvements—mainly those related to health, education, etc. — for workers in the copper industry.

f. There are plans for production of copper products able to compete in the international markets in price and quality. This step will be developed in collaboration with Anaconda.

2. BENEFITS FOR CHILE

(Calculated for a copper price of $0.29 per pound):

a. Greater fiscal receipts of $47 million per year;

b. Greater direct revenue of $68 million per year;

c. Greater foreign currency entrances of $115 million.

Thus in 1970 the country will have:

$134 million in fiscal receipts and

$167 million in revenues.

This represents foreign currency receipts of $301 million instead of the $189 million in 1963.

The new investments by themselves will realize approximately $50 million toward the balance of payments — this for a period of 40 years. Actually, much of the new investments will be in machinery. Financing in escudos will be obtained from contributions and loans from the government.

3. GOVERNMENTAL RESPONSIBILITY

To attain these objectives the government grants:

a. Active financing of part of the investment;

b. Stability in the system of profit taxes and revenues;

c. No tax discrimination;

d. Maintaining the franchise for imports of equipment and material not available inside the country.

CONCLUSIONS

The new policy for copper represents tangible and important benefits for the country.

It means greater tax collection, thus allowing greater fiscal expenditures. It also means a greater entrance of foreign currency, thus allowing a greater volume of imports—a vital consideration at the present moment, and vital in the long-run for the effective functioning of a market economy.

In addition the new investments will incorporate a considerable number of employees in activities which are characterized by their high productivity and relatively high wages, with the consequence of a multiplier effect on other sectors of the economy, due to the greater consumption and savings originated by the new activity.

On the other hand, the new investments require not only more labor but also *considerable amounts of materials* that increase the demand for national industries.

Also important is the permanent demand for imports required for the attainment of the proposed objectives; e.g., steel, explosives, etc. This new demand will surely encourage new investments in the industries presently supplying the copper mining activities, thereby improving their productivity.

Furthermore, the President stated the possibility of *promoting* the development of *new industries supplying the copper activities,* if quality, efficiency, and a price that will make them competitive with foreign industry are achieved. It can be said that the new policy is clearly and decidedly profitable for Chile, in terms of an expansion of its national product.

From private enterprise's general point of view, some of the new policy statements are of undoubted value, not only because they represent economic benefits for different sectors of production but also because they imply a clear and strict acceptance of two basic principles of policy enunciated by President Frei in his speech of December 21, 1964:

1. "Stability in the system of profit taxes and in the administration of revenues, for without these conditions, it is not possible to estimate the bases for financial development of these enormous investments nor to count on foreign financing . . .

2. "Concerning other taxes and economic and administrative conditions, the general guarantee that there will be no adverse discrimination against these investments as opposed to other national economic activities. This is a basic principle of our constitutional and financial system."

The evident public acceptance of these fundamental principles of the National Christian Democrat leader lends hope that the foundations of the private enterprise system will be maintained.

The funds for financing the obligations contracted by the government in copper mining will be obtained in part directly from the companies through taxes on company earnings and through the government's shares in company profits—this kind of financing being made possible due to the medium-term nature of the debts owed to the companies for the government's newly purchased shares in them. Another part will be obtained from external credits to the government contracted for that purpose. Still another part will be obtained from current fiscal receipts. Unfortunately the project does not contemplate the possibility of Chilean private capital's forming part of the new companies, thus avoiding for the government problems of financing that in the end will have to be met, directly cr indirectly, through the tax system. Likewise, the new policy for copper must be considered as a dangerous advance of the state's economic power. This implies a new step toward socialistic forms of government.

The solution adopted by the Chilean government is not the optimum one from a social standpoint, but is satisfactory as a workable economic policy. The Chileanization of Copper bill which was first introduced in December, 1964, still had not come into force in March, 1967. After a long political debate which lasted over a year, the Chamber of Deputies and the Senate authorized the government to associate itself with the copper companies. Its implementation has encountered many difficulties. The delegation of management functions to the companies has been the bone of contention. In the case of *El Teniente,* it was proposed that the government would own 51 per cent of the stock, but it had guaranteed that managerial control would go to the Braden Copper Company for the duration of the association. Later, this guarantee was reduced to twenty years, and the Christian Democrats even pressed for ten years. Many problems still must be solved before the agreement becomes a reality. There is no way of forecasting accurately when the new investment policy can be initiated.

Copper Production Over The Past Few Years

In 1964 the country's production was 621,000 tons, declining to 586,000 in 1965 and climbing to 657,000 in 1966. The low 1965 figure was the result of long strikes which had repercussions in all large mining operations.

The mean price per pound of Chilean copper over the past four years has averaged (in U. S. money) the following:

1963 — 31¢ per pound	1965 — 36¢ per pound
1964 — 33¢ per pound	1966 — 54¢ per pound

As can be seen, copper prices during recent years have steadily mounted, the trend being more pronounced in 1966 as a result of the Vietnam war. The top price in 1966 was 70 cents per pound in July.

The high copper prices have had a favorable impact on balance of payments. Total exports increased to $684 million in 1965 and $987 million in 1966. Imports were $732 million and $858 million respectively. Therefore, exports increased 61 per cent and imports 17 per cent between 1965 and 1966. The balance of payments surplus and the net balance of capital movements amounted to $116 million.

3. The Role of Agriculture

Agriculture in Chile is the sector upon which the nation's political, social, and economic problems converge. It is a key sector because of the emphasis placed on its problems in domestic politics and because the policies proposed for it undoubtedly affect other sectors.

While approximately one-third of the Chilean population is engaged in agriculture, workers in this sector have incomes below the national average, and the sector as a whole represents only 12 per cent of the total Chilean domestic product. In addition, the sector's growth has not been high enough to absorb the increase in internal demand, caused by population growth, greater incomes, and changes in the structure of total demand due to the increase of urban population. As a result, the volume of agricultural exports has been diminishing, while the volume of imports has been increasing.

This adverse situation in agriculture has coincided with the entry of rural workers on the political scene. The result has been that the sector has become the center of a struggle for political power. Extremist groups in this struggle have succeeded in creating a social unrest that seems to keep increasing.

It has been suggested that agriculture is a deadweight for the country's economic development because of:

1. Rural workers' low levels of income, causing a depressed demand for goods produced in other sectors, especially for manufactured goods;

2. An inadequate rate of growth in agriculture, resulting in greater food imports, and thereby tending to worsen the already chronic deficit in the balance of payments;

3. Serious political problems related to demands for a redistribution of land—demands which often degenerate into attacks against the private property system;

4. The political instability of the sector, which affects the whole country inasmuch as the agricultural areas elect more than half the members of the Parliament.

The agricultural problem is a difficult one to define and summarize since it is simultaneously economic, social, and political. A separate analysis of each of these aspects of the problem is important in order to arrive at adequate solutions for the complex situation. However, before passing on to such an anlysis, it seems appropriate to give a general picture of Chilean agriculture.

Agricultural Land

Continental Chile (excluding the Antarctic Zone) has a surface area of 74,177,000 hectares[11], which can be divided into:

Agricultural land:	27.7 million hectares
Forest land:	21.4 million hectares
Barren land:	25.0 million hectares
	74.1 million hectares

The 27.7 million hectares of agricultural land can be subdivided, according to quality and possible uses, into:

Irrigated land:	1,099,000 hectares
Arable land:	5,543,000 hectares
Uncultivable land:	21,070,000 hectares
	27,712,000 hectares

The uncultivable land is located in mountainous regions or regions having excessive humidity. This type of land can be used, depending on the region's climatic conditions, as temporary or permanent grazing land. For the most part, these lands are of very low productivity and subject to constant climatic problems. This situation is little known to the majority of people and leads to great confusion when problems related to land ownership are considered. Discussion generally centers on the physical size of properties, while ignoring the fact that a large part of the major farm estates are mountainous and practically barren.

The 25.0 million hectares of barren land are for the most part the mountainous territories of the Andes, deserts in the north, mountains and dunes on the coast, and swamps and forests in the south.

The 1 million hectares of irrigated land constitute the productive nucleus of the country's agriculture. They are situated

---

[11] A hectare is approximately 2.5 acres.

in the better climatic regions forming the central part of Chile. It is important to realize that over 60 per cent of the country's production comes from irrigated lands, which have high productivity due to the temperate climate and the fertility of the soil. In the northern and central parts of the country, there is practically no rain during the summer; this makes irrigation indispensable. The absence of irrigation would convert this into a semi-desert, good only for grazing and very limited farming.

On the other hand, the cost of irrigation is enormous. Great investments are required to overcome the obstacles presented by a mountainous country whose haphazard topology includes rivers in deep canyons and steeply sloping plains. This is why during the years 1940-60 the increase in irrigated land was small —a great part of the lands easily irrigated had already been so, while the remainder required large investments. During the years 1960-64 the government began constructing major irrigation works in projects which will cover approximately 400 thousand hectares in the next ten years.

The nonirrigated arable lands, amounting to 5.5 million hectares, are located in the central and southern zones of the country. The lands in the central zone are good for sheep grazing and for some crops requiring little moisture, such as wheat, barley, chick-peas, etc. Nevertheless, climatic problems greatly affect the production of this region, and the frequent years of drought cause considerable decreases in production. The southern zone has more frequent rain during the spring and summer, and considerable rain in the winter; thus it is excellent cattle territory. Toward the extreme southern parts of the country the climate becomes inclement; it is good only for sheep grazing.

The land situation can be summarized as follows:

	Per Cent of the Total
Irrigated land	1.3
Arable land	7.5
Uncultivable land	28.4
Forest land	28.9
Barren land	33.8
TOTAL	100.0

Land Ownership

Because of its constant recurrence in agricultural debates, the question of land ownership must first receive our attention. The typical reference to a feudal system in which, by a long tradition of inheritance some few people own great expanses of land, has created both at home and abroad the image of an archaic agricultural system. High increments of production, it is argued, could be obtained only by breaking down the "traditional structures" that supposedly block access by vast sectors of the population to ownership of land. Even some foreign authors, badly informed, make reference to regions in Chile where, they claim, the law of primogeniture is still in effect.

Attention must be called to the fact that among the first laws of independent Chile, pronounced by the O'Higgins government, was the abrogation of the system of primogeniture and of the use of titles of nobility (1818). Later Bello's Civil Code established that legacies should be divided equally among the sons.

According to censuses of agriculture and a study by Hugo Trivelli ("Agrarian Structure and Expansion"), the number of agricultural land owners has increased impressively, as indicated by the following table:

Table 17 **EVOLUTION OF THE NUMBER OF FARMS IN CHILE**

YEAR	NUMBER OF FARMS
1855	32,800
1875	47,000
1911	70,000
1920	95,000
1930	146,000
1961	261,374

The figure for 1961 is the latest available and was taken from official speeches made by the Ministros de Tierras y Colonización (Ministers of Land and Colonization). These figures show that over the past century there has been a process of land division resulting in an 800 per cent increase in the number of farms.

Nevertheless, such data do not give an adequate picture of the way in which farms are distributed, since there are differences in size and value of farms. Table 18 shows farm distribution according to fiscal evaluations, which correspond in general to 20 per cent of commercial values. (The figures refer to 1961, when the rate of exchange for Chilean currency was $1.00 = 1.053 escudos.)

Table 18 **DISTRIBUTION OF LAND ACCORDING TO THE 1961 FISCAL EVALUATIONS**

FISCAL EVALUATION (E°)	NUMBER OF FARMS	% OF TOTAL NUMBER OF FARMS	TOTAL EVALUATION	% OF TOTAL EVALUATION FOR ALL FARMS
0- 999	220,529	84.37	46,912,485	11.11
1,000- 1,999	14,819	5.67	21,215,083	5.02
2,000- 2,999	6,361	2.43	15,625,903	3.70
3,000- 4,999	6,275	2.40	24,375,467	5.77
5,000- 6,999	3,003	1.15	17,974,846	4.26
7,000- 9,999	2,588	0.99	21,811,576	5.17
10,000- 19,999	3,600	1.38	50,299,099	11.91
20,000- 39,999	2,351	0.90	66,576,306	15.77
40,000- 59,999	805	0.21	39,120,809	9.26
60,000- 79,999	441	0.16	30,419,077	7.20
80,000- 99,999	225	0.08	20,070,089	4.75
100,000-199,999	292	0.11	38,451,571	9.11
200,000-299,999	48	0.02	11,217,417	2.66
300,000-399,999	20	0.01	6,695,800	1.59
400,000-499,999	4	0.01	1,885,653	0.45
500,000 and over	13	0.01	9,624,327	2.27
TOTALS	261,374	100%	422,275,508	100%

The above data show a great number of owners with farms valued at less than 1,000 escudos. These are small farms equivalent to less than five hectares of irrigated land, and include the minifundia, that is, farms so small that they do not cover the owners' subsistence needs. These come from the repeated subdividing of medium-sized family farms. The inheritors of these diminished tracts of land, instead of selling them, settled on them, thus creating a group of small farmers, far from urban centers, with few possibilities of work and little access to culture. This type of farmer constitutes one of the most serious problems of agriculture because of his low income and productivity.

The minifundia problem is extremely grave in some of the provinces, where such holdings are common. For example, in Tarapaca the minifundia comprises 54.3 per cent of the total fiscal evaluation of the land; in Antofagasta the figure is 63.7 per cent; in Maule, 38.5 per cent; in Concepción, 39.5 per cent, in Aracuo, 24.3 per cent; in Llanquihue, 20.3 per cent; in Chiloé, 63.7 per cent; and in Aysén, 56.3 per cent. There is a high degree of correlation between the incidence of minifundia and cultural, social, and economic backwardness. Especially significant is the fact that rates of production per hectare in these regions are considerably lower than those in other similar regions lacking minifundia.

To complete our picture of land ownership in Chile, we must consider the relationship between the size and the quality of farms, as shown in Table 19 taken from the last census (1955). (These figures cannot be accurately correlated with those in the previous table because of differences in the definitions of terms and in the years under consideration.)

Table 19
AVERAGE SIZE AND QUALITY OF FARMS IN CHILE

SIZE OF FARM (HECTARES)	NUMBER OF FARMS	AVERAGE TOTAL AREA (HECTARES)	AVERAGE AMOUNT OF ARABLE FARMLAND (HECTARES)	AVERAGE NUMBER OF IRRIGATED HECTARES
Less than 1	28,245	0.3	0.2	0.1
1 to 9.9	47,381	4.4	3.0	0.9
10 to 99.9	53,766	34.1	18.7	2.6
100 to 499.9	15,240	214.2	101.7	21.8
500 to 999.9	3,076	683.1	250.6	58.5
1,000 to 4,999.9	2,554	2,009.1	539.7	105.1
5,000 or more	696	21,788.3	982.9	191.4
TOTAL	150,959	183.6	36.7	7.3
TOTAL HECTARES IN COUNTRY		27,712,308.9	5,543,380.7	1,097,984.9
PERCENTAGE OF TOTAL EXTENSION			20%	4%

The above figures indicate that even the larger farms have only a proportionately small amount of cultivable land relative to their total extension. This is important, since we wish to emphasize the fact that in Chile the problem of the latifundia (excessively large farm) is of no great importance, unlike the very real problem of the small farm.

The Economic Problem of Agriculture

The economic problem has been defined primarily as the slow growth of total agricultural output. Frequent criticism is made of national agriculture for its failure to produce the food the country needs, thereby being responsible for the constant increments in food imports. A detailed analysis must be made of this argument so often cited by politicians and journalists.

From 1950 to 1959 population rose by 23.4 per cent, from 6 million to 7.5 million. During this same period total agricultural production rose by 26.4 per cent, including a 48.4 per cent rise in crop production and a 4.3 rise in the production of livestock.[12] These figures clearly show that the main problem of food scarcity is to be found in the meat categories. The figures at least weaken the thesis of a stagnating and decaying agricultural sector.

Other sources indicate that between 1940 and 1959 the increments in production were the following:

Table 20
INDICES OF AGRICULTURAL PRODUCTION

YEAR	CROP INDEX	TOTAL AGRICULTURAL INDEX	LIVESTOCK INDEX	POPULATION INDEX
1940	100	100	100	100
1959	173	156	138	148

Source: *La Economía Chilena,* University of Chile.

Thus, in terms of available food per capita, crops and total agriculture have evolved favorably, while livestock has evolved unfavorably. It can be inferred also that the balance-of-payments

---

[12] *Análisis de Producción,* Ministry of Agriculture.

problem imputed to agriculture does not correspond so much to a backward agricultural sector as to increments in per capita consumption due to higher incomes.

It is also useful to notice that, according to studies done by the Instituto de Economía Universidad de Chile (Institute of Economics of the University of Chile), the output per sown hectare increased from 1940 to 1949 by 18 per cent, and from 1950 to 1959 by 34.2 per cent. These figures show clearly the increasing productivity which has resulted from technological innovation.

Nevertheless, this situation of unmistakable growth in the agricultural sector contrasts with the gross domestic product generated by agriculture. In fact, the contribution of agriculture to the national product (in 1960 escudos) was 547 million escudos in 1950 and 545 million in 1959. Thus between these years the absolute contribution of agriculture decreased by 0.4 per cent.

This apparently paradoxical situation has its explanation in the declining prices for the sector's products, as confirmed by the following table:

Table 21   **PRICE INDICES FOR AGRICULTURE BY SECTORS**

YEAR	CROP REAL PRICE INDEX	LIVESTOCK REAL PRICE INDEX	TOTAL AGRICULTURE REAL PRICE INDEX
1950	100	100	100
1959	75	86	81

Source: *La Economía Chilena,*   University of Chile.

These figures show that agricultural prices have declined in real terms, causing the sector's real income to decrease in spite of the physical increments of production. The situation can be seen to be even more serious if consideration is taken of the increase in real terms of the prices for agricultural inputs. Agricultural price indices show an average increment of 384.5 per cent between 1951-55 and 1956-60 whereas over the same period the price indices of inputs show an average increment of 407.8 per cent.

Thus it is possible to assert that the agricultural sector, as a result of inflation, price controls, and other forms of government intervention, has fallen behind, and that if the situation is not changed, a crisis in agriculture will be inevitable.

A major share of agricultural price policy had its origin in pressures from urban areas, and was justified to the public by presenting farmers as rich and powerful landowners. This argument may be judged in the light of the data on land ownership given in the preceding pages.

Under the Frei government, there has been some effort to improve the farmer's relative position. As previously noted, the 1965 price policy contemplated a general price increase of 25 per cent, with a maximum increase of 19 per cent for the industrial sector. But for agriculture a rise of 25 per cent was permitted. In other words, an effort was made to protect the latter sector against negative effects of the stabilization program to avoid the pitfalls of previous programs.

The price of wheat, one of the basic items, was increased 44 per cent. The wholesale price index was increased 36.3 per cent for agricultural products, 28.0 per cent for industrial products, and 8.0 per cent for imports. The average index rose 24.5 per cent. These figures indicate that the agricultural position, in real terms, had improved.

In 1966, the government decided to reduce inflation to the 15 per cent level. Therefore, prices on industrial products could not climb more than 13 or 14 per cent, and agricultural products not more than 17 per cent or 18 per cent. In 1966 the general price index increased 19.6 per cent on the average, while the agricultural sector registered a 24.9 per cent rise, the industrial sector 24.0 per cent, and imported products 9.6 per cent. Mining products were readjusted so as to have a 16.7 per cent increase.

Consequently, the general price policy has been rather favorable to agriculture. Nevertheless, price increases have not meant greater production. For the last two years, weather conditions have been unfavorable. During this period in rural areas an atmosphere of political and social unrest has also prevailed. This climate of fear and instability cannot help the development of agriculture.

Agricultural Imports and Exports

In recent years imports of agricultural products accounted for about 23 per cent of the total—a high proportion for a country suffering from a chronic shortage of hard currency. Agricultural exports amounted to 8 per cent of the total.

Although this leaves agriculture on the debit side of the balance-of-payments picture, a thorough study shows that a very high percentage of these products cannot be cultivated in the country because tropical climate conditions are required to grow rubber, coffee, bananas, etc. In 1964, agricultural imports totalled $156 million, of which $76 million were products that could not be grown in Chile. That year, agricultural exports were $50 million. Thus, the net deficit attributable to Chile's agricultural situation amounted to $30 million. Although some politicians tried to argue the point, one cannot measure the efficiency of an economic sector in terms of balance of payments.

However, agricultural production indices have declined in the past few years, while food imports have been rising. In 1965, agricultural imports were close to $180 million and in 1966, although exact figures are not available, the figure may well exceed $200 million.

This situation is particularly dangerous if the trend in the United States to eliminate agricultural surpluses is taken into account. Chile has not experienced difficulties because higher copper prices have alleviated the traditionally unfavorable balance-of-payments position.

Social Problems

Declining agricultural incomes are also the cause of acute social problems.

Though the number of agricultural laborers rose from 620,000 in 1940 to 648,000 in 1960, this represents a declining agricultural share in the labor force from 35 per cent to 27 per cent. These figures indicate a strong emigration from the rural to the urban sector.

In 1960, agriculture produced 12 per cent of the national domestic income. Because 50 per cent of Chile's national income derives from commercial and social institutions and 50 per cent from labor, those who till the soil represent 27 per cent of the active population but they receive less than 6 per cent of the national income.

Unfortunately, there is no adequate statistical information on agricultural wages, but they are equivalent to the industrial minimum salary, and in some cases are even lower. Although agricultural labor as a sector represented 27 per cent of the population in 1960, its income may be very roughly estimated at about 6 per cent of national income.

In addition, rural workers have been short-changed in comparison with urban workers in the development of public services. For instance, the per capita budget for health, hospitals, and related services for rural workers is less than a third of the corresponding budget for urban workers. Similarly, only 10 per cent of rural workers have access to electric lighting, as opposed to 73 per cent of urban workers. Of housing built by the government during 1960-1964, 97 per cent was in urban areas; but estimates showed that urban areas needed to replace 30 per cent of their houses, while 75 per cent needed replacement in rural areas.

In education, although great efforts have been made to increase the number of schools, the agricultural sector has been left behind in comparison with urban sectors.

This situation is aggravated by the isolation of agricultural groups, which are usually far away from the big urban centers, in areas where good roads are lacking. Great efforts have been made in recent years to integrate every region of this long and narrow country by means of better roads. Nevertheless, there are still vast regions, especially in the south, the Andean range, and the coastal zone, which are isolated during the winter because of the lack of good roads.

All the above facts give a fair picture of the social problems of the peasants: low incomes, cultural and sanitary backwardness, and generally abject conditions.

The agrarian policy attempted to favor rural workers, agricultural workers, and small landowners. In fact, the minimum wage policy represented an increase of approximately 70 per cent in 1965 and over 35 per cent in 1966. Both figures are higher than the cost-of-living rise for the same period. Credit institutions have augmented their activities in the field of agriculture more than 50 per cent in real terms during the last two years. Also the Agricultural Development Institute, one of the principal national bureaus that serves agriculture, has enlarged its coverage to 80 offices.

Political Problems

After years of passiveness, the rural workers, despite the adverse conditions described above, have begun to take an active part in political life. This is of great significance, since rural areas, with approximately 30 per cent of the population, are decisive in the election of over 50 per cent of Parliament. For this reason great importance is attached to political strategies in these areas. Since growth rates have been greater in urban sectors, the marxists, as well as the Christian Democratic and other left-center parties, have reoriented their efforts at political penetration of the rural areas.

In past years rural areas had elected the parliamentary majority of the Radical and right-wing parties. Thus a big change in the rural electorate will also mean a big change in the national structure of political power.

The rural sector's emergence as the center of the fight for political power not only increases present anxiety, but also forces every political party to propose concrete solutions for rural problems in order to attract the voters' sympathy. These circumstances have moved every party to propose agrarian reform as the only way out. Agrarian reform was initiated during the Alessandri Administration and each party has its own approach to the problem, ranging from the acute demagoguery of marxists to the moderate and gradual solutions of the right-wing groups. It must be pointed out that, although the left-wing groups have made a strong penetration in the rural areas, they have not produced violent situations as in other countries.

After the 1964 presidential elections, the rural areas with their majority moved toward the Christian Democratic Party, thus almost causing the extinction of the right-wing parties and greatly diminishing the parliamentary representation of the Radicals. As a result, the Christian Democrats have obtained the executive and legislative powers that will permit them to develop their proposed plans, among which is agrarian reform.

Agrarian Reform

When President Frei took office in 1964, he sent a new agrarian reform bill to Congress. He also proposed a constitutional amendment modifying the legal nature of property rights to facilitate drastic measures for expropriation of land.

After a long debate, this amendment was passed in 1966. The new agrarian reform law is reaching its final stages but it has not been actually approved. The new law will be very hard on landowners due to the expropriation methods contemplated. All properties smaller than the agricultural basic unit (80 irrigated hectares) cannot be expropriated. In exceptional cases, where the land is well cultivated, the maximum size can be 320 basic hectares. The law favors eliminating commercial agriculture, and the creation of small, one-family type units. The Chilean approach advocates a drastic division of all land, quite contrary to the trends in Europe and the United States, where an effort is being made to increase the average size of agricultural lands as a means of greater productivity.

The Chilean law goes even further—forbidding creation of new agricultural enterprises, such as corporate farms. This type of concern was not too common, but constituted an interesting solution because land cultivation would have characteristics similar to those of modern industry.

The Chilean agrarian reform law not only covers size limitation of agricultural land but also the methods of expropriation and repayment. The payment can be deferred up to 30 years. The cash pre-payment is only 5 per cent. Since inflation is so prevalent in Chile, a clause on payment adjustment was included, but this covers only 70 per cent of the inflationary process, and the farmer loses some of his capital. Furthermore, the payment will be in bonds which yield only 3 per cent interest, while stocks average much more. In addition, the transfer of these bonds is extremely difficult.

Under such circumstances, many of the persons or institutions whose lands are to be expropriated will, in fact, lose part of their capital. The amount recovered represents a fixed income, but since the bonds have very limited liquidity, the principal cannot be used in new economic ventures. The causes for expropriation are broad and varied. A large part of Chilean land, if not all of it, can be subject to expropriation.

It is of interest to point out that a new 1965 law does not allow a voluntary division of a property or its sale to a third party unless 40 per cent of its value is donated to its rural workers. In this way, the private initiative which had contributed to a greater distribution of farmland was eliminated.

According to provisions of the reform, the state will take over the irrigation systems built by the national private sector. Consequently, the new agrarian reform has created an atmosphere of great uncertainty and instability for the whole corporate agricultural sector. The new law has adversely affected investment in agriculture, which often produces benefits only after a long period of time, as in the case of irrigation or orchards.

In 1965-1966, the Agrarian Reform Corporation took over 1,000,000 hectares. Considering the area that can be cultivated in Chile, this figure is very high. A million hectares represents between 10 per cent and 15 per cent of all property that could be expropriated. The lands have not been turned over directly to rural workers, but continue to be operated as a unit in accordance with a system of settlement. The corporation looks after the administration and management of the farms. It also advises rural workers until they are capable of taking over and cultivating their own individual plots.

As this is written, there was no complete study of the corporation's operations, and its results in real economic terms are not known. As it is natural to expect contradictory opinions on the subject, partisans of the reform maintain that production has not decreased in the estates taken over, and that in some of them it has even been increased. Opponents say that even if this were so, the land's productivity is lower and that in many respects the lands under the Agrarian Reform Corporation receive subsidies.

4. Education and Economic Development

Among the most important factors influencing the economic, political, and social development of Chile has been the development of education, which has made positive contributions to: the social integration of the country; the raising of the technical knowledge and cultural levels of the people; the development of an extensive and dynamic middle class; the improvement of income distribution; and the spread of civic-mindedness, which has given stability to the democratic political system.

The durability of our governmental system, with its periodic free elections, is due mainly to three of the above factors: social integration, civic-mindedness, and the development of the middle class. Our political stability, unequaled elsewhere on the continent, not only has brought fame to Chile; it also has been a decisive factor in her development. The political stability and democratic continuity of the country, unmarked by the bloody revolutions or *coups d'etat* so common in other parts of the continent, has created a favorable climate for both national and foreign investors, founded on the security inherent in a consistent legal system.

The institutional stability, however, has not been translated into stability in economic policies, due to the constant advance of statist ideas. This has been an unfortunate negative effect of education up to the present. On the other hand, educational programs have provided a large part of the population with basic schooling, which is indispensable for achieving higher levels of efficiency in labor and in the economy as a whole. Another positive educational factor which should be singled out is the training of technicians and specialists, without whom it would have been impossible to reach the levels of industrialization and mineral and agricultural development achieved by the country.

Primary Education

The concern of the government and of social groups in general for solving the country's educational problems is shown forcefully by the rise in the number of students enrolled in primary education, as well as by the numbers in secondary, special-ized, and university education. The evolution of total enrollment in public and private primary schools is shown in the following figures:

YEAR	ENROLLMENT IN PRIMARY SCHOOLS	% INCREASE OVER 1940
1940	524,125	......
1950	652,082	22.5
1960	1,125,400	114.7
1962	1,324,200	152.6

Enrollment in primary education—grades one through six—in the period 1940-62 increased by 152.6%, an average annual increase of 6.6%. In 1964-65 a school construction plan was put into effect; it will result in a total primary school enrollment of more than 1,500,000, which means that practically all Chilean children will have access to basic education. It should be noted that the state is not alone in providing education for young people; an important share of the burden is carried by private schools and institutions, which enroll about 30 per cent of primary school students.

Secondary Education

Secondary education comprises the six years which follow primary education, during which time students complete their studies of humanities and are prepared for entrance into the universities. Total enrollment in public and private secondary schools has evolved as follows:

YEAR	ENROLLMENT IN SECONDARY SCHOOLS	% INCREASE OVER 1940
1940	44,055	......
1950	70,055	59.0
1960	182,800	314.9
1962	197,800	349.0

It can be seen that secondary education has expanded at a faster rate than primary education, with enrollment averaging an annual increase of 15.2 per cent. However, the actual capacity is still far from sufficient to satisfy the needs of the population.

Specialized or Professional Education

Parallel to the system of secondary education, a system of specialized or semi-professional education has been developed, with the purpose of training skilled workers, laboratory technicians, etc. As in the case of secondary schools, these schools are designed to meet the needs of youth of less than 18 years of age. Total enrollment in public and private professional schools has evolved as follows:

YEAR	ENROLLMENT IN SPECIALIZED SCHOOLS	% INCREASE OVER 1940
1940	32,360	......
1950	60,009	85.4
1960	99,330	206.8
1962	104,800	223.8

As in the case of other branches of education, specialized or professional education has grown rapidly, averaging a 9.7 per cent annual increase in enrollment. Concentration in this area of education will be intensified in the next few years, since it constitutes the basis of solid economic development by promoting technological progress and by raising per capita productivity. In particular, it is hoped the new teaching methods will be developed that use, in part, the industrial equipment actually in the factories, with the intention of achieving a rapid increase in the efficiency of manual labor. An example of what can be done in this field may be seen in the branch schools of the University of Santa María, which operate in close collaboration with industry.

It should be added that the relative number of private schools participating in specialized or professional education is small in comparison with other branches of education; more than 80 per cent of the students in this area are in government-operated schools.

University Education

Chilean universities, unlike universities elsewhere on the continent, have a selective admissions policy, based primarily on scores received in the high school graduation qualifying examination. Thus, since admission is dependent on individual capability, the universities have been able to maintain high scholastic levels and to produce a technical and intellectual elite that has been the foundation of the nation's technological and cultural development. Private and public university enrollment has evolved as follows:

YEAR	ENROLLMENT IN UNIVERSITIES	% INCREASE OVER 1940
1940	7,846	......
1950	14,917	90.1
1960	23,300	197.0
1962	24,700	214.8

While university education has grown rapidly, averaging a 9.3 per cent per annum increase in enrollment, the rate is lower than that for secondary education, which is the college preparatory stage.

Conclusions Concerning the Growth of Education

The above figures on enrollment show that efforts made in favor of Chilean education have been of considerable magnitude, and that during the more than twenty-year period analyzed here, extremely successful growth rates have been achieved. How well these rates compare with the 2.5 per cent population growth rate may be appreciated from the following recapitulation, showing per annum rates of growth of population and of enrollment in each sector of education between 1940 and 1962:

Population	2.5%
Primary education	6.6%
Secondary education	15.2%
Specialized education	9.7%
University education	9.3%

In 1965 and 1966, the Frei government made an extraordinary effort in the field of education. The first goal was to provide basic or primary education for all Chilean children. The education deficit was eliminated to a great extent because enrollment rose in 1965 to 175,000 students. Secondary education increased 30 per cent and specialized education 12 per cent. Construction and renovation of schools proceeded at a very rapid pace and had an added impetus with 1,535 new schools. Adoption of modern methods has been accelerated with the aim of improving the quality of education; new programs have been introduced and old ones reshaped. At present, 8,000 teachers participate in advanced teacher-training programs. The educational system encompasses more than 2,000,000 young students.

Deficiencies in the Educational System

Although in quantitative terms educational development has proceeded at a satisfactory pace, qualitatively it has had some deficiencies with respect to social and economic development. These will have to be overcome if the educational system is to adapt itself better to the needs of the country.

In the first place, education at both primary and secondary levels in Chile has been inspired by the French canons of the past century, centered on a humanistic, encyclopedic approach to learning. Major changes in this approach are needed at the high school level to make room for the important advances of the twentieth century, especially in the area of technology. The principle criticism of Chilean education is that it is directed exclusively toward the university and that it puts an extremely heavy emphasis on the humanities.

Another fundamental flaw in Chilean education is that for all its humanistic orientation, emphasizing literature and history, it has not inculcated in its students those fundamental values needed for a modern society, such as an incentive to work, a sense of responsibility, and so on. Chilean liberal education also tends to depreciate the technical professions and manual labor.

At present, along with the great efforts being made to give all children a basic education, efforts must be made at providing widespread technical education, particularly in order to prepare skilled workers, foremen, and technicians, for whom there is a great demand in the industrial sectors.

An education reform plan was finally approved in 1965 with more emphasis on science and technical education—a break with traditional patterns.

Economics is another aspect of education in need of improvement. Youth must be taught the meanings of basic economic concepts, such as savings, the various forms of capital formation, the nature of enterprise, the functions of enterprise and the ways in which they contribute to economic development. A number of entrepreneurs are presently concerned about this very problem and are looking for ways of spreading economic knowledge among the nation's youth. Advocates of an economy based on free enterprise must accept, as a fundamental truth, the fact that their future in developing countries is closely linked with the image the public has of private enterprise and of the system of economic freedom. If citizens are not given an adequate economic education in their youth, spurred on by their own hopes and aspirations, they will choose the apparently easy road to economic betterment: state ownership, sudden and massive redistributions of income, price controls, and so forth.

Public Recognition of the Importance of Education

It should be pointed out that concern for education and recognition of its importance for economic and social advancement have increased in all sectors of the nation in recent years. This new awareness has been manifested at several distinct levels:

1. In the lower classes the children are taking education seriously as necessary for a more promising future. This, together with the accelerated growth of population, has placed enormous pressure on the government to provide new schools.

2. Political and intellectual circles rank education first among national objectives, thereby promoting national recognition of its importance.

3. Business groups see in education an effective means for

achieving political stability, social progress, and economic development.

Another aid to education, especially at the university level, is the scholarship plan approved in 1963 by Parliament, which voted a special fund for this purpose. The universities themselves have developed their own scholarship systems. It should be noted that education is free at all levels except in a few private schools.

Several business groups are financing and offering their personal services to the literacy campaign. Other groups, coming from teachers, the police corps, the armed forces, and philanthropic organizations, have followed the businessmen's example. The results of this private initiative have been astounding: in the first year, 120,000 illiterates were taught to read. It is expected that if the literacy campaign is maintained at this pace, illiteracy will have disappeared in Chile by 1970.

Despite the development of a system of free or nearly free education (with a $10 enrollment fee at the universities), much has been made recently of the system's inherently discriminatory nature. By the time they reach college age (18-25), students from low-income families feel obligated to go out and work to help support their families, which in any case cannot afford to support their children through four more years of education. Because of the frequency of such situations, Parliament has approved a program of financial aid, based on loans to be paid back in installments once the student has left the university.

The profound interest in education comes not only from the desire for greater culture, but also from the deep conviction that education contributes to raising an individual's income. The effect on income is clear from the analysis of the difference between the incomes of an unskilled laborer and a professional. Additionally, education eases access to higher social levels, thereby contributing also to the reduction of social tensions.

On a more general level, it is evident that increased specialization and technological advance require that the country have as many adequately educated people as possible, in order that new production methods may be introduced to raise productivity and thereby to promote industrial growth and economic progress.

CONCLUSION

Wherever change occurs, there is naturally some degree of uncertainty, a condition that is compounded in Chile's case by the instabilities that have long characterized its economy. As might be expected under such circumstances, the outlook for private savings and investment in Chile is not too favorable. Given the ideological spectrum represented in the present Parliament, for example, it is politically impossible to guarantee the copper companies that nationalization will not take place. Such uncertainties obviously inhibit the development of private enterprise.

In Chile, and to a lesser degree in other Latin American countries, there is a lack of well-defined political thinking that is able to provide clear and positive alternatives to the different forms of socialism, to give priority to private enterprise, and to establish basic conditions for its further development.

Public opinion is attracted by an approach that is statist, socialist or marxist. Private enterprise can be criticized to the hilt, and demagogues can exploit aspirations, resentments, and frustrations. The masses have a total ignorance of the true nature of the economic process, and politicians, many times in good faith, offer unrealistic solutions based more on ideals than on concrete, positive facts. This explains why certain political slogans have gained importance through the years. They were first used by marxist elements, then adapted by other brands of democratic socialism, including the Christian Democrats in Latin America. These slogans, favoring nationalization of oil, copper, and financial institutions, and drastic agrarian reforms, have been repeated ad infinitum; as a result, they have been accepted as absolute and irrefutable truths.

It is not surprising, therefore, that certain economic policy solutions are politically heretic. To make politically feasible and to implement such solutions, a long, patient, and systematic educational process is needed, because only then will the Latin American masses come to understand the basic characteristics of a private enterprise system.

Judging from recent events in Chile, as well as from political developments along similar lines in other Latin American countries, public opinion must be well-informed about basic economic concepts. The task is urgent and cannot be postponed.

———

Appendix

Table A   **INCREASE IN THE SUPPLY OF MONEY:**

1940-1966

END OF YEAR	MONEY IN CIRCULATION (MILLIONS OF ESCUDOS)	ANNUAL VARIATION (PER CENT)
1940	3.2	18.7%
1941	3.8	18.7
1942	4.6	21.1
1943	5.8	26.1
1944	6.8	17.1
1945	7.7	13.2
1946	9.3	20.8
1947	12.0	29.0
1948	15.0	25.0
1949	18.1	20.7
1950	19.1	5.5
1951	24.6	28.8
1952	31.5	28.0
1953	48.5	54.0
1954	69.7	43.7
1955	114.8	64.7
1956	164.6	43.3
1957	211.8	28.7
1958	279.9	32.1
1959	331.6	18.5
1960	477.2	43.9
1961	531.6	11.4
1962	755.6	42.1
1963	972.5	28.7
1964	1,476.1	51.8
1965	2,251.1	52.5
1966	3,323.7	47.6

[a] Includes checks as well as bills and coins in circulation, calculated as of December of each year.

Table B   **VELOCITY OF MONEY IN CIRCULATION**

YEAR	FIRST HALF	SECOND HALF
1940	1.58	1.63
1941	1.71	1.89
1942	1.80	1.88
1943	1.80	1.88
1944	1.83	1.92
1945	1.91	1.91
1946	1.82	1.97
1947	2.00	2.26
1948	2.19	2.23
1949	2.23	2.24
1950	2.28	2.61
1951	2.59	2.71
1952	2.63	......
1953	2.49	2.67
1954	2.55	2.73
1955	2.71	3.36
1956	3.30	3.54
1957	3.63	3.96
1958	3.68	3.47
1959	3.46	3.03
1960	2.73	2.67
1961	2.61	2.86
1962	2.39	2.55
1963	2.56	2.80
1964	2.94	2.97[a]
1965	......	2.70
1966	......	2.64

[a] Third quarter of 1964.

Source: *Boletin Mensuel,* Central Bank.

Table C   **AVERAGE RATE OF INTEREST**
(Percentage)

YEAR	FIRST HALF	SECOND HALF
1950	10.38%	10.98%
1951	11.43	12.02
1952	12.16	12.12
1953	12.05	12.54
1954	12.91	13.41
1955	13.52	13.82
1956	13.82	13.96
1957	14.11	14.61
1958	15.47	15.90
1959	16.25	16.40
1960	16.55	16.74
1961	15.88	15.27
1962	14.62	14.20
1963	14.21	14.39
1964	14.63	15.09
1965	15.30	15.86[a]
1966	15.84	15.86[a]

[a] In 1965 and 1966, taxes were levied on interest rates, which amounted, in fact, to a rate increase of 50 per cent. In 1966 the average interest rate was 23 per cent for borrowers.

Source: Boletin No. 438, Central Bank.

Table D   **SUPPLY OF CREDIT**

(In thousands of 1964 escudos)

END OF YEAR	COMMERCIAL BANKS	STATE BANK	TOTAL
1940	796,889	264,798	1,061,687
1941	743,394	259,566	1,002,960
1942	652,127	254,548	906,675
1943	688,546	288,890	977,436
1944	710,563	294,834	1,005,397
1945	818,492	304,973	1,123,465
1946	773,636	316,704	1,090,340
1947	774,050	309,488	1,083,538
1948	850,398	333,091	1,183,489
1949	830,506	369,054	1,199,560
1950	764,827	319,042	1,083,869
1951	747,738	325,734	1,073,472
1952	891,706	369,008	1,260,714
1953	680,175	424,823	1,104,998
1954	533,658	387,855	921,513
1955	416,727	303,849	720,576
1956	387,094	332,955	720,049
1957	457,270	405,339	862,609
1958	429,364	374,106	803,470
1959	691,782	403,569	1,095,351
1960	760,866	438,131	1,198,997
1961	919,841	549,579	1,469,420
1962	964,555	493,902	1,458,457
1963	877,589	491,299	1,368,888
1964	869,369	554,650	1,424,019
1965	901,712	654,944	1,556,656
1966	906,288	671,184	1,577,472

Source: Superintendent of Banks.

Table E   **BOND ISSUES**
(In thousands of 1964 escudos)

YEAR	VALUE
1940	54,293
1941	53,029
1942	61,671
1943	81,383
1944	115,256
1945	121,883
1946	106,517
1947	62,296
1948	58,658
1949	56,932
1950	54,866
1951	46,099
1952	53,127
1953	42,122
1954	21,086
1955	14,991
1956	9,351
1957	27,895
1958	7,642
1959	7,181
1960	7,392
1961	12,761
1962	9,935
1963	3,929
1964	1,470

Table F   **STOCK TRANSACTIONS ON THE SANTIAGO STOCK EXCHANGE**

YEAR	VOLUME (SHARES)	VALUE (THOUSANDS OF 1964 ESCUDOS)
1940	14,100,246	220,781
1941	30,275,632	519,815
1942	25,084,398	279,295
1943	32,663,208	315,305
1944	19,541,740	160,704
1945	16,382,452	123,183
1946	26,547,553	199,094
1947	42,414,219	238,594
1948	33,250,079	147,591
1949	40,297,187	119,564
1950	39,562,291	117,755
1951	83,688,034	258,788
1952	73,177,736	278,693
1953	68,960,037	149,299
1954	147,796,964	213,033
1955	234,706,726	377,560
1956	126,690,384	152,344
1957	163,331,952	114,339
1958	176,440,500	105,854
1959	201,242,825	110,124
1960	114,833,566	66,867
1961	94,611,871	56,092
1962	146,988,964	71,015
1963	209,133,607	106,836
1964	87,716,822	99,851
1965		91,344[a]
1966		46,204[a]

[a] The 1965 and 1966 figures include transactions of the Valparaiso Stock Exchange as well as those of Santiago Stock Exchange.

Table G   **BOND TRANSACTIONS ON THE
SANTIAGO STOCK EXCHANGE**
(In thouands of 1964 escudos)

YEAR	MUNICIPALS AND GOVERNMENTS	MORTGAGES, INDUSTRIALS, "NITRATES"	TOTAL
1940	19,403	34,890	54,293
1941	18,489	34,540	53,029
1942	20,838	40,833	61,671
1943	28,852	52,531	81,383
1944	64,090	51,166	115,256
1945	70,036	51,847	121,883
1946	69,929	36,588	106,517
1947	36,010	26,286	62,296
1948	36,644	22,014	58,658
1949	29,317	27,615	56,932
1950	37,913	16,953	54,866
1951	32,662	13,437	46,099
1952	32,379	20,748	53,127
1953	23,846	18,276	42,122
1954	13,865	7,221	21,086
1955	5,977	9,014	14,991
1956	3,113	6,238	9,351
1957	1,928	25,967	27,895
1958	1,378	6,264	7,642
1959	1,320	5,861	7,181
1960	968	6,424	7,392
1961	282	12,479	12,761
1962	123	9,812	9,935
1963	57	3,812	3,869
1964	40	1,430	1,470
1965	48	730	778
1966	39	479	518

Table H

NATIONAL PRODUCT AND INCOME, 1950-1963

(In 1964 escudos)

YEAR	DOMESTIC INCOME		NATIONAL INCOME		GROSS DOMESTIC PRODUCT		GROSS NATIONAL PRODUCT	
	TOTAL (MILLIONS)	PER CAPITA	TOTAL (MILLIONS)	PER CAPITA	TOTAL (MILLIONS)	PER CAPITA	TOTAL (MILLIONS)	PER CAPITA
1950	7,351	1,225	7,208	1,171	8,438	1,385	8,294	1,385
1951	7,595	1,226	7,433	1,183	9,207	1,445	8,651	1,402
1952	8,180	1,283	8,027	1,283	9,406	1,496	9,252	1,461
1953	8,738	1,367	8,650	1,339	10,043	1,566	9,954	1,538
1954	8,909	1,352	8,831	1,335	10,101	1,523	10,021	1,386
1955	8,749	1,288	8,608	1,269	10,315	1,526	10,174	1,497
1956	9,307	1,340	9,088	1,308	10,589	1,524	10,370	1,492
1957	9,616	1,352	9,450	1,328	11,106	1,588	10,941	1,535
1958	9,530	1,307	9,393	1,288	11,383	1,558	11,245	1,539
1959	9,931	1,327	9,708	1,297	11,564	1,546	11,341	1,516
1960	9,744	1,271	9,550	1,246	12,228	1,595	12,034	1,571
1961	10,360	1,320	10,176	1,295	12,579	1,601	12,395	1,579
1962	11,217	1,392	11,009	1,366	13,421	1,667	13,213	1,641
1963	11,642	1,410	11,412	1,383	13,830	1,676	13,600	1,648

Table I **CHILEAN COPPER PRODUCTION IN RELATION
TO WORLD PRODUCTION**
(In thousands of short tons)

REGION	1948 PRODUC-TION	% OF WORLD PRODUC-TION	1963 PRODUC-TION	% OF WORLD PRODUC-TION	% INCRE-MENT BETWEEN 1948-63
Chile:					
Large-scale mining..	468.4	18.18	590.0	11.93	25.96
Total production	490.6	19.04	662.1	13.39	34.96
Peru	19.9	0.77	195.5	3.95	888.41
Canada	245.3	9.52	461.8	9.34	88.26
United States	855.2	33.20	1,208.2	24.44	41.27
Rest of Latin America	89.7	3.48	70.4	1.42	21.51
Total for Americas	1,700.7	66.01	2,598.0	52.54	52.76
Total Europe	127.8	4.96	170.7	3.46	33.67
Total Asia	74.4	2.88	261.9	5.30	252.96
Total Africa	461.1	17.90	1,072.2	21.69	132.53
Australia	13.8	0.54	118.8	2.40	760.87
Total Free World	2,377.8	92.29	4,221.6	85.39	77.94
Soviet Bloc	198.4	7.71	772.6	14.61	264.21
WORLD TOTAL	2,576.2	100.00	4,994.2	100.00	91.94

Source: *Metals Year Book.*

Table J

COPPER RESERVES OUTSIDE UNITED STATES

COUNTRY	MILLIONS OF SHORT TONS
Canada	7.0
Chile	46.0
Northern Rhodesia	24.5
Congo (Katanga)	20.0
Peru	12.5
Yugoslavia	1.5
South Africa	1.1
Philippines	1.0
Australia	1.0
Others	7.4
Sino-Soviet bloc	16.0
TOTAL	138.0

Table K

TAXES ON COPPER MINING IN DIFFERENT COUNTRIES FOR COMPANIES SIMILAR TO BRADEN COPPER COMPANY OF CHILE — 1963

(In millions of U.S. dollars)

	BRADEN		USA	RHODESIA	CANADA	CONGO	PERU
	CHILE (1960)	CHILE (1963)					
A) Profits	44.5	44.5	44.5	44.5	44.5	44.5	44.5
B) Deduction for exhaustion	....	....	13.3	....	14.8	....	13.3
C) Other taxes	....	....	....	9.5	....	13.3	
D) Taxable income [A−(B+C)]	44.5	44.5	31.2	35.0	29.7	31.2	31.2
E) Tax rate	72.7%	84.7%	52.0%	44.8%	50.0%	18.8%	41.2%
F) Tax amount	32.4	37.7	16.2	15.7	14.9	5.6	12.9
G) Total Taxes	32.4	37.7	16.2	25.2	14.9	18.9	12.9
H) Real rate of taxation (G divided by A)	72.7%	84.7%	36.4%	56.6%	33.3%	42.5%	29.0%

Table L   **PLAN FOR MEETING NEW OBJECTIVES
IN THE COPPER INDUSTRY**

1. INCREASE OF PRODUCTION

Production increments will be obtained in the following way:

MINE	CHILEAN BRANCH	AMERICAN COMPANY	INCREMENT IN PRODUCTION (TONS)
Rio Blanco	Minera Andina	Cerro de Pasco	60,000
Chuquicamata and Salvador	Chile Andes	Anaconda	190,000
El Teniente	Braden Copper	Kennecott	90,000
Exótica		Anaconda	100,000
Mediana y Pequeña Minería		Private Chilean Enterprises	100,000
Other companies		Foreign companies	65,000
TOTAL			605,000

The country's production is the following (in tons):

Large-scale mining	524,000
Medium- and small-scale mining	93,000
TOTAL	617,000

Projected production for 1967-1970 is:

Large-scale mining	964,000
Medium- and small-scale mining	258,000
TOTAL	1,222,000

2. COPPER REFINING

Increments in refined copper will be obtained in the following way:

PROJECTED REFINING FOR 1970 (IN TONS)				
COMPANY	FIRE REFINING	ELECTRIC REFINING	BLISTERS	TOTAL FIRE + ELECTRIC REFINING
Anaconda	....	445,000	111,000	445,000
El Teniente	82,000	....	127,000	82,000
ENAMI[a]	....	170,000	....	170,000
	82,000	615,000	238,000	697,000

[a] ENAMI (National Mining Enterprise) will receive ores from El Teniente, from Andina, and from the smaller firms.

3. ASSOCIATION

The following relationships between private companies and the government have been agreed upon:

Cía. Minera Andina: a branch of Cerro de Pasco and owner of the Río Blanco mine. The state contributes 25 per cent of the capital, and ENDESA (National Enterprise of Electricity) supplies the electrical services.

Cía. Explotadora de Exótica: a branch of Anaconda and owner of the Exótica mine. The state contributes 25 per cent of the capital. It was also agreed in conjunction with the Anaconda group to form a new association to study the prospecting and exploiting of new copper ore deposits. The state will own 49 per cent of this company. The copper ore from Exótica is refined at Chuquicamata, and the mine is rented to Anaconda.

El Teniente S.A.: established by Braden, a branch of Kennecott. The state acquired 51 per cent of the new incorporated company for $80,000,000. In addition, the new company will have recourse to foreign credits of $100,000,000 and internal credits from the state of $20,000,000. El Teniente S.A. will have a board of directors composed of five persons: two representatives of Kennecott, two of the Chilean government, and one representative from the international financial organizations supplying the credits — this last will be elected by the government in the future. The new tax rate will be 20 per cent on profits, with an additional 30 per cent on distributed profits.

4. AMOUNT OF INVESTMENT
   Projected investments are:

	TOTAL INVESTMENTS (MILLIONS OF DOLLARS)
Anaconda Group (incl. Exótica)	135
Minera Andina	81
El Teniente S.A.	200
	416

Of these investments, Government's holding will be:

in *Minera Andina:*
   25% of shares   bought for only. $1.5 million

(The Government will also supply the Company with a loan of $15 million.)

in *El Teniente S.A.:*
   51% of shares   bought for only $80.0 million

(The Government will also supply the Company with a 20-year loan of $20 million.)

in *Exótica:*
   25% of shares   bought for only $3.75 million

(Figures for a possible governmental loan to Exótica or to another Anaconda subsidiary are not available.)

5. OTHER MEASURES

A complementary measure is the transformation of the Department of Copper into the Copper Corporation, with a greater range of responsibilities, especially in the fields of commercialization and financing of copper production.

Several other measures concern health, housing, and education of miners. Another interesting subject is the expansion of copper production to be able to compete in price and quality on the international market. This phase will come about with the participation of Anaconda, private Chilean companies and possibly the Corporación de Fomento.

138.

ECONOMIC

DEVELOPMENT

OF

COLOMBIA

Hernan Echavarría

140.

The Author

HERNAN ECHAVARRIA, who was appointed Colombian Ambassador to the United States in February 1967, is an industrialist with a background in economics. He is the president of two Bogotá companies, Lamines del Caribe and Cerámica Corona Ltda., and is a member of the boards of directors of various other enterprises. He studied at the Victoria University of Manchester and the London School of Economics and is the author of several books dealing with economics. He also has been president of the Economics Association. Prior to his Washington appointment, Mr. Echavarría served as Minister of Public Works (1943 and 1959) and Minister of Communications (1959).

Contents

Economic Development of Colombia / *Hernan Echavarría*

142.

Introduction

Few people would deny that in recent history most South American countries have been deliberately following economic policies that create excess demand, followed by regulations and controls that seek to maintain stability. This has certainly been the case in Colombia, Chile, Argentina, Uruguay, and Brazil. With slight local variations, the characteristics of these policies, the methods used to carry them out, and the results obtained have been remarkably similar in each case.

These policies were initiated just after World War II, and during the past two decades they have undergone a process of development and adaptation to specific situations, but at no time have they been abandoned or substantially modified. They emerged as a response to the new concept of the modern state as the responsible agent and prime mover of economic development. No doubt the economic development success story of the Soviet Union contributed much to their nearly universal acceptance. Although no longer such a clear-cut solution, at the end of World War II firm government intervention in the elaboration and execution of development plans seemed the obvious answer to existing economic problems. And perhaps it still does seem so to a large portion of Latin American public opinion.

In economic systems based largely on private enterprise, the state's most important activity is necessarily oriented toward the creation of social capital — that is, capital for large scale public works to benefit all society. Therefore, as a corollary of the new theory, which holds the state to be the principal agent of economic development, high government expenditures have been generally accepted without question. The argument starts with the unquestionable assumption that social needs in Latin American countries are unlimited. Among many other things, there exists a gross shortage of good highways and railroads, power plants, schools, and public health and sanitation facilities. Actually, even in the richest and most developed countries the needs of the state seem unlimited.

In view of these obvious needs of the modern state, Colombians have accepted constant growth in public spending, whether financed by foreign loans, increased taxes, or the issue of additional currency. To govern is to spend, according to popular wisdom, and since World War II the criterion of good government has been the amount of money spent by successive administrations. Neither the way in which funds have been accumulated, nor whether they have been efficiently invested, has seemed to concern either the general public or government officials. Nearly all of the latter have belonged to the "Kubitschek" or "proyectista" schools. They consider grandiose state projects not only the source and the very essence of economic development, but the only possible way of helping the masses. These ideas have been clearly expressed by distinguished Colombian statesmen and, for that matter, are shared by many foreign economic experts who have been assigned to Latin American missions. The truth is, however, that they are in large part hangovers from liberal thinking popular during the 1930's. Oversimplifying, the thesis contends that anything the state does automatically benefits the general public, whereas the activities of private enterprise benefit only individual entrepreneurs. Politically, then, development is dependent exclusively on the formation of social capital, and productive enterprise is practically irrelevant.

There are obvious limitations to the amount of foreign aid and internal taxes the state may obtain to finance its projects. But another resource — on which there is no real limit — is the issue of currency. Theoretically, the Colombian constitution forbids the government to print money without proper reserves. Theoretically, too, the Central Bank is a private institution empowered to lend money to the state as it sees fit. In practice, however, the Ministry of Finance can obtain whatever capital it needs to finance fiscal deficits. Thus the government can initiate all kinds of new projects, merely issuing the necessary currency to pay for the expenses.

The concept of the modern state as a prime mover in economic development, together with the ease with which the state can issue the money it needs, necessarily leads to inflation. Public opinion has come to accept, or at least tolerate, this inflation, and many well known economists still maintain that inflation is inevitable as long as the need for social capital is so great. This way of thinking suggests the state can simply conjure up at the mint the material resources that the country lacks.

No doubt monetary expansion has permitted public works that never would have been realized had the state conformed to more orthodox fiscal policies. This is the argument of the inflationists. They claim that the end justifies the means: even though accomplished through inflationary measures, in the final analysis the works remain, despite the accompanying inflation. The problem of inflation is then met by direct controls and state intervention in an attempt to maintain the standard of living of the masses. Prices and the rate of monetary exchange must be artificially kept down, and successive salary boosts must be decreed.

This, in short, is the economic policy Colombia has adopted during the last two decades. As mentioned above, the policy has been deliberate; moreover, it has been generally accepted by public opinion. Only recently has there been an awareness of the dangers of inflation. Nevertheless, inflation in Colombia has not reached the proportions it has in other South American countries. Measured by the rise in the cost of living, the Colombian peso has averaged an annual decrease in purchasing power of 10.4 per cent over the last ten years.[1] But this moderate figure obscures the drastic proportions reached in specific years, such as 21.4 per cent in 1957 and 35.4 per cent in 1964. At this rate, inflation in Colombia has been sufficient to create economic problems and considerable social unrest.

Undoubtedly experience has begun to raise questions about the efficiency of inflation as a positive tool for economic development. Of course, many times an identical set of facts can be used to argue an economic question one way or another, but there are indications that fewer people persist in believing that monetary expansion can make up for a lack of the material resources a country needs for development. Experience has shown, moreover, that inflation is easily touched off but it is very difficult to check. Once excess demand creates unbalances

---

[1] The data in this paper extend through 1964.

in production, it is nearly impossible politically to establish the discipline that is necessary for the return to an efficiently functioning economy.

But even though ranks of the inflationists have thinned, many people still adhere to the notion that a high level of public spending is indispensable to national development. This idea is naturally based on the "proyectista" thesis that grandiose state projects are not only indispensable to and synonymous with rapid development, but that they are the only possible means of benefiting the general public. Colombian economic literature is full of allusions to ambitious projects intended to cure economic ills and raise the general standards of living — housing, power, irrigation projects, and so forth. But interestingly enough, very rarely does one find mention of production goals for rice or corn, or of plans for the construction of textile plants for increased cloth production, or projects for new brick plants necessary for eventual housing construction. Rather than concerning itself with directly productive enterprise, the economy remains oriented toward ambitious government projects, and public opinion complacently approves the ever-increasing allocation of funds necessary to carry them out. Society's most liberal factions base their hopes in these state works to achieve a higher standard of living for the public at large, but they give only passing consideration to what happens meanwhile in the field of production.

1. Social versus Private Capital

Now, it is obvious that any development process requires the allocation of a reasonable proportion of the national income for the needs of the state and for the formation of social capital. However, the available statistics on Colombia's economy indicate that the government must have been siphoning off a very high percentage of available resources. It is very difficult to make a sound analysis of what actually has been happening in Colombia's economy because of the lack of reliable statistics on production, from which could be calculated the national income. Exact production figures even for such basic items as potatoes and corn simply do not exist. Estimates of the number of head of cattle in the country run from a low of 8 million to a high of 15 million. Under these conditions, any estimate of the national product is nearly worthless. Even ostensibly reliable statistics appearing in international publications are taken from local sources that cannot be trusted.

The annual increase in public expenditures by the Colombian government[1] over the last ten years has been 13.6 per cent. In 1964 it reached 5 billion pesos. It is difficult to say just what proportion of the total national income this figure represents; estimates run between 10 per cent and 20 per cent. Judging from the total output of the coffee industry, which is also about 5 billion pesos annually, the latter figure is probably closer to being correct. The coffee industry — by far the most important in the country — sustains some three million Colombians or about 20 per cent of the population. This group enjoys a relatively high standard of living compared with the population at large; in fact, a good proportion of the remaining four-fifths of the population does not even operate within the money economy of the country. Therefore, 5 billion pesos must be at least 20 per cent of the total GNP and must be more than 20 per cent of the market economy, which is what really counts.

The magnitude of the sum devoted to social overhead, as well as the annual rate of this figure is a result of the "proyectista"

---

[1] State and municipal governments have their own separate budgets.

school of thought, which recommends high taxation to implement development. This idea has been reinforced by administrators of foreign aid, whose point of view is that there should be equitable distribution of the tax load. Since they are distributing money supplied by the United States taxpayer, they obviously want the Colombian citizen to share the burden, too. However, the contributions of the Colombian taxpayer cannot satisfactorily replace United States aid. The essence of foreign aid lies in the fact that it is administered in dollars, which permit the importation of commodities not produced in Colombia. Since development is the goal the actual effect on development strategy takes priority over the fairness of relative tax burdens as a criterion for judging tax merits of higher or lower domestic taxation.

The question of what influence vigorous public spending may have on economic development can be argued with equal logic to entirely different conclusions. On the one hand, it can be said that high state expenditures, by creating demand and opening new internal markets, are therefore an important factor in development. But it is also reasonable to conclude that the high taxes necessary to allow this spending diminish resources available for private investment, thus impeding the growth of directly productive capital.

Which of the two viewpoints is correct depends on the particular case and situation. In a rural, agrarian economy that operates largely without money, state expenditures may indeed act as catalyst for the process of monetization and modernization. In this case the government is putting existing but unused or under-utilized resources to work. But in a developed economy with full employment, state spending may merely compete with the investments of private industry, thus hindering the continued growth of productive enterprise.

Colombia is a mixed case. A good proportion of the economy is scratching for subsistence outside the monetized sector, while another part is as economically developed as an industrialized nation. During the 1930's, government with its accompanying taxation undoubtedly did exercise a salutory effect on the development of the economy; a little extra demand and a higher level of monetization helped Colombia recuperate from the deflation caused by the Great Depression. Postwar and present day conditions are very different, however. The accumulation of foreign reserves during World War II produced monetary expansion that successively has worsened each time currency has been issued to cover fiscal deficits. The ensuing expansion of demand has brought about full utilization of the monetary portion of the economy, and this has created shortages of certain resources, as well as of foreign exchange and technical and administrative know-how.

In such circumstances, additional demand must necessarily force prices up. And any transference of economic activity from the private sector to the government can only produce a decline in private investment, thus inhibiting the growth of means of production. Hence, it really becomes a question of which deserves priority at the present time: More social capital for social projects or more investment to satisfy consumer demand? Is there greater need for new highways or for more consumer goods?

But it is a little more complicated than merely deciding between consumption and capital accumulation — it is more a question of development strategy. Some people think that the formation of social capital is the key to development and accordingly deserves top priority, even to the point of absorbing virtually all available resources. Others consider that while social capital is basic, it needs to be balanced by the simultaneous growth of private investment to meet the demands of the consumer and to strengthen means of production through the purchase of tools and industrial equipment.

The difference in approach seems to be the difference between those who consider that ambitious public works make a nation great and those that believe that a great nation can carry out great works. That is, the former believe that grandiose public works provide an initial, external push to start the process of modernizing the economy. The latter contend that it is the "internal combustion," or general economic activity, that generates the drive and the resources necessary to increase levels of consumption, as well as to create a broad social infrastructure to support the developing economy.

2. The System of Taxation

The question of taxation, necessary for social projects, is a difficult one. Unfortunately, political emotions color the economic problem, and the tendency is to adopt a criterion of equity rather than choosing the most appropriate means for attaining the fastest economic development possible, within a framework of political freedom. In all fairness, any system of taxation should be progressive. But even such democratic countries as the United States, England, and Sweden recognize that there are limits beyond which progression cannot be carried within free enterprise without having negative effects on economic growth.

In any system of free enterprise, private capital accumulation is obviously necessary, and the rate of growth of means of production (and therefore of the general standard of living) is dependent upon the magnitude of such savings. Under these circumstances it is not hard to understand why a dilemma arises in every progressive movement, including the Alliance for Progress. How can economic growth be encouraged without making the rich even richer?

The argument can be made that high taxes do not necessarily reduce the rate of private capital investment, but that they may merely curtail the taxpayer's consumption of nonessential luxury items. Which of these two occurs depends on the historical background and on the present circumstances of each country. If the society is entrepreneurial-minded and if the social climate is generally favorable, it is quite possible that the affluent classes hardest hit by a progressive tax schedule will prefer to reduce their consumption of luxury items and maintain or even increase their level of investment. But if a sizable portion of the population is not thus phychologically oriented, or if the social and political atmosphere is unfavorable, it is more than likely that increases in taxes on those who accumulated capital will cut levels of investment more than consumption. The way a tax system is conceived and applied also plays an important role in determining the taxpayer's reaction.

The case of Colombia is illustrative. The progressive tax schedule established in 1935 was designed to tax all types of property and income, but in effect it has taxed only property and income belonging to the monetized sector of the economy. Capital invested in real estate is usually protected from high taxes by artificially low appraisals. And since the entire agricultural and livestock industries of the country are operations carried on by individual landowners, the taxation on incomes from these activities has been, and is even today, very difficult. In contrast, effective taxation is possible on industrial and commercial operations, particularly on incorporated organizations, since the value of the capital investment and of the annual income can be directly determined from the enterprise's books.

Hence, the first tax law was relatively burdensome for industrial and commercial activities, compared to the effect of the taxation of real estate and the attemped taxation on activities operating outside of the monetized sector. Through the years this unequal situation has become more severe due to successive increases in the progressive tax schedule and due to inflation, which by itself exaggerates the tax progression. Today personal income taxes in Colombia are higher than those in the United States (except in the highest brackets in the United States, at levels where there are none in Colombia).[2] Corporation income tax rates are lower, but after excess profit taxes and other supplementary excises are added, the tax liabilities of profitable corporations are higher in Colombia than in the United States.

---

[2] A group of outside experts who recently studied Colombia's tax system consider it quite satisfactory, recommending that rates be made even more progressive. They base their conclusions mainly on criteria of social justice and emphasize the pressing needs of government. These experts even go so far as to claim that tax rates on real income should be higher in Colombia than those on equivalent real income in the United States; taxes in Colombia, they say, should be related to the social position of the taxpayer. A manager of a business enterprise in Colombia consequently should pay the same rate as a manager in the United States, aside from consideration of his real earnings. The same would apply to physicians, lawyers, and other occupational social groupings. Whatever foundation this approach may have from a perspective of social justice, such approaches ignore the fact that Colombia is not an isolated entity, that it has close ties with other countries. These ties involve international migrations as well as trade and political relations. In view of these ties, Colombia can hardly afford higher progressive tax rates since the result would inevitably be an emigration of her qualified personnel and the loss of potential immigrants possessing needed skills. I cannot imagine that these experts believe Colombia can or should effectively isolate herself from the rest of the world.

Particularly burdensome is the excess profits tax, which applies to all earnings running over 12 per cent of an enterprise's total capital investment. Bank loans presently carry interest rates of 12 per cent and are moving toward 14 per cent. Moreover, continuing inflation has increased profits in devalued currency, which are calculated as a rate of return on the cost of investment made years ago. The result is that every day more companies become subject to the excess profits tax, and, in view of the continuing inflation, this tax becomes more burdensome.

We thus can see that Colombia's present system of taxation and government expenditure is working against the best interests of rapid national development. On the one hand, it favors the non-monetized sector and non-productive activities, such as speculation in real estate; it also favors small individual production units as against corporate organizations. On the other hand, it allocates too great a proportion of the national income to the formation of social capital and to public services, thereby limiting the growth of directly productive enterprises and creating shortages of goods and price increases. It would come as no surprise if under these conditions increases in taxation would reduce investment rather than the consumption of luxury items, which would be desirable.

At first glance it might appear that tax reform aimed at real estate speculation and small, unincorporated business activity might produce beneficial results. This could have been the case three or four years ago, before the high levels of public spending and inflation that we see today had been reached. But under the present circumstances, with the economy already overly strained, any further increase in taxes or in public spending can only aggravate the existing shortage of goods, thus creating even greater social problems.

Here again we have a case in which it is possible to argue with logic from different perspectives. One line of argument has it that inflation is brought about by the government's lack of revenues. To curtail inflation, it would be necessary only to increase revenues through higher taxation. Moreover, with this added revenue the government could undertake additional welfare projects to promote the country's economic development and social progress. The other line of argument is that beyond some point, greater state expenditures necessarily result in a lower rate of growth of private investment in productive enterprise and therefore eventually in less production of consumer goods. The automatic market reaction to this scarcity of goods is a corresponding rise in prices, adding to the spiraling inflation, even if the quantity of money is kept more or less stable.

3. The Effects of Foreign Aid

We can see which of these two mechanisms has been operative by a brief review of Colombian economic history. From 1926 to 1929, Colombia received considerable foreign aid, in compensation for the loss of its Panama territory and through loans from the United States. In a little over two years a total of some $100 million poured into Colombia, a substantial sum considering that only about $80 million were in circulation in the country at the time. The arrival of these funds permitted extraordinary state expenditures, which resulted in a sharp rise in the cost of living and social unrest very similar to that which Colombia has experienced in the last few years. Eventually it became necessary to pass emergency laws for the importation of food and other consumer goods. The government projects had reduced agricultural production by absorbing a sizable share of the country's already scarce productive resources. This may sound strange, since theoretically the public works being carried out by the state — mostly highways and railroads — must have helped to augment agricultural production. But it was a question of timing: the social overhead investment was being made faster than the economy could expand to take advantage of it.

It is this slow capacity for expansion in the Colombian economy that Colombian "proyectistas" and foreign experts have not taken into account once again in recent years. Though Colombia today enjoys many more resources than in 1929, it is still severely limited compared to larger or more industrially advanced nations. This means that any sharp increase in demand tends to immediately produce a rise in prices. The corresponding increase in production, necessarily lagging behind, cannot meet the demand with sufficient speed.

The Colombian economy reacts in this way due to weaknesses in organized, monetized industry, and commerce. These areas of the economy lack sufficient organization, technically trained personnel, and machinery to respond rapidly to increases in demand. Government-induced increases in demand draw people from the non-monetized, subsistence economy, converting them into consumers in the national market. This precisely is the role that the state should assume to stimulate a traditional, stagnating economy. It can be argued then that such government action is beneficial provided it proceeds *pari passu* with the general expansion of the economy, so that increased production may satisfy the increased demand. If, on the other hand, the increased demand outstrips the economy's capacity to meet it with correspondingly increased production, the result is a scarcity of goods and a rise in the cost of living.

This is what happened in Colombia in 1929 and again in recent years. The government draws people from rural subsistence economy areas at an ever-increasing rate. These groups cease being producers of consumer goods (though the goods may have been only for their own consumption) and become consumers in the monetized sector of the economy. Organized Colombian commerce and industry are unable to meet the increased demand, due partly to their relatively small size and to the high rates of taxation which have considerably reduced private capital accumulation. Furthermore, government controls on foreign trade — a subject to be discussed later — do not allow the increased demand to be satisfied through the importation of goods.

The expansion of state activities also encourages increasing urbanization. The Colombian government, like that of all Latin American countries, is highly centralized and bureaucratic. Much of the demand created by the state is therefore concentrated in the capital and in two or three other large cities. The concentration is such that the capital, Bogota, represents from 40 per cent to 50 per cent of the country's purchasing power for industrial goods. In contrast, such rural zones as the departments of Cauca and Nariño account for only about 2 per cent. This centralization of demand naturally produces a movement of economic activity from rural areas to the cities. In view of the administrative centralization of the government, the greater the state expenditures, the greater the circulation of money in the nation's capital and in the other few cities that produce items demanded by the bureaucratic middle class. This greater circulation of money makes economic activity in these centers more profitable than similar activity in rural areas. Hence the tendency is to abandon agricultural production in favor of urban commerce and industry to meet the demands of the upper and middle classes. Such a transformation in economic activity can result only in a greater shortage of basic consumer goods and an even higher cost of living for the lower-income groups.

The experience of Colombia has demonstrated the economic and social effects of high government expenditures. The results in 1929, when state spending was made possible by foreign aid, were the same as those in 1962, when public works were financed by issuing currency and by taxation. In both cases Colombia suffered economic dislocations such as inflation, rapid urban growth, greater concentration of wealth, and reduction of mass consumption. And, as was to be expected, the higher cost of living provoked great social unrest.

Contrary to popular opinion in most Latin American countries, the value of foreign aid can be a limited one, for the very reasons we have just seen in the case of Colombia in 1929. Aid money, coming from outside and spent within the country, creates demand for many goods and services that are locally produced. If the demand can be met by the national commerce and industry, then the whole economy benefits from foreign aid and can accelerate its resulting growth and integration. But if a greater, excessive demand is created, bottlenecks inevitably hinder efficient production.

It may be argued that the public works financed with foreign aid should facilitate increased production, which in turn would break down bottlenecks. While this is true in theory, of course, in practice the results depend on the balance of growth among the different areas of the economy. What has happened to Colombia in the last four or five years is a practical demonstration of the cost that results when the growth is unbalanced. Excessive public expenditure has been followed by excessive urbanization and price increases of consumer goods. We now have serious economic distortions that result in social cost which is borne by the consumer, giving rise to social unrest.

Depending on regulations governing the country's international trade, foreign aid may, of course, be used to finance importation of commodities necessary to break down production bottlenecks created by the excess demand brought about by excessive state spending. This has not been possible in Colombia, however, due to trade policies that are geared to bring about self-sufficiency by prohibiting the importation of anything even remotely capable of being produced within the country. The truth is that Colombia has tried to do everything simultaneously; it has sought to invest in vast social overhead and in all types of private industry at the same time. The restriction of imports has undoubtedly stimulated industrialization, and at the same time has made industrialization more difficult and expensive due to the lack of equipment, raw materials, and consumer goods.

It must be remembered that foreign aid has two mutually supporting aims. The one most frequently mentioned is that of enabling the country to import the capital goods that it does not produce and that are indispensible to its development. Since these capital projects bring about a higher level of economic activity, there is need for the importation of additional commodities. The other aim of foreign aid therefore is to provide the foreign exchange to finance these imports. This second objective has been forgotten in recent years in Colombia, and as a result foreign aid has been subjecting the economy to serious strains. Foreign aid has financed many capital projects, but the autarkic policies of the government have not permitted the importation of goods necessary to meet the new demand created by the projects.

It is obvious that increased economic activity creates needs for more raw materials, tools, and machinery. Many of these, even if they are produced within the country, must still be imported to meet the additional demands created. The sources of production within a country cannot expand or re-tool overnight to deliver the needed goods at a moment's notice. As a result, if government control blocks their importation, the national production is put under stress, and bottlenecks inevitably form. This further aggravates the inflation already stimulated by the issue of currency made necessary by high state expenditures.

In a case such as the one we are analyzing, the importation of consumer goods, as well as that of machinery and raw materials, is also essential. Important construction projects financed with foreign aid can be carried out only if balanced by a greater supply of consumer goods on the market to meet increased consumer demand. If the need for more consumer goods is not taken into account, shortages develop, with corresponding rises in the cost of living. Hence, importations of articles in short supply are the key to economic and social stability during periods of vigorous public spending.

4. The Effects of Inflation

This detailed analysis of the inflationary ills Colombia has suffered in recent years might be interpreted as an argument in favor of stability, even at the expense of economic growth. This argument is not widely accepted. The general view is that any serious attempt at development necessarily produces economic tensions that result in inflation. Such has been the experience in many parts of the world, and it has naturally served to strengthen the arguments of Latin American inflationists. But for the very reason that special development efforts do tend to produce inflation, it is essential for Latin American countries to adopt policies that will counteract this tendency. Yet the very opposite has been done. The adverse effects of inflation have been taken lightly, and it has been thought that direct state controls could re-establish lost economic equilibrium and at the same time protect the general standard of living menaced by currency depreciation and autarky.

But aside from the social injustices it creates, inflation undoubtedly hinders economic development as well. Contrary to traditional public opinion in Latin America, inflationist policies that may initially stimulate the economy soon became a formidable obstacle to all growth. Only now are Latin Americans beginning to appreciate that arguments against inflation are not arguments in favor of stagnation or stabilization as such.

Inflation has not been feared as it should have been in Latin America, perhaps because Latin Americans have not realized the nature and the administrative complexity of the economies of well-organized, highly developed nations. The general public identifies economic development with the abundance of consumer goods and social services, whereas these are really only the end products of development. No connection is made between the desire for these goods and the necessity of creating and administering the mechanism by which these goods are produced.

Many modern economists also tend to refer to economic development as some vague, indefinite, and abstract process that somehow materializes. But there is nothing abstract or mysterious about economic development. The only mystery seems to be why some countries succeed in launching themselves toward rapid development while others do not. But the means are perfectly clear: It is necessary to create an efficient organization of production, which is easier said than done. Whether production is coordinated by state administration or private entrepreneurs, their roles as managers is to seek out labor, train it, assign rights and obligations to it, and supply it with raw materials and equipment. The means of production are thus integrated and organized for the subsequent production in abundance of goods desired by consumers, and the process is always the same whether under capitalism or socialism.

The operation described above is a well-defined administrative and technical process. If it is carried out rapidly and efficiently, the country experiences economic development and enjoys an abundance of consumer goods. If it is not achieved, there can be no development nor goods for consumption, whatever social policies the state may adopt or whatever the magnitude of the public projects it may undertake.

Inflation makes the process of integration and organization of the means of production difficult if not impossible. It must not be forgotten that in a free enterprise system production derives from the initiative of individuals or groups motivated by expectations of profit. Therefore anything that distorts the relative values of commodities must hinder the rational growth of productive organization.

In an economy suffering inflation, as we have seen in Latin American countries, excess demand not only causes all kinds of distortions, inefficiency, and waste of resources, but also orients individuals toward non-productive activities. An excess of currency destroys interest in greater efficiency and economy in the use of materials and labor, and it encourages monopoly and the hoarding of specie. And, as we have seen, the relatively high purchasing power in cities adds to urban growth at the expense of rural areas. This economic concentration in urban centers encourages entrepreneurs to abandon production in favor of increasingly profitable — but non-productive — speculative activities.

Moreover, once a certain degree of inflation is reached, truly productive enterprise suffers decapitalization, while capital invested in real estate remains safely protected. In such a situation a highly progressive tax schedule — especially one with an excess profits tax, like Colombia's — becomes confiscatory and discriminatory against any monetized activity producing taxable profits. It is not surprising, then, to find more and more businessmen abandoning productive activity for more profitable speculation.

Perhaps even more serious are the political consequences of inflation. Confronted with constantly rising prices and the ever-increasing cost of living, the public tends to blame everything on speculation and on greedy profiteering. Colombian government officials echo this chorus — and no political leader in recent years has admitted that the government bore any responsibility for inflation. The government, hearing the complaints of the populace, willingly responds by freezing prices so that the working classes may consume what is not being produced!

But the consuming public's excess purchasing power cannot be checked, controls or no controls. Apparently the consumer is unable to keep his excess purchasing power in his pocket. If the price of milk or some other commodity is kept artificially low, or is not to be had, then the consumer finds something else — a phonograph or a transistor radio, for example — to buy with his nominally higher wages. These items then rise in price, directly or indirectly dragging the prices of everything else up with them. Worse still, production then has no incentive to increase the nation's milk yield, but turns instead to meet the newly created demand for phonograph records and transistor radios.

5. The Exchange Rate and Import Controls

In an economy like Colombia's, which depends to a great degree on foreign imports, the creation of excess demand is immediately reflected in an increase in the rate of exchange. There is an almost direct relationship between internal demand and the demand for foreign currency for financing imports. This explains why the government has to freeze the exchange rate whenever it increases internal demand excessively through the issuance of more currency.

As we have already seen, traditional political and economic thinking has approved of these policies. Public opinion also has accepted them because of the extraordinary prestige of state intervention in economic management.

Moreover, like the man in the street, government naïvely associates increases in the cost of living with increases in the exchange rate. Since the value of foreign currency is seen to rise as internal prices rise, popular logic has it that, to curb inflation, forestall price increases, and assure continued abundance of essential articles, it is only necessary to freeze the rate of exchange. It is presumed that controlling the exchange rate will boost the purchasing power of increasing money incomes, thus allowing the consumer to buy more goods at the same price as before, even though their importation is strictly limited.

The truth of the matter is that as inflation progresses, the rate of exchange can be maintained at a stable level only through the imposition of the strictest import controls. The experience of Colombia since 1945 has demonstrated the functioning of this mechanism on more than one occasion. As the government-fixed rate of exchange becomes less and less realistic compared to the ever-increasing rate on the free market, any further pressure exerted on the balance of payments makes the artificial support no longer tenable. Finally the dam breaks, and the value of the peso is sharply devaluated.

Political resistance to monetary devaluation is strong, yet, interestingly enough, there never seems to be much resistance to inflation and to other government policies that make devaluation inevitable. Colombian popular feeling ran so high after the devaluation of 1962 (which reduced the peso from 6.70 to 9.00 per dollar), that no future devaluation now seems possible without an extraconstitutional change in government. This is explained by the serious consequences of the inflation-producing measures taken by the state at the same time of the devaluation. A general wage increase of 30 per cent was decreed, shortly followed by the issue of currency to finance new state projects.

Obviously Colombia's dilemma is difficult to solve. The "Kubitschek" and "proyectista" schools demand inflationary policies, or at least lean toward such policies. Meanwhile, a good proportion of public opinion is opposed to rising prices at the same time that it is dead set against any new devaluation. The true causes of the low standard of living are not recognized, and the price increases and scarcities are blamed on speculation. Public opinion, which is generally against free enterprise, favors government intervention as a means of curbing speculation.

The managers of production, that is, private businessmen, thus become the scapegoat for Colombia's economic ills.

Moreover, interventionists persist in believing that controls are the key to the rational and efficient organization of production. But these actually make the whole system of production less efficient. Colombia's experience, particularly with imports, clearly shows the undesirable results of policies that encourage excess in demand, and utilize direct controls to prevent price increases.

Since 1945, the rate of exchange in Colombia has been held by the government at artificially low levels on several occasions. The first time was in the years immediately following World War II, when the country refused to take steps to correct the inflation produced by the increase in foreign reserves which had been accumulated during the war. After the devaluation of 1952, in which the peso fell from 1.95 to 2.52 per dollar, government issue of currency touched off a new period of inflation which was soon made even worse by the increase in the price of coffee following the Korean War. In 1957 there was a further devaluation to 6.40. Continued money issues to finance public expenditures finally and inevitably led to the previously mentioned devaluation of 1962. Hence, for the last two decades the country has followed a policy of stimulating excess demand, and of placing rigid control on imports and of freezing the exchange rate. These controls are exceedingly tight at the present time, as indicated by the disparity between the official rate of exchange for paying for imports at 9 pesos per dollar and the free market rate at 14.

Interventionists do not see any disadvantage in the administrative direct control of imports, since they consider decisions by the state on what kinds and amounts of commodities should be imported more efficient than determination by market forces. But in fact, government import controls which ignore the relativity of prices are inefficient to the point of chaos. This is true enough in a centralized economy; in a decentralized democracy such as Colombia, with no integral plan for national production, it is even more so.

The present situation in Colombia points up the impracticability of the proper regulation on imports by the government. The country is suffering shortages of practically all imported goods: car and tractor replacement parts, seeds, industrial raw materials, tools and machinery, etc. Applications for import licenses run two and three times higher than the available currency allocated for imports. The government can no longer choose between essential and non-essential goods for import, but is now forced to decide among a number of absolute essentials.

But in some cases there are no rational guidelines. Are replacement parts for tractors more important than those for cars? Or even more difficult, should the import license be granted to a John Deere or Fordson agent? Government employees, having to constantly make completely arbitrary decisions, are left open to bribery, which frequently leads to administrative inefficiency and high costs.

One of the most evident and costly distortions that have followed policies of import control is over-investment in industrial equipment. A high percentage of installed equipment remains unused, not because of lack of demand but due to the lack of available foreign exchange for the importation of needed raw materials. Nevertheless, since internal demand is excessive, industrial profits are exaggeratedly high, while artificially low exchange rates create windfall profits for those granted import licenses. Regardless of unused installed capacity, it becomes highly profitable to import more and more competitive capital equipment. Continued profits, even at a low level of production, are assured by increasing inflation and the ever-tighter import controls which result.

Evidently, a realistic official rate of exchange is the only way to prevent industrial over-investment in an inflationist regime. Since a non-controlled rate of exchange would rise in direct proportion to the increasing inflation, there would be no particular incentive to import excessive amounts of industrial equipment. This self-regulating mechanism is more efficient than arbitrary decisions made by government officials.

Moreover, it is only with a relatively stable rate of exchange that a nation can organize its imports so that the economic strains brought about by ambitious projects do not bear too heavily on the consuming public. A system of strict import controls does not properly take into account the strain placed on the economy by large-scale social overhead projects, and therefore it cannot produce balanced growth.

At a meeting of the Inter-American Committee for the Alliance for Progress (CIAP) in Mexico in 1964, the economies of Latin American countries were outlined as suffering from "a considerable under-utilization of existing capacity, slow growth of agricultural production and income, and a growing gap between the levels of development in urban and rural areas."

In view of the economic policies followed by these countries since World War II, this outcome is not surprising. High public expenditures financed with taxes, foreign aid, and the issuance of currency, in conjunction with government controls, necessarily have produced greater demand in cities than in rural areas. And the combination of import controls and artificially low rates of exchange could only produce the industrial over-investment that characterizes most South American countries.

6. Summary

An impartial observer would have to admit that the present economic and social situations in Colombia are entirely unsatisfactory. Due to severe shortages of imported commodities, the economy is under considerable stress and is functioning with great inefficiency. The rational and efficient organization of means of production will continue to be extremely difficult as long as an artificially low official rate of exchange is maintained, and goods to be imported are determined by government decree rather than by market forces. But, as noted, any exchange reform in Colombia is now practically impossible politically.

What, then, have been the advantages of the economic policies adopted by Colombia over the last two decades? The country chose the construction of grandiose public works projects as the means to faster development. To achieve results, it has not hesitated to create an almost permanent state of excess demand. Then to counteract the effects of inflation, it has applied rigid controls that have thrown the economy into chaos.

It might be more useful to inquire whether Colombia's rate of economic growth during the last ten years has been higher than that of Latin American countries following more orderly economic policies. In view of the distortions and social unrest created by Colombia's policies, even if its growth were higher than that of countries enjoying relative political and social stability, it would be difficult to decide if it had been worth the price.

We have already mentioned the difficulty in measuring Colombia's economic growth due to the lack of accurate statistics, particularly in the area of agricultural production. An important school of Latin American economists holds that missing statistics can always be obtained by "interpolation," that is, by approximation. For determining general results or tendencies, this is a perfectly acceptable technique. But there is a constant danger of forgetting that the results of interpolation are only approximations and proceeding to base more sophisticated calculations upon them, which are then presented as exact figures.

For this study, only actual statistical data have been used. Colombia's performance between 1955 and 1964 shows substantial variations from year to year, including retrogression. The tables in the Appendix are mainly devoted to mass-consumption manufactured products, with an annual growth rate of between 3 and 8 per cent. There is little reliable data for agricultural production, which is probably expanding at an even more limited rate. The consumption of beef shows an average annual rate of growth of only 2.7 per cent. Industries related to construction, such as bathroom fixtures and asbestos cement, indicate a somewhat higher rate of 6 per cent to 14 per cent. The consumption of steel shows a growth of 11 per cent, undoubtedly due to the relatively high number of reinforced concrete buildings being constructed to meet the concentration of demand in urban centers.

The generation of electric energy has shown a very appreciable annual growth of 13.7 per cent. This is slightly misleading, however, since in some areas there is not sufficient industrial activity to utilize the available energy. True, the production of many basic sectors of the society's substructure remains unknown due to the lack of statistics, but the low growth rate figure for the consumption of gasoline — 4.8 per cent — certainly does not indicate a considerable increase in highway transportation.

In considering the statistics, we must be wary of the possibly misleading figures relating to industrial development. Colombia may produce three times as much caustic soda today as it did ten years ago, and it may also produce enough steel to meet all construction needs. But the country is not necessarily any better off since this was achieved only by restricting important areas of agricultural growth or other industries that are perhaps more essential — even though they are less dramatic — in the long run for supplying the consumer with a higher standard of living. In the final analysis, the success of an economic policy must be judged by the economy's total production, and, in the case of a country like Colombia, this can only be measured in terms of increases in the supply of consumer goods.

Appendix 1955-1964

Table 1   ECONOMIC INDICATORS

	1955	1964	AVERAGE YEARLY RATE OF CHANGE %
Means of payment in circulation (Colombian pesos)	1,933,000,000	8,351,000,000	15.8%
Public expenditures (Colombian pesos)	1,328,000,000	4,736,000,000	13.6
Cost of living index (July 1954-June 1955 equals 100)	101.7	274.4	10.4
Foreign credits (U.S. dollars)[a]	$ 56,000,000	$110,000,000	0.6
Exports (U.S. dollars)	$533,000,000	$470,000,000	− 1.3
Imports (U.S. dollars)	$664,000,000	$518,000,000	− 0.2
Electric power generation (KWH)[b]	1,180,085,000	4,271,887,000	13.7
Steel production (metric tons)	77,489	162,402[c]	11.5
Cement production (metric tons)	1,046,294	1,964,616	6.4
Gasoline production (barrels)	4,929,000	11,688,000	4.8
Fuels, production (gallons)	384,075,000	745,274,000	8.6
Sugar production (tons)	233,066	395,279	5.4
Salt production (tons)	209,242	288,960	3.3
Barley production (tons)	60,000[d]	110,000	6.2
Cotton production (metric tons)	24,672	63,382	9.9
Cotton fabric production (yards)	98,713,000	187,997,000[e]	8.4
Wool cloth production (meters)	4,033,000	5,227,000	3.3
Cigarette production (gross)	4,625,000	6,258,000[e]	3.8
Beer sales (dozens of ⅓ liter bottles)	103,521,000	149,585,000[f]	4.2
Soft drink production (liters)	258,900,000	401,500,000[e]	5.6
Chocolate production (tons)	32,500	39,300[e]	2.4
Pastas (macaroni, spaghetti, etc.) production (tons)	9,200	20,800[e]	10.7
Rice production (tons)	320,200	600,000[g]	6.5
Meat consumption (head)[h]	2,255,000	2,957,000	2.7

[a] More than one year; excludes Internaitonal Monetary Fund loans, bank acceptances, and "swaps."   [b] Excludes private companies.   [c] January to October.   [d] 1957.   [e] 1962.   [f] 1963.   [g] Estimate.   [h] Beef cattle, pigs, lambs, and goats.

Sources: Central Bank, *Boletin Mensual de Estadística,* Report of the General Comptroller of the Republic, *Anuario de Comercio Exterior, Anuario General de Estadística, Procebada,* Instituto de Fomento Algodonero, Distribuidora Bavaria S.A., Federacion Nacional de Arroceros.

Table 2   MONEY SUPPLY, PUBLIC EXPENDITURES, COST OF LIVING

YEAR	MEANS OF PAYMENT IN CIRCULATION		PUBLIC EXPENDITURES		COST OF LIVING (END OF YEAR)	
	MILLIONS OF COLOMBIAN PESOS	ANNUAL CHANGE (%)	MILLIONS OF COLOMBIAN PESOS	ANNUAL CHANGE (%)	PRICE INDEX (BASE = JULY 1954–JUNE 1955)	ANNUAL CHANGE (%)
1955	1,933	—	1,328	—	101.7	—
1956	2,415	24.9%	1,465	10.3%	110.0	8.2%
1957	2,744	13.6	1,379	5.9	133.5	21.4
1958	3,318	20.9	1,718	24.6	144.0	7.9
1959	3,716	12.0	1,891	10.0	155.1	7.7
1960	4,103	10.4	1,891	- 0 -	166.8	7.5
1961	5,112	24.6	3,615	91.2	176.0	5.5
1962	6,169	20.7	4,021	11.2	186.7	6.1
1963	6,922	12.2	4,690	16.6	252.8	35.4
1964	8,351	20.6	4,736*	1.0	274.4	8.5

*Approximation.

Sources: Central Bank (money supply); Central Bank and Report of the General Comptroller of the Republic (public expenditures); *Boletin Mensual de Estadística* (cost of living)

Table 3   EXPORTS, IMPORTS, AND FOREIGN CREDIT

YEAR	EXPORTS		IMPORTS		FOREIGN CREDITS*	
	MILLIONS OF U.S. DOLLARS	ANNUAL CHANGE (%)	MILLIONS OF U.S. DOLLARS	ANNUAL CHANGE (%)	MILLIONS OF U.S. DOLLARS	ANNUAL CHANGE (%)
1955	533	—	664	—	56	—
1956	476	− 10.7%	523	− 22.4%	40	− 28.6%
1957	449	− 5.7	437	− 16.5	194	385.0
1958	409	− 8.9	308	− 29.5	80	− 58.8
1959	417	1.9	403	30.8	77	− 3.8
1960	382	− 8.4	488	21.1	23	− 70.1
1961	374	− 2.1	524	7.4	78	239.1
1962	401	7.2	455	− 13.2	135	73.1
1963	363	− 9.5	556	22.2	133	− 1.5
1964	470	29.4	518	− 6.8	110	− 17.3

*More than one year; excludes IMF loans, bank acceptances, and "swaps."

Source: Central Bank.

Table 4   **ELECTRIC POWER GENERATION***

YEAR	THOUSANDS OF KWH	ANNUAL CHANGE (%)
1955	1,180,085	—
1956	1,276,440	8.2
1957	1,379,496	8.1
1958	1,515,178	9.8
1959	1,666,271	10.0
1960	1,894,026	13.7
1961	1,973,442	4.2
1962	3,381,406	71.3
1963	3,819,409	12.9
1964	4,271,887	11.8
Average annual change, 1955-1964		13.7

*Excludes generation by private companies.

Source: *Boletin Mensual de Estadística.*

Table 5   **STEEL PRODUCTION AND IMPORTS**

YEAR	METRIC TONS			ANNUAL CHANGE (%)
	PRODUCTION	IMPORTS	TOTAL	
1955	77,489	473	77,962	—
1956	90,166	1,155	91,321	17.1
1957	114,384	1,081	115,465	26.4
1958	121,053	1,315	122,368	6.0
1959	108,821	1,421	110,242	− 9.9
1960	156,760	2,161	158,921	44.1
1961	176,090	3,559	179,649	13.0
1962	136,507	5,950	142,457	− 20.7
1963	201,127	5,577	206,704	45.1
1964*	162,402	6,513	168,915	
Average annual change, 1955-1964				11.5

*January to October.

Sources: Central Bank (production); *Anuario de Comercio Exterior,* and *Boletin Mensual de Estadística* (imports).

Table 6   **CEMENT PRODUCTION**

YEAR	METRIC TONS	ANNUAL CHANGE (%)
1955	1,046,294	—
1956	1,220,456	16.6
1957	1,208,357	− 1.0
1958	1,213,262	0.4
1959	1,347,619	11.1
1960	1,384,921	2.8
1961	1,569,173	13.3
1962	1,719,186	9.6
1963	1,769,570	2.9
1964	1,964,616	11.0
Average annual change, 1955-1964		6.4

Source: *Boletin Mensual de Estadística.*

Table 7   **GASOLINE PRODUCTION AND IMPORTS**

YEAR	THOUSANDS OF BARRELS			ANNUAL CHANGE (%)
	PRODUCTION	IMPORTS	TOTAL	
1955	4,929	2,348	7,277	—
1956	5,401	2,237	7,638	5.0
1957	5,956	1,085	7,041	− 7.8
1958	7,817	209	8,026	14.0
1959	8,287	80	8,367	4.2
1960	9,201	312	9,513	13.7
1961	10,744	12	10,756	13.1
1962	11,072	- 0 -	11,072	2.9
1963	10,891	- 0 -	10,891	− 1.6
1964	11,688		11,688	7.3
Average annual change, 1955-1964				4.8

Sources: Central Bank (production); *Anuario de Comercio Exterior* (imports).

Table 8   **COTTON: PRODUCTION, CONSUMPTION,
IMPORTS, AND EXPORTS**

| YEAR | METRIC TONS | | | | ANNUAL CHANGE IN PRODUC- TION (%) | ANNUAL CHANGE IN CONSUMP- TION (%) |
	PRODUC- TION	IMPORTS	EXPORTS	CONSUMP- TION		
1955	24,672	2,404	......	27,076	......	......
1956	22,529	12,407	......	34,936	− 8.7	29.0
1957	20,573	14,738	......	35,311	− 8.7	1.1
1958	25,873	10,864	......	36,737	25.8	4.0
1959	56,408	6,181	......	62,589	118.0	70.4
1960	68,732	717	29,113	40,336	21.8	−35.6
1961	71,509	337	23,608	48,238	4.0	11.9
1962	80,050	627	28,910	51,767	11.9	10.7
1963	64,507	2,940	10,400	57,047	− 19.4	11.0
1964	63,382	......	2,925	60,457	− 1.8	6.0
Average annual change, 1955-1964					9.9	8.3

Sources: Instituto de Fomento Algodonero (production and imports);
Federacion Nacional de Algodoneros (exports).

Table 9   **RICE PRODUCTION**

YEAR	THOUSANDS OF TONS	ANNUAL CHANGE (%)
1955	320.2	—
1956	342.5	7.0
1957	350.2	2.2
1958	380.4	8.6
1959	422.1	10.9
1960	450.0	6.6
1961	473.6	5.2
1962	585.0	23.5
1963	550.0	− 6.0
1964	600.0*	9.1
Average annual change, 1955-1964		6.5

*Estimate.

Source: Federacion Nacional de Arroceros.

ECONOMIC

DEVELOPMENT

OF

Gustavo Romero Kolbeck

MEXICO:

Financing the Infrastructure

The Author

GUSTAVO ROMERO KOLBECK is professor of economics at the National School of Economics of the National University of Mexico and at the University of the Americas in Mexico City. He is also head of the Economic Research Department of the National Bank of Mexico and director of the Investment Commission of the President of the Republic. He has served as delegate to various international conferences, including the 1964 United Nations Conference on Trade and Development in Geneva. His books and articles have mainly dealt with economic development. He is general director of *Business Trends,* an economic bulletin. He is a director of the Confederación de Cámaras de Comercio and of the National University of Mexico.

Economic Development of Mexico / *Gustavo Romero Kolbeck*

Contents

176.

Introduction

That less-developed countries share certain general features in common is hardly a sufficient basis for making universal prescriptions about their economic growth. It is true that these countries are generally characterized by low levels of per capita income, an economic structure in which primary economic activities of low productivity predominate, and a labor force in which large numbers are underemployed. But it is hard to conceive how comprehensive development formulas are to be designed that will apply to low-income countries everywhere, if we take into account the possible economic, political, social, and institutional aspects of underdevelopment. What fuller awareness of development experience in these countries can contribute is better insight into the formulation of specific criteria for policy applicable to individual cases.

Against this background, the present study emphasizes the contribution of two key factors in the economic development of Mexico: the creating of the country's basic economic infrastructure and the financing of economic development. Evaluation of the contribution of these factors is undertaken in the belief that even though error and waste, some of it serious, have been present in Mexican development, the over-all results are encouraging in contrast to experiences in less-developed countries generally. In the last twenty years, Mexico's gross national product (GNP) has increased at an average annual rate of 6 per cent. In 1964, the production of goods and services rose by 10 per cent over the previous year. Presently, per capita income is above $400, as compared with the 1950 level of $183, also measured in current dollars.[1]

[1] This refers to 1964, the latest year for which data was available when this paper was written.

1. Key Factors of Mexico's Economic Development

We were asked by the Committee for Economic Development to make a brief study of Mexico's policy toward the formation of infrastructure and the financing of development. Accordingly, this paper concentrates on these topics. Nevertheless, we want to note that Mexico's economic development has been brought about by the dynamism of the private sector and by the friendly relationship between public and private sectors. It is important to stress this relationship and the contributions made by each sector.

Economic development is a highly complex phenomenon. But the view taken here is that in the most fundamental sense development proceeds from the determination by a society — or at least by an influential section of it — to attain higher standards of living. In Mexico, this attitude has grown steadily in importance, and it has been particularly characteristic of the public sector since 1925. Up to 1940, the Mexican economy was dominated by primary industries, but it has become semi-industrialized since then. The entrepreneurial class has taken advantage of the external economies created by the public sector's investments in the economic, social, and institutional infrastructure, which is described in detail in later chapters.

The private sector has invested its resources in the expansion of existing industries and the establishment of new ones. Modern techniques of commercial banking and commercial distribution have been introduced. The sustained growth of the economy reflects the successful adaptation of the private sector to the changing economic needs of the economy.

Government has facilitated private industrial growth directly and indirectly. Indirectly, development has been aided by social and political stability; by stable exchange rates and by improvements in the public financial institutions, the tax system, and the administration of public expenditures. Direct assistance to the private sector has resulted from policies regarding social security, tax exemptions, and tariff protection; and quantitative controls on imports have promoted production of import-substitutes.

However, despite the cordial relations between the public and private sectors, there are still problems that have to be solved. Perhaps the most important one is the lack of a clear definition of the boundaries of each sector, though it should be pointed out that this condition also exists elsewhere in the world. As in other nations, there is competition in Mexico between the two sectors in certain fields of economic activity. We may state, however, that there is a growing recognition that the public sector should devote its efforts to infrastructure work.

It is likewise true that the country's accelerated growth rate has caused an unbalanced growth of different sectors of the economy, thus creating bottlenecks. Currently, Mexico has sectors that are highly developed and productive as well as those that admittedly are underdeveloped. This situation did not prove to be a serious obstacle to development until recently. Among the key obstacles and limitations are these: a) the small size of Mexico's domestic market, especially the rural market; b) the lack of integration and efficiency in certain industrial sectors; and c) the secular disequilibrium in the balance of payments.

The public and private sectors have a clear awareness of these problems and are making constant efforts to find solutions. Nevertheless, it is necessary to adopt aggressive policies and measures based on more carefully prepared and integrated programs.

Although we will not dwell on the major role played by the private sector in Mexico's present economic position, private enterprise — at times working under adverse conditions — took full advantage of new opportunities and may claim the merit and responsibility as equal partner with the public sector in reaching today's position, a mere starting point for future growth and improvement.

2. The Infrastructure

From the end of the armed conflict of the Revolution of 1910 until well into the 1930's, Mexico's basic infrastructure was totally inadequate to permit the realization of the hopes awakened by the Revolution. The dynamism that the revolutionary movement had brought to society could not be exploited to maximum advantage when the only major element of infrastructure was a railroad system that had been severely damaged in the Revolution. To be sure, there had been some irrigation and port facilities, but these too had thoroughly deteriorated by the end of the Revolution. What was needed was a program of public works and other efforts to create an infrastructure that would promote economic development.

The creation of infrastructure greatly expands the scope of private investment by increasing profit-making opportunities for private business. With such an incentive, businessmen increase their investment in the economy by creating enterprises based on fields opened by public works. When these private firms develop to the point of integration or of forming industrial complexes, they generate new external economies. All this contributes in turn to increase output in the same way that external economies were generated earlier by public works. As we shall observe later, Mexico's public policy in this area was adapted to prevailing conditions, placing emphasis pragmatically on those sectors of the infrastructure that would give the greatest impulse to economic development, at times through promoting higher output, or at other times through changing the structure of production.

Mexico created its infrastructure through the public sector, and especially by the use of a sustained program of public works. These public works permitted the gradual realization of the aspirations of important groups and facilitated geographic and social mobility introduced by the Revolution.

As soon as armed hostilities ended and some measure of confidence was restored, the railroads were rehabilitated, and the basic plant, together with the capital at hand, was used to pull output up to pre-Revolutionary levels. But the railroad system was oriented toward export markets and could not sustain further expansion, and there was a general lack of efficient basic industrial plant. These inadequacies held back economic development between 1921 and 1934.

After 1925, the production of goods and services tended to stagnate, due both to a general lag in national economic activity and to the Great Depression of the 1930's. Public investment also stagnated between 1925 and 1934, averaging about 2.5 per cent of gross national product annually, or 92.8 million pesos adjusted to current prices.

The consolidation of revolutionary political groupings and the laying of the institutional foundations on which the future progress of the country would rest was the outstanding achievement of the period 1921-1934. Major banks were created in this period: the Central Bank of Mexico (Banco de México), National Bank of Agricultural Credit (Banco de Crédito Agrícola), National Urban Mortgage and Public Works Bank (Banco Nacional Hipotacasio Urbano y de Obras Públicas), National Industrial Development Corporation (Nacional Financiera). The basis for establishing additional financial institutions was also provided. Two key specialized agencies were created, The National Irrigation Commission, (Comisión Nacional de Irrigación), and National Highway Commission (Comisión Nacional de Caminos), both destined to play an important part in the construction of public works.

Beginning in 1935, public investment increased dramatically, being channeled mainly into the rebuilding and reconditioning of the railroads and, to a lesser extent, into irrigation and highway construction. In terms of 1950 prices, public investment moved from 417 million pesos in 1934 to 887 million pesos in 1940, or from 2.5 per cent to 4.3 per cent of national product. This facilitated the movement of products; it also encouraged productive enterprise that had been released both as a consequence of agrarian reform and of the breakdown of old barriers impeding social and economic mobility.

The increasing number of small individual farmers — who represent private enterprise at its best — was the main factor in halting the descending trend in agricultural production and in pushing it beyond the point of self-sufficiency in foodstuffs. Mexico has now become an important exporter of cotton, coffee, fruits, vegetables, and other products previously imported for internal consumption. This was especially true for commercial farming. Notwithstanding the depression in the United States and expropriation of the Mexican petroleum industry, between 1935 and 1940 Mexico's national product expanded at an annual average rate of no less than 4.4 per cent. Public investment increased at an average rate of 10 per cent a year.

This six-year period had great importance in the modernization of Mexico's economy. In taking on a dynamic role as an investor, the state contributed to the growth of wider markets in a political and institutional setting consistent with Mexican realities. In so doing, it provided adequate incentives to private businessmen and thereby stimulated further investment in productive activities, accelerating the whole process of industrialization. This is reflected in the growth of gross national product since 1935, which has increased at an average yearly rate of 5.9 per cent in constant prices. Public investment rose at an even higher rate — 10.2 per cent yearly — increasing its share of GNP from 3.5 per cent in 1935 to 8.2 in 1963. This reinforces the view that public investment acquired the most dynamic position in the Mexican economy.

Public investment between 1925 and 1934 was used principally for the improvement of transportation and communications. Rehabilitation and expansion of the railroads accounted for 62.3 per cent, and highways, which the country sorely needed, accounted for 12.4 per cent. Improvement of port facilities accounted for an additional 2.3 per cent. Thus, transportation and communications absorbed no less than 77 per cent of total public investment; the remaining 23 per cent was divided equally between allocations for irrigation and social welfare in agriculture. In this ten-year period, public investment climbed to 928 million pesos but tended to remain stationary as a per cent of GNP.

In the following six years, from 1935-1940, public expenditures on improvements in the nation's railroad system were maintained at a high level, as were those for highways and irrigation. A new dimension of public investment was added, however, with the financing of electric power development. Up to this time, investment in electric power generation was wholly accountable to foreign enterprises. Public investment in this sector of economic activity arose out of the belief that it would promote political and social integration and encourage greater mobility of productive factors in all parts of the country.

The general lines laid down in this period carried forward into the next six-year period (1941-1946), although public investment increased at a slower rate, the annual average in those years being 5.88 per cent in contrast to the 9.9 per cent average of the previous period.

Since 1946, the allocation of public investment by sectors of economic activity had undergone significant changes. A great deal having been accomplished in the development of nation-wide railroad and highway networks, expenditures for transportation declined. They now account for only 3.2 per cent of public investment. On the other hand, investment in electric power and petroleum has been increasing to meet changing industrial needs — so much so, that from 1959 to 1963 these two activities accounted for 32.4 per cent of public investment. Another upward trend is seen in the provision for social welfare, which accounted for 21.5 per cent of public investment in the 1959-1963 period.

The profound effects that investment in basic infrastructure have had on the whole process of economic development are difficult to identify in their entirety. Modernization of the country's basic communications system has led to greater integration of people. It has facilitated the expansion of markets. It has made possible the development of certain resources that were previously uneconomic. It has accelerated the mobility of productive factors. The promotion of agriculture, stock-raising, and irrigation projects has changed Mexico's export structure radically by expanding exports of agricultural commodities at the same time that mineral exports have decreased. Meanwhile, increasing agricultural income has enlarged the internal market. The expansion of electric power capacity has been sufficient to take care of increased industrial demand. All this has given other basic industries a forward push, has encouraged the economic development that we now see, and has brought about many other results that are too numerous to list here.

Despite the fact that Mexico is now endowed with an infrastructure designed to give rise to higher living standards and to reduce the underemployment of the nation's resources, there are naturally many things that remain to be done. There is a serious lack of feeder roads. The illiteracy rate is still very high. The scarcity of trained manpower keeps industrial production costs too high. In many regions of the country, farm output is much too low. It is likely that at least one-third of the 350,000 new workers being added to the nonagricultural labor force every year are grossly underemployed and will remain so.

3. Financing Development

Once the armed stage of the revolution ended, the government's main task was to establish a basic political, economic, social, and institutional structure. The nation's financial system was in a chaotic condition: Numerous banks had gone into bankruptcy; confidence in paper money had been lost because the contending revolutionary factions had abused the power of issue; not only had service on the foreign debt been suspended but there was virtually no prospect that payment would be resumed. Under these circumstances, the government decided to give primary attention to monetary policy and reorganization of the banking system. By creating adequate financial channels, the government hoped to facilitate the construction of basic infrastructure projects, whose necessity was clear to all, as well as lend assistance to the private sector. Creation of the Central Bank (the Banco de México), with exclusive power of issue; the National Banking Commission (Comisión Nacional Bancaria); and other governmental financial institutions laid the groundwork for a financial system that would contribute notably to improvement in the use of Mexico's resources. Between 1925 and 1934, financial authorities tried to create an aura of confidence through primary reliance on balanced budgets, nonexpansionist monetary policies, and other orthodox financial practices. Public investment drew its funds from resources that had previously been earmarked for military and administrative expenditures. (The latter amounted to less than 1 per cent of public investment in the period from 1925 to 1934, as against 32 per cent in 1909 and 1910.) Mexico set about to create a truly modern financial structure based on sound financial and fiscal policies. Confidence in the banking system was restored, while the reforms of 1913-1932 strengthened the position of the Central Bank. The country was taken off the gold standard.

In the period from 1935 to 1940, as economic policy was released from restrictions imposed by strict nineteenth century monetary orthodoxy, the government launched an aggressive public works program. Since it was virtually impossible to obtain foreign credits, the program was financed exclusively from domestic resources. It is important to remember that service on the foreign public debt had been suspended since 1924 and that Mexico's relations abroad had deteriorated as a result of conflicts over the petroleum industry. To make matters worse, international money markets were generally weak and few new credit lines were being opened. Under these circumstances, public expenditures in Mexico had to depend exclusively on tax revenue and public borrowing at home. (Tax evasion in one form or another constituted a truly chronic problem for economic development when taxes were between 7.5 per cent and 8.5 per cent of GNP.) It was fortunate that deflationary effects of the world-wide depression of the 1930's and other conditions combined to prevent inflationary price increases.

In the following years, from 1940 to 1963, a great deal of dynamism characterized development of the Mexican economy. Gross national product increased at an annual average rate of 6 per cent and gross investment at 10 per cent. Mexico's credit standing in international money markets was strengthened — a very positive factor in Mexican development. Investment was still financed mainly from domestic savings. However, during the early years of World War II, foreign investment began to assume significant proportions in manufacturing and service industries, and in recent years it again increased perceptibly, this time largely in the form of indirect investment. Over the entire 14 years, foreign investment accounted for somewhat less than 10 per cent of gross investment. The conditions placed on foreign loans also became increasingly more favorable to Mexico as soon as foreign financial sources began to judge the country as a safe credit risk. More favorable evaluation of Mexico's debt capacity was based on Mexico's rapid growth and political stability; its liquidation of old debts and record for punctual payment of new ones; the existence of an integrated program of public works; the establishment of a sound financial structure; and, as a consequence of greater exports and tourist receipts, an expansion of foreign reserves. Despite the increase in the ratio of foreign investment to total investment in recent years, internal savings have also increased — from 9 per cent of GNP in 1963, to 12 per cent in 1950, to 12.5 per cent in 1963.

Meanwhile, sources of public investment adjusted to changing economic developments. Between 1939 and 1964 no less than 94.2 per cent of public investment was financed out of domestic resources. Such a high level of domestic saving was due in part, as noted earlier, to the extreme difficulty Mexico encountered in seeking credits abroad. It would have been even higher if the country's ability to obtain foreign credits had not improved so markedly after Mexico resumed service on the nation's foreign debt in 1941. This was faciliated by a consolidation of the debt through agreements reached with the United States government and the International Committee of Bankers. In 1942 Mexico received some initial foreign credits. In the total public investment of this period, besides the contribution from foreign sources, taxes accounted for 43.9 per cent, enterprises owned wholly or partly by the state accounted for 30.2 per cent, and government borrowing for 20.1 per cent. Looked at another way, government relied on public loans at home and abroad for 25.9 per cent of total public investment.

Mexico's desire to maintain high rates of growth caused public investment to grow at an average annual rate of 15.1 per cent. But Mexico's tax system was unable to finance such an expansion. The percentage of public investment financed out of tax revenue rose as high as 56.4 per cent from 1947 to 1952, followed by a sharp drop to 35 per cent from 1959 to 1963. Meanwhile, public investment financed by foreign credits rose to 26.4 per cent in the period from 1959 to 1963.

External funds were available but costly. Initial efforts to obtain loans were rather disappointing, since the government was able to obtain only small loans that were generally subject to relatively stiff conditions (tied, short-term loans at a high rate of interest). It is understandable, therefore, that the lion's share of external funds first came in the form of direct investment. From the Mexican point of view, however, direct investment in one way or another was excessively oriented to the needs of the country of origin and did not necessarily accommodate itself to urgent development needs. What is more, the servicing of this class of investment in the forms of dividends, royalties, and other items was more costly to Mexico than the servicing of loans, especially of long-term loans.

In recent years, Mexico's economic strength and political stability have permitted the country to negotiate foreign credits on much better terms and to channel these credits into the financing of basic economic plant. Indicative of the country's stronger position was the result of an "international competition" that the government initiated in 1960 among foreign suppliers of equipment, requesting quotations from them on local costs as well as on the other usual costs. The first bids received included offers to finance only 10 per cent of the purchase price of equipment. The most recent bids offer no less than 14 years' credit on the *total* cost of the installation. When international financial institutions became aware of this situation, they too finally changed their policy against the financing of local costs.

If we consider that local costs raised a serious obstacle to development, one which the country hesitated to tackle at the expense of monetary stability, consequences of the "international competition" have had certain decided advantages for public investment in Mexico. Backed up by the strong credit position of the country and a reputation that it meets foreign obligations punctually, Mexico gained access to new and even larger sources of foreign credit. Included among these recent sources is the placing of Mexican government bonds in international markets, under conditions equal to those enjoyed by bonds of wide acceptance. Conditions like these naturally serve to facilitate rapid growth in Mexico.

But to think that borrowing abroad, even on optimum terms, could take the place of domestic saving is ridiculous. It is obvious that effects of applying this line of thinking to Mexican development would tend to hold back the country's growth. Sustained growth requires a heavy reliance on domestic saving; outside capital should merely complement domestic saving. In effect, Mexico must take care that the servicing of foreign investment, both direct and indirect, will not reduce the capacity of the country to import. Even a beginning student in economics knows that foreign exchange is the normal means for financing imports and for servicing foreign investment.

The servicing of foreign investment, including amortization and interest, dividends, and royalty payments, is a steadily rising item in the country's balance of payments. In 1950, it equalled 12.7 per cent of Mexico's foreign exchange earnings; the figure for 1963 was 27.4 per cent. If we look at only that part involving service on the public debt held abroad, the figures are 4.8 per cent in 1950 and 16.7 per cent in 1963. Measured as the amount of new credits (one year or longer) that the public sector contracted abroad, the respective figures are $105.8 million for 1950 and no less than $1.5 billion for 1964. With the servicing burden rapidly approaching a level that will correspond to one-third of Mexico's total annual foreign exchange earnings, there is certainly room for serious concern.

Finally, let us shift our attention to other sources of public investment. First of all, funds originating from state enterprises have remained at a relatively constant level of about 28 per cent. In view of the spectacular expansion of state enterprises in recent years, it is rather remarkable that this source was able to supply the amounts it did. Second, even though government borrowing from domestic savings has declined as a source of public investment, the capital that it has provided was obtained without causing significant inflationary pressures. To strengthen this situation the government's borrowing powers were consolidated in the Central Bank. The bank used its powers to place a significant volume of government securities in private financial quarters and in public agencies such as social security institutions. Another key contributing factor was the success of financial authorities in attracting private capital to invest in securities of the National Industrial Development Corporation (Nacional Financiera). For Mexico, the latter achievement would appear to represent a solid step toward the creation of the kind of capital market characteristic of those found in advanced industrial countries.

4. Allocation of Public Investment

The country's economic growth has been self-generated in the sense that there have been no national programs seeking specific goals. Nevertheless, the government has tried several times to formulate an order of priorities, coordinating and directing investment in the public sector along lines that would guarantee maximum profit. These programs have not been complete since they are directed only toward the regulation of public expenditure.

Because of the characteristics of Mexico's economic and social structure, the policies outlined by a state program cannot be imposed on the private sector. The state has frequently tried to direct private investment toward lines considered basic to economic development. However, private plans have never been included in the state's development programs.

Systematic efforts to plan the country's economic and social growth were introduced during the Six-Year Plan of 1934-1940, which was outlined by the National Revolutionary Party (Partido Nacional Revolucionario). This plan covered important aspects of government activities, such as foreign relations, national economy, and economic development; it was the empiric answer to the country's needs of that time. It was not a complete plan since it did not interrelate the several programs, and most important, it did not offer a financial program capable of supporting the proposed policies that required increases in public expenditure. For these reasons, accomplishments fell short of the desired goals.

Between 1941 and 1946 there were no significant attempts to program economic activity. A government action plan for 1947-1952 was proposed by the Banco de México in 1948. This program was formulated in the belief that a loan of $250 million would be granted by the International Bank for Reconstruction and Development (World Bank). However, only a very small fraction of the amount requested was granted, so the Six-Year Plan of 1947-1952 was not put into practice.

This new attempt to program the economy offered rather

incomplete guidelines for government economic and social policies. A large number of the figures on expenditure were only estimates, and the several proposed policies were not interrelated and coordinated in a technical way.

The main cause of these failures was the lack of adequate instruments. In order to formulate a realistic and complete plan it is essential to have adequate statistics, to know the potentiality of the available resources and the different ways they can be utilized. As long as necessary investigations are not undertaken and adequate information is not compiled, the formulation of a realistic plan will be difficult.

Even though the six-year program did not have the success desired, it became a technique for evaluating key national problems and determining the orientation of public investment. Considerable advances were made in the construction of public works, and the attitude that anything done was a positive contribution was overcome.

After this, the federal government realized that the formulation of an order of priorities and the coordination of public investment was necessary in order to find the most efficient way to utilize its scarce resources. Thus, at the beginning of 1948, the National Commission of Investment (Comisión Nacional de Inversiones) was set up under the Ministry of Finance and Public Credit (Secretaría de Hacienda y Crédito Público). Its duties were to control, supervise, and coordinate the organizations referred to in the Law for the Control of Decentralized (e.g. autonomous) Organizations and State Enterprises.

The main goal of the National Commission of Investment was to obtain maximum benefit out of the large financial resources, which at that time were being administered by autonomous organizations and state enterprises; its action, however, was not directed toward the formulation of investment programs for these organizations. An attempt to impose a rigid control through the Ministry of Finance was made, but it created such strong opposition on the part of the most important organizations that the duties of the commission were reduced to a study of some autonomous organizations. By the end of 1949 the Law establishing the Commission was repealed.

By the Presidential Act of June 9, 1953, the State Ministries, Federal District Department, decentralized organizations, and state-owned enterprises were required to submit their investment programs for the 1953-1958 period to the Ministry of Finance. With this information the Ministry of Finance would outline a program coordinating the investments of the public sector. This program would be used as an instrument for outlining the economic policy most adequate to the country's economic and social development. A Committee of Investments (Comité de Inversiones), created under the Ministry of Finance was responsible for the corresponding studies.

Upon considering the wisdom of increasing the rights and responsibilities of the Committee of Investments, the President issued the Presidential Act of September 7, 1954, creating the Commission of Investments (Comisión de Inversiones), an organization under the President. Its duty was to submit to him a coordinated program of public investment according to priorities and to suggest changes that should take place. The work of the Commission of Investments permitted a higher degree of coordination in public investment and a more efficient utilization of resources by the establishment of a system of priorities.

The Commission continued to function until 1959, when the Presidential Ministry was created, which, while retaining the Commission as part of its structure, substantially revised its functions. Thus, the Commission ceased acting as a direct consultative body to the President and its place in the government became simply that of an additional auxiliary organization, while it still retained influence in the determination of work programs of the Ministries, decentralized organizations, and state-owned enterprises.

This outline will not be complete if we do not analyze the efforts made in the key branches of infrastructure. Every one of them shows outstanding aspects of the country's economic development. In the beginning, the development of infrastructure did not take place in an integrated way; nevertheless, the economic policy achieved a certain balance. Therefore, we believe it necessary to make a brief outline of the work done in irrigation, communications, petroleum, and electric power.

It should be pointed out that while the communications and transportation sector received the major share of Mexico's public investment during the earlier post-revolutionary period, this share has declined. The sector absorbed 77 per cent of total public investments between 1925 and 1934 and 30 per cent between 1959 and 1963. Between 1925 and 1929, 270 million pesos out of 478 million pesos of total public investment were assigned to this section, while in the 1949-1963 period only 15,078 million pesos out of a total investment of 49,925 million pesos were assigned to communications and transportation. In recent years, increasing sums in absolute terms have been invested in this sector, but these increases have been considerably smaller than those of other sectors.

Irrigation

The basis of modern Mexico was established as a consequence of the revolutionary movement of 1910, which changed the country's economic and social structure radically. One of the accomplishments of this movement was the disintegration of the semi-feudal structure that characterized agriculture by eliminating latifundia (large haciendas), which accounted for a large percentage of Mexico's cultivable land. This spurred the development of the domestic market, which later became the base for the country's industrialization.

Mexico's natural resources are scarce, and nearly 90 per cent of the country's cultivable area requires irrigation in order to be used efficiently. According to estimates, 14.9 per cent of the land can be used for agriculture. But 8.5 per cent of this land is pasturage located on prairies, 35.2 per cent is pasturage located on mountains, 33.7 per cent is forested, and 7.7 per cent is not available to agriculture. It is estimated that the country's water resources could support permanent irrigation of 10 to 15 million hectares — that is, less than half of all workable land (29.3 million hectares).

The distribution of water resources is very uneven. Fifty per cent of the estimated annual drainage (357,257 million cubic meters) is located in the South Gulf zone, which accounts for 13 per cent of the total land surface. For this reason there has been a need for irrigation in Mexico since pre-Colombian times. Several irrigation works were built during the Colonial period (1545 to 1810) and in the Independent era. The haciendas started irrigation projects between 1880 and 1910. In 1910 it is estimated that nearly 1 million hectares were improved by irrigation, but a high percentage of these projects were merely temporary.

In 1925, following the revolutionary movement's policy of redistribution of land, the government set up the National Commission of Irrigation (Comisión Nacional de Irrigación). This Commission issued the Irrigation Law, which took into account the public benefit of irrigation.

The construction of irrigation projects was started in 1928; however, it was not until 1932 that studies and projects were formulated and the construction of these works was undertaken by Mexican engineers and contractors. Between 1924 and 1929, 70 million pesos were invested on this sector, and between 1930 and 1934, 50 million pesos were invested. As a result, an area of 83,900 hectares was opened to cultivation during that period and 62,700 hectares of land were improved.

According to the principles of the Agrarian Reform, no property within the irrigation districts could have over 100 hectares. This restriction took into consideration the high productivity that can be obtained in such lands as compared to other lands that usually allow only one crop a year. In 1935 the limit was reduced to 50 hectares, although landowners who had already been alloted 100 hectares were allowed to keep them as long as they paid a compensation fee for the irrigation works. Preference was given to *ejidatarios*[1] in the distribution of land located in the irrigation districts, with the result that by 1958, 42 per cent of the irrigated land belonged to *ejidatarios,* 37 per cent to small landowners, and 21 per cent to larger land owners. According to the 1958 census, 52 per cent of the irrigated land was accounted for by properties of 20 or less hectares, belonging to 250,000 farmers; 23 per cent was accounted for by properties of 20 to 50 hectares, belonging to 16,000 farmers.

---

[1] Semi-collective agricultural units whose land was owned in perpetuity by the state.

After 1935 the irrigation policy acquired a more social sense. Since then, there has been a tendency to aid the most underdeveloped regions. Productivity and average costs of the hectare are not only taken into consideration when evaluating the projects, but the social benefit generating from the work is considered as well.

The irrigation policy received a decisive impetus during the 1935-1940 period. A large number of projects were started, 206 million pesos were invested in irrigation, 63,466 hectares were opened for cultivation, and 55,029 hectares were improved. Between 1941 and 1946 investment increased even more: 649 million pesos were invested (62 million of which were assigned to small irrigation projects), 272,501 hectares were opened for cultivation, and 276,628 hectares were improved. A study was undertaken to determine the nation's water resources, and irrigation works were programed. This plan has been improving gradually but, at that time it was a valuable instrument in classifying public investment in this sector according to priorities. During the same period, the International Water Treaty with the United States was signed. This agreement permitted major extensions of irrigation along the northern frontier.

In 1947 the National Commission of Irrigation was transformed into the Ministry of State. Its responsibilities were broadened to cover construction of water and sewage installations, as well as to provide flood protection, etc.; all projects were to be guided by the principle of efficient utilization of the country's water resources. The government introduced a program for the complete development of several river basins, establishing for this purpose the Papaloapan and Tepalcatepec commissions. The construction and operation of irrigation works was not the only goal sought; the commissions also undertook the construction of additional infrastructure (roads, electrification, drinking water, schools, etc.) necessary for balanced development of those regions, and the creation of a framework for the development of private activity in agriculture, industry, trade, and services.

Between 1947 and 1952, 2,159 million pesos were invested in irrigation. (1,991 million pesos were assigned to large irrigation works and 587 million pesos to small irrigation works),

286,668 hectares were opened for cultivation, and 276,628 were improved.

During the 1953-58 period, a heavy emphasis was placed on the efficient use of the country's existent resources in an effort to obtain a more balanced regional economic development. The commissions for the Fuerte, Grijalva, and Lerma-Chapala-Santiago regions were created. An order of priorities of the country's needs was followed in the construction of these works. Public expenditure was organized and programed in order to obtain the greatest efficiency possible, and the use of international loans for the financing of specific projects was introduced. During this period, 3,585 million pesos were invested (3,075 million for large irrigation works and 510 million pesos for small irrigation works), 576,868 hectares were opened for cultivation, and 200,206 hectares were improved.

Between 1959 and 1963, 4,378 million pesos were invested, the use of foreign resources increased considerably, and great projects were undertaken that will increase the irrigated area in the very near future. While only 288,621 hectares were improved in this period, large investments were made that will benefit a large portion of the southern and southeastern territory in the coming years.

The irrigation policy followed after 1925 made possible the transformation of the country's economic and social structure, which has been dominated by subsistence agriculture. The irrigation of extensive regions facilitated the commercialization of agricultural activities. Rural productivity has increased considerably, new techniques and procedures were adopted, thus making competition in international markets possible. There has been a consequent diversification of production and exports, with the result that the country has not been so severely affected by international price fluctuations.

Public investment in irrigation (11,097 million pesos between 1925 and 1963) has been financed by taxes and water quotas paid by the farmers. Nevertheless, agriculture is still the main national economic problem. There is still low farm output and an excessive farm population whose absorption by other sectors seems very distant. (Nearly 60 per cent of the economically active population is engaged in agriculture.) Therefore, it will be necessary to allocate increasingly larger investments to this sector — especially to small irrigation projects — in order to raise the standards of living of the rural population.

The irrigation program has been financed principally by resources made available in the current budget. During the 1939-1963 period, 81 per cent of total investments were financed by these resources, 12 per cent by budgetary deficits, and 7 per cent by resources from abroad.

International loans granted for irrigation were first made available in 1950; the use of these resources has not been continuous and, as we have already mentioned, they have only been used on specific projects. By December 31, 1962, the Export-Import Bank (Eximbank) had granted loans for $31 million (at that time there was an outstanding debt of nearly $11.5 million); the World Bank had granted a loan for $30.5 million, which had still not been used; and the Inter-American Development Bank had granted a loan for $28.9 million, of which only $1.5 had been used.

Railroads

Though a few railroads were built before the last quarter of the nineteenth century, the Mexican railroad network came into being between 1876 and 1910. The view that the state should finance the construction of railroads was replaced during this period by the belief that the network should be developed by subsidies and franchises granted to foreign companies because the state lacked the necessary financial resources. No economic development plan was followed in granting these franchises, and serious problems resulted. With the exception of the railroad between Mexico City and several border cities in the north and south, railroads were financed and operated by foreign investors. However, this plan was disastrous to the country: In addition to the exploitation right granted to foreign companies, the government heavily subsidized the construction of railroads and also permitted the expropriation of all land necessary and the importation of all the equipment and material required free of duty.

Ownership and control of the railroads changed several times before the industry was nationalized completely in the 1930's. The anarchy prevailing in the construction of railroads forced the government to acquire most of the shares of the three principal firms operating in the country, and in 1908 these merged into an autonomous organization called the National Railroad of Mexico (Ferrocarriles Nacionales de México). During the revolutionary period, most of the equipment and several rail lines were destroyed, so the government decided to nationalize the firms in order to rebuild them. This huge investment, together with the large interest payments on the bonds, increased the public debt from 82.5 million pesos to 121 million pesos between 1917 and 1921. Therefore the government decided to de-nationalize the railroads, although it retained the majority of the shares. In 1920 the network had 20,880 kilometers as compared with 19,770 kilometers in 1910. The labor-management conflicts, the world crisis of 1929, the competition of highway transportation, and the increasing operating deficits forced the total nationalization of the railroad industry in 1937. However, the industry was not integrated into one company because of administrative problems.

Between 1935 and 1963 public investment in the railroads amounted to 15,122 million pesos. Among the lines built were the Chihuahua-Pacific, the Pacific, the Southeast, and the Sonora-Baja California. Money was also assigned to the repair of lines, the maintenance of workshops and terminals, and the acquisition of equipment — primarily diesel engines. In 1963 the network had 23,735 kilometers.

The railroad system has operated with an annual deficit since 1943, and these deficits have been increasing since 1953. This has been due partly to the heavy outlays for modernization, partly to government policy on tariffs. Whereas export products were given priority before 1908, the recent rate structure has favored consumer products, and some products have even been subsidized. Furthermore, rates have remained stable despite considerable increases in merchandise prices — a consequence of the view that railroad transportation is a public service that should encourage economic development in every possible way.

Railroad freight has increased very rapidly. From an annual average of 5 million kilometer tons between 1908 and 1910, freight traffic increased to 9,390 million kilometer tons in 1950, and in 1963 it reached 14,939 million tons. Before 1910, the bulk of the freight consisted of minerals, agricultural, and forest products, while in recent years industrial products have accounted for 30 per cent.

Passenger transportation has increased at a much lower rate because of the marked preference for road transportation. The figure for passengers per kilometer increased from 1,962 in 1928, to 2,523 in 1960 and to 3,886 in 1963.

Investments in the railroad system have been financed by the resources coming from the operation of several lines, from the budgetary resources of the federal government, from domestic bonds, and from loans granted by international organizations such as the World Bank and the Eximbank.

Roads

Mexico's irregular topography and the uneven distribution of population has created a need for a vast network of roads. In the earlier years of the revolutionary movement, several roads were built in an attempt to integrate the country socially and politically. Since 1940, the promotion of economic development has been a determining factor in deciding which roads should be built. Highways integrated large regions that were outside the market economy or could not develop their natural resources because of the lack of communications.

The road construction program began in 1925 with the creation of the National Commission of Roads (Comisión Nacional de Caminos). The first highways (Mexico City-Pachuca and Mexico City-Cuernavaca) were built by foreign contractors, but since 1928, all roads have been built by national firms and engineers. (Open bids from foreign contractors are invited, however, in the case of roads financed by international organizations.) The national network has grown considerably since 1930, when there were only 1,426 kilometers; in 1950, the network had 21,422 kilometers; in 1963, 57,038 kilometers, of which 31,477 kilometers were paved roads.

Public investment for the construction of roads has increased considerably. Investment between 1925 and 1929 was 41 million pesos (only 8 per cent of total public investment), while between 1959 and 1963, 11.5 per cent (5,732 million pesos) were assigned to this sector.

The highway policy has been changed several times. Before 1934 the construction of main roads was financed by the government alone, but in that year the Law of Construction of Roads in Cooperation with State Governments was passed, stipulating that the construction of main roads should be financed by the federal government, while secondary roads should be financed by the federal and state governments with each paying for half the cost. This system permitted the gradual integration of the network and resulted in great savings on administrative expenditures; furthermore, it provided an order of priorities for the construction of roads. In order to complete the institutional structure, the federal government created the National Committee of Feeder Roads (Comité Nacional de Caminos Vecinales), in 1947. This committee supervised the construction of feeder roads financed jointly by the federal and state governments and by the private sector, although a contribution could be accepted in the form of labor from the private sector in lieu of the financial contribution.

Finally, in 1958 a decentralized organization (Caminos y Puentes Federales de Ingreso) was created to build and operate toll roads that were necessary because of the congestion of some highways, especially those leading to Mexico City and others connecting key production centers.

The government started the construction of new roads because of the need to link up key production centers and to develop potential production zones. But because it neglected the maintenance of those already built, a review of the highway policy became necessary in 1955 in order to solve the problem of "deferred maintenance." Since then, increasingly larger investments have been earmarked for the maintenance and reconstruction of the network, but these expenditures must be increased considerably more in order to avoid a deterioration of national assets.

Before 1925, the construction of roads was financed by private capital, and the government also attempted to finance this through external debt. However, investments in this sector were very small. The roads were built to low specifications, and constant transit was impossible. A federal sales tax on gas was levied when the National Commission of Roads was created in order to obtain resources for the Commission. In 1934, when the law was passed providing for joint federal-state cooperation on highway construction, it was established that the federal government would get two-thirds of the proceeds of the tax and state governments one-third.

Nevertheless, this tax has not been sufficient to finance the construction of roads. Between 1925 and 1963, investments in this sector amounted to 13,475 million pesos, while tax revenue amounted to only 9,169 million pesos; thus, the gas tax financed only 68 per cent of road construction. The issue of domestic highway bonds, authorized in 1934, was another source of revenue. Bonds amounting to 663 million pesos, which were redeemable in 5, 10, or 20 years, had been issued by 1947. Since 1947, bonds guaranteed by the gas tax have been issued.

A special tax on diesel fuel and 20 per cent of the sales tax on autos, trucks, and tires were allocated in 1954 for the National Committee of Feeder Roads, which would take care of the construction of feeder roads.

In addition, external loans were granted by the Eximbank for the purchase of machinery and equipment and by the World Bank for the construction of new roads. Thirty-four per cent of the investments were to be financed by the World Bank and 66 per cent by government funds. By December 1962, the Eximbank had granted loans for $47.2 million, of which $3.5 million had not been paid. Of the $25 million credit granted by the World Bank only $640,000 had been used.

Aviation

The federal government has encouraged civil aviation by granting special franchises and subsidies. In the beginning, private companies built their own airports, but since 1940 the federal government has been in charge of building airports in the principal cities. Nevertheless, it was not until 1959 that investments in this sector were encouraged. Between 1940 and 1963, investments amounted to 835 million pesos, of which 670 million pesos were spent during the last five years of the period. Today, the government is operating Aeronaves de México, S.A., due to a financial crisis in the company. Aeronaves de México, S.A. and Compañía Mexicana de Aviación are Mexico's most important airlines. In 1960, there were more than 300 companies licensed to operate airlines in the country. International routes are operated by more than 20 companies.

Maritime Commerce

It was not until 1958 that steps were taken to form a national merchant marine. In 1950, the national fleet had 173,000 gross tons; by 1963 it had increased to 455,000 tons.

The government started giving serious thought to the construction and restoration of ports and docks after 1947. Between 1925 and 1963, 2,008 million pesos were invested; 79 per cent was spent in the last 15 years of this period. The restoration of docks in Veracruz, Tampico, and Coatzacoalcos in the Gulf of Mexico and in Salina Cruz, Acapulco, Mazatlan, and Ensenada in the Pacific has absorbed most of the investments.

Marine traffic has increased considerably. In 1950, 6,253 thousand tons were transported in international trade and 1,552 thousands tons in coastal trade; in 1963, international trade had risen to 8,528 thousand tons, while coastal trade came to 6,302 tons.

Communications

In 1865, the telegraph service became a monopoly of the state and the entire network was nationalized. By 1910, the network had 35,295 kilometers, but since then it has grown at a much slower rate. Investment has gone into modernization of equipment, replacement of lines, and construction of offices. In 1959, the telegraph network had 46,294 kilometers. The government invested 326 million pesos between 1925 and 1963;

investment amounted to 210 million pesos between 1958 and 1963. This sum was used almost entirely for the installation of a Telex electronic system.

Telephone service was introduced in 1878, two years after its introduction in the United States. Almost all urban areas have telephone service; but needs have still not been satisfied. The service is operated by private companies with special franchises so no public investments are necessary. Large sums of money have been invested during recent years for the installation of micro-wave systems.

Commercial radio was introduced in 1923. In 1960 there were 301 commercial stations and 1,081 amateur stations. Television is also operated by private companies, so no public investment is necessary in this sector.

Petroleum

Economists have pointed out that Mexico's economic development has been the result of three fundamental factors: a) the agrarian reform, b) the formation of its basic infrastructure, and c) the nationalization of the petroleum industry. Undoubtedly, these factors have contributed in a very special way to the formation of a domestic market that has been adequate for the growth of the manufacturing industry and the expansion and improvement of service industries.

Foreign companies, mainly British and North American, took care of the exploitation of petroleum before its nationalization on March 18, 1938. At that time, crude oil was exported, and the embryonic refining industry, which chiefly produced for the export market, could barely supply the domestic market.

The organized exploitation of oil began in 1901. Foreign private investment as well as production increased considerably. Production reached a peak of 193 million barrels in 1921, then decreased gradually until 1937, when it amounted only to 47 million barrels.

Foreign companies were not concerned about Mexico's interests in exploiting its petroleum resources. There was an increasing need for fuel all over the world at that time, and these firms tended to maximize profit. Their increasing influence in internal affairs and mistaken attitude during labor-management conflicts forced the government to nationalize the industry.

After nationalization of the industry, production was directed toward the domestic market. This change was possible because of the fast growth of road transportation and the development of the electric power and manufacturing industries.

It is difficult to conceive the country's present development if the structure of the petroleum industry had not been changed. Mexico's energy requirements are mostly taken care of by the use of petroleum. In 1930, 65 per cent of the energy was generated from petroleum; in 1940 it increased to 80 per cent; and in 1960 to 92 per cent.

Large investments for the construction of refineries, expansion of the transportation system (pipelines, trucks, tanker ships) and storage capacity, and increase of production were required in order to organize and integrate the industry and to satisfy internal needs. Between 1938 and 1963, 15,400 million pesos were invested in the autonomous government dependency, Petroleos Mexicanos (Pemex); 64 per cent of this was financed with the industry's own resources, 5 per cent with internal borrowing, and 31 per cent with foreign credits. Eighty-three per cent of these foreign credits were granted between 1958 and 1963, when Pemex began to engage in petrochemical activities.

Pemex has been one of the most dynamic factors in Mexico's economic progress. For example, in 1938 crude oil production was 38.4 million barrels while in 1962 it increased to 121.6 million barrels. Refined products in 1938 amounted to 33.7 million barrels as compared with 116.2 million barrels in 1962. Over the same period production of natural gas rose from 683 million cubic meters to 10,515 million.

There has been a heavy emphasis on exploration. In 1938 reserves amounted to 814 million barrels, while in 1962 they amounted to 2,775 million barrels. Meanwhile, daily refining capacity rose from 92 million barrels to 406 million barrels.

The expansion of the domestic market has required a continuous expansion of the oil distribution system. In 1938, there were only 1,717 kilometers of pipelines and 327 kilometers of gas lines, and the fleet consisted of one large and 146 small tanker ships (36,000 gross tons). In 1963, there were 3,811 kilometers of pipelines (of which 3,247 kilometers were usable for the transmission of oil), 4,491 kilometers of gas lines, and the fleet comprised 18 large tankers (224,000 tons).

Domestic consumption of oil increased 383.4 per cent, from 22 million barrels in 1938 to 107 million in 1962.

The petrochemical industry was started in 1951 with the production of anhydrous ammonia and fertilizers made with natural gas. However, the basis for the integration of this industry was not established until 1959. According to certain laws, only the government — through Pemex or autonomous organizations with no private participation — could manufacture basic products. ("Basic products" means those produced in the first stages of the petrochemical industry.) These basic products could then be manufactured by private industries to obtain other sub-products, which now include propylenes, ethylenes, natural gas, aromatics, and butylene. By February, 1964, 29 special franchises had been granted to private companies, which had a total installed capacity of 602,630 tons. As of that date, the investment in the petroleum industry, already committed or planned came to 4,047 million pesos — 2,330 from the public sector and 1,717 from the private sector. All projects undertaken have been designed to supply domestic demand, and as a consequence imports are expected to drop considerably.

Electric Power

The country's electrification was undertaken at the beginning of this century by the Compañía Mexicana de Luz y Fuerza and Impulsora de Empresas Eléctricas. These companies were financed by foreign capital which managed to acquire the small private companies that were operating in Mexico at that time. The electric power industry developed remarkably well between 1910 and 1930. Total capacity increased from 120,000 kw in 1920 to 510,000 kw in 1930, 80 per cent being accounted for by the two big foreign utilities. This demonstrated that large companies operate more efficiently than small companies.

These companies were only required to meet certain specifications under special franchises granted by the government. Therefore, electric power plants were not built as part of a coordinated program. Serious problems resulted; the systems were technically incompatible, making integration difficult, and service was unreliable. There was a general shortage of power because new facilities were built only when demand existed; they were not planned with future requirements in mind. Moreover, the industry was unbalanced by its concentration in the large population centers, where there was a guaranteed demand.

In 1933, the government designated the electric power industry as a public service and a monopoly of the state. The implied threat of nationalization — which did not actually occur for a quarter of a century — together with the control imposed on tariffs, reduced incentives for private investment in the industry; as a consequence, supply lagged behind demand.

For political reasons, governments are generally reluctant to grant tariffs high enough to produce satisfactory returns of investment, with the result that rising costs reduce profits and eventually eliminate them. (The New York City subways offer a good example of this squeeze.) This condition prevents necessary financing to take care of future requirements. In fact, between 1930 and 1934, total installed capacity increased only by 9 per cent, and between 1937 and 1943, it increased by a mere 1 per cent.

Thus, during a period when Mexico's economic development was receiving a big push, electric power generation became an obstacle to growth. In 1937, the government created the Federal Commission of Electricity (Comisión Federal de Electricidad) which was given priority on the use of hydroelectric resources; it was also empowered to revoke special franchises if they interfered with its own development.

This organization outlined and developed programs to carry electric power into additional areas, thus permitting a more balanced regional growth. On the other hand, due to the stagnation of private investment, the government had to build several plants to satisfy the increasing demand of some industrial centers. These plants sold the energy to the private companies for distribution through their systems, thereby surmounting obstructions to the country's economic growth.

In this way the electric power industry experienced an accelerated growth. Its installed capacity increased from 680,000 kw in 1940 to 1,235,000 kw in 1950 and 3,021,000 kw in 1960; that is, installed capacity increased at an average annual rate of 6.4 per cent during the 1940-1950 period, and at a rate of 9.4 per cent between 1950 and 1960.

The installed capacity of thermal electric power has increased more rapidly than that of hydroelectric power. This is despite a national policy favoring the use of hydroelectric resources and also despite the fact that thermal power is normally more costly to produce. One factor working in the other direction is the remoteness of major urban centers from hydroelectric locations. More important has been the availability of cheap fuel from the nationalized oil industry. As a consequence, hydroelectric capacity as a percentage of total installed capacity dropped from 49 per cent in 1910, to 44 per cent in 1960, to 37 per cent in 1963.

Hydroelectric resources are not being neglected, however. Two big projects that will increase the installed capacity by 1,528,000 kw are under construction. One of them, Infiernillo, located in the limit of Michoacan and Guerrero, will have four 164,000 kw generators; the other, Malpaso, located between Tabasco and Chiapas, will have four 218,000 kw generators. These plants will increase the supply of electric power to key population centers and at the same time permit rural electrification and the creation of new industrial centers in underdeveloped regions.

Despite the dynamism shown by the electric power industry during the last few years, only a very small percentage of Mexico's population is supplied with electricity. This percentage increased from 21 per cent in 1950 to 26 per cent in 1960.

The country's urban population represented only 29 per cent of the total in 1950 and 38 per cent in 1963. This distribution has prevented a more intensive electrification of the country. In the beginning, the great demand in consumption centers and the rigidity of government tariffs directed private investment principally toward those markets that could guarantee efficient operation of the plant and possibility of profit. After the nation-alization of the industry, the majority of its resources were allo-cated to great electric power projects, which soon will supply electric power to extensive regions. Nevertheless, the problem is not solved yet, since the scarcity of resources and the lack of a national electric power program will prevent the most efficient utilization of the available resources.

Between 1950 and 1960, electric generation increased at an average annual rate of 9.2 per cent and from then on at a rate of 8.8 per cent. The principal consumer is the industrial sector (44 per cent in 1958), followed by the residential sector (16.5 per cent), and the commercial sector (16.1 per cent). Public lighting represents 6 per cent of the total.

Though the most urgent needs have been satisfied, there is need for a plan that would eliminate the obstacles that hold back demand and that would encourage conditions for continuous economic growth. Such a plan ought to increase consumption by expanding output and distribution and to give preference to those areas of potential growth, even though consumption would have to be subsidized by the tariff system.

There remains the problem of integration of the existent electric systems. This will entail large investment to make service uniform and to balance and regulate the rate structure. Utiliza-tion of hydroelectric resources, rather than thermoelectric power is needed, because even though cheap fuel supplied by Pemex is available, thermoelectric generation is still more expensive than hydropower.

The stagnation of private investments in the electric power industry was caused principally by the government's policy on tariffs. What was not politically possible with private ownerships became readily possible with government ownerships; in other words, under government operation there is no longer a barrier to higher tariffs. Whereas in 1950, investment in the industry was 236.8 million pesos, in 1961 it was 2,518 million pesos; in 1962 2,291 million pesos; and in 1963, 1,760 million pesos. During the 1959-1963 period, these investments represented 17.6 per cent of total public investment.

The nationalization of the industry, when it finally did occur, did not take on the character of an expropriation but rather that of a commercial transaction. In 1960, the government acquired the two large privately owned foreign companies. The purchase of these companies did not require large expenditures because, as has been noted, these companies were not making sufficient investment and also were supplying the market with energy bought from plants built by the Federal Commission of Electricity. This way, the government purchased plants with a total installed capacity of 954,000 kw (31 per cent of the country's total) and a great deal of the country's distribution lines.

Between 1940 and 1960, the private companies were financing their operation by earnings and foreign loans (guaranteed by the government most of the time); thus an increase of capital by the issuance of new stock did not take place. The public sector financed its investments with its own resources, budgetary resources, and external loans, principally from the World Bank and the Eximbank. Under these circumstances, the nationalization of the electric power industry did not represent an increment in Mexico's foreign obligations but rather a change in the form of ownership — from a foreign private enterprise to a state enterprise, with all the advantages and the disadvantages derived from this.

Finally, it must be noted that almost all the distribution equipment and part of the generation equipment is now produced in the country, while before 1940 the machinery and equipment used was imported.

210.

ECONOMIC DEVELOPMENT OF PERU

Rómulo A. Ferrero

The Author

ROMULO A. FERRERO has had a varied career as agricultural engineer, economist, cabinet minister, and banker. After attending the National School of Agriculture in Lima, he worked for the Agricultural Experimental Station at Cañete, farmed for a while, then joined the staff of the Agricultural Bank of Peru in 1933. He became professor of money and banking at the Catholic University of Peru in 1940, and two years later was made Dean of the Faculty of Economic Sciences. Mr. Ferrero served as Peru's Minister of Finance and Commerce in 1945 and 1948 and as Minister of Agriculture in 1948. At present he is chairman of the Lima Savings Bank and director of the Cartavio Sugar Company. He has served on a number of commissions, boards, and advisory bodies, and as president of the Agricultural Commission of the International Labor Organization. Mr. Ferrero has written numerous articles and books on economics.

Economic Development of Peru / *Rómulo A. Ferrero*

Tables

Appendix Table

Table of Franchises and Benefits of Industrial Promotion Law (No 13270, November 30, 1959) for Peruvian and Foreign Capital.

Introduction

In the past 25 years, and particularly since 1950, Peru has experienced considerable population and economic growth, accompanied to a lesser degree by social gains. Population has expanded at an accelerated pace, with the largest relative increases occurring along the coast and in urban areas. Accompanying this has been an even greater growth of the gross nation product (GNP), and thus a rise in per capita income and standards of living. As might be expected, the growth of the national product has not been uniform — periods of rapid development have alternated with periods of stagnation or slow growth, while certain economic activities and geographic areas have grown faster than others.

The most important factor behind both economic growth and its uneven rate appears to have been exports: When exports have increased rapidly, so has the gross national product, and when exports have stagnated or diminished, the growth in GNP has stopped or even has turned down. Furthermore, since the growth of exports has been greater than that of the GNP, it is clear that internal economic sectors have been lagging, while the relative importance of trade as a component of the GNP has grown. The rapid development of exports has been qualitative as well as quantitative. New export products have emerged, and in some cases have overtaken traditional exports as earners of foreign exchange.

Besides the growth of trade, major influences on the GNP have included the relative decline in agricultural production, the development of industry, and particularly the expansion of governmental activity. Unfortunately, this last has been at the cost of large fiscal deficits, covered by loans from the Central Reserve Bank (Banco Central de Reserva del Perú). The resultant monetary expansion, inflation, and devaluation in the international market will be discussed later.

With the exception of a brief period following World War II, Peru has maintained a relatively high level of economic freedom, particularly in the areas of international trade and payments. This has enabled Peru to expand production and exports, and to attract foreign capital. In addition, economic freedom has helped to maintain general stability, since other South American countries that have maintained long-standing policies of economic controls have been subject to far worse inflation and have had to undergo far more serious currency devaluations in the international market.

Despite the encouraging statistics on economic growth, Peru is in many ways a typically underdeveloped country, undergoing changes and suffering from problems that are current in most of South America: growing urbanization, industrial development, lag in food production, increased economic intervention by the state, inflation, currency devaluation, very uneven distribution of incomes aggravated by inflation, the "revolution of rising expectations" among the poorer classes, and social tensions sometimes intensified by political demagoguery.

In view of this, it seems most appropriate to open the present study with an analysis of the evolution of major indices of economic development over the period 1950-65, followed by a comparison with similar data for other South American countries. Two final chapters are included: one on chief positive factors of Peruvian development, and the last on chief negative factors or chief obstacles to development.

1. Indices of Economic Development

(1950-65)

Population

According to census data for 1940 and 1961, the population of Peru grew from 6.2 million to 9.9 million between those years, an annual increase of 2.3 per cent. Estimates for the period covered by the present study show population increasing from 7.4 million in 1950 to 11.1 million in 1965, an annual rate of 2.6 per cent.[1] In the last few years, the growth rate has risen to about 3.0 per cent yearly, a rate that probably will not be substantially exceeded in the future. An explanation for the rising growth rate may be found in the declining rate of mortality, which fell from 33 per thousand in 1940 to 18 per thousand in 1960. The birth rate, on the other hand, has remained close to its average level of approximately 48 per thousand.

The growth of total population has been accompanied by a marked shift toward urban areas, which advanced in population from 36 per cent of the total in 1940 to 48 percent in 1961.[2] The urban growth rate has been 3.7 per cent annually. Over the same period, rural population averaged a growth rate of only 1.3 per cent, declining from 64 per cent to 52 per cent of the total.

The present population of Peru is "young," with 43.3 per cent less than 15 years old, another 52.9 per cent of "working age" (15-64 years), and the remaining 3.8 per cent 65 or over.

Employment in 1961 was highest in primary production (agriculture and mining), which accounted for 52 per cent of the total. Secondary activities (industry, construction, electricity, water, etc.) accounted for 17 per cent of the total. Another 27 per cent were employed in a third level of activities (com-

---

[1] The census figures omit certain groups, mainly the native population in the jungles (población selvatica). If these groups were included, Peru's total population would have been 8.1 million in 1950 and 11.8 million in 1965.

[2] A better and more restrictive definition of "urban population" (residence in localities of two thousand or more inhabitants) shows this segment increasing from 25 per cent to 39 per cent of the total between 1940 and 1961.

merce, transportation, warehousing, communications, and services). This leaves 4 per cent in unspecified employment.

Gross National Product

Between 1950 and 1965, gross national product (in constant 1963 prices) more than doubled, rising from 39.0 billion
to 88.5 billion soles. This was an average annual rate of 5.6
per cent. But the growth rate was not steady over the whole
period; it averaged 6 per cent in 1950-55, 4.3 per cent in 1955-60,
and 6.6 per cent in 1960-65. Per capita GNP over the whole
period rose from 4,824 soles to 7,532 soles (in 1963 prices),
an average increase of 2.6 per year.

While inflation and changing exchange rates make it impossible to compute an exact figure for GNP in dollars, the range
can be determined by computing the 1965 GNP in constant
1963 soles and in current soles, and then converting both figures
to dollars at the prevailing 1965 exchange rate. This calculation
puts GNP between $3.2 billion and $4.3 billion and per capita
GNP between $280 and $360. Thus it is safe to say that per
capita GNP is now on the order of about $320 a year.

Table 1 shows this growth of GNP during the period under
consideration:

Table 1   **GROSS NATIONAL PRODUCT**

(In billions of soles)

YEAR	1963 PRICES	CURRENT PRICES
1950	39.0	15.6
1955	52.1	28.9
1960	64.2	55.5
1965	88.5	114.7

Source: Central Reserve Bank.

This growth has been accompanied by changes in the composition of the gross national product. Between 1950 and 1963,
agriculture dropped from 35 to 22 per cent of the total (if fish-

eries are excluded, the figure for 1963 is 20 per cent). Meanwhile, manufacturing rose from 15 to 17 per cent, commerce from 11 to 16 per cent, and government from 7 to 10 per cent, while mining maintained its share at about 5 per cent. Investment as percentage of GNP averaged 24 per cent over the period, ranging from 18 per cent to a high of 28.4 per cent in 1954.

Foreign Trade

The period 1950-65 was marked by rapid expansion in the volume of trade, as well as by substantial changes in the composition of trade. Exports grew by 245 per cent, or from $194 million to $667 million, an average increase of just over 9 per cent a year. This growth rate is well above that of the GNP, and it is far higher than the growth rates for both Latin American and world exports. Imports grew at a higher rate than did exports, increasing by 317 per cent, or from $176 million to $734 million.

Table 2 **GROWTH AND BALANCE OF FOREIGN TRADE**

(In millions of dollars)

YEAR	EXPORTS	IMPORTS	EXPORT SURPLUS
1950	194	176	18
1955	269	300	− 31
1960	432	373	59
1965	667	734	− 67

The importance of trade may perhaps best be appreciated in the light of its relationship to GNP. Exports grew from 13.5 per cent of GNP in 1950 to a peak of 23 per cent in 1961 and 1962, while imports increased from 16.2 per cent to 22.6 per cent in 1963.

The composition of exports has changed drastically since 1950. Agriculture, which comprised well over half of all exports at the beginning of the period, appears to have fallen to little more than one-half of that relative level by 1964. Fishing, on the other hand, grew from a level of relative insignificance to a point where it now represents more than a quarter of total exports. The third major category, mining, experienced sharp relative fluctuations while apparently improving its initial position.

Table 3   **COMPOSITION OF EXPORTS**

(per cent of total)

YEAR	AGRICULTURE	FISHING	MINING	OTHER
1950	57.1	3.0	37.9	2.1
1955	47.4	4.7	45.3	2.6
1960	35.7	12.1	49.4	2.8
1963	37.2	22.6	38.4	1.8
1964	32.1	25.0	41.3	1.6
1965	25.8	26.0	45.4	2.8

Source: National Planning Institute.

The composition of imports was relatively stable over the 15-year period, the most important changes being the relative rise in capital goods and the decline in consumer goods. Raw materials and foodstuffs fluctuated without any discernibly significant trend.

Table 4   **COMPOSITION OF IMPORTS**

(per cent of total)

YEAR	CONSUMER GOODS	FOOD-STUFFS	RAW MATERIALS	CAPITAL GOODS	MISCEL-LANEOUS
1950	27.3	2.0	30.2	39.2	1.2
1955	26.5	3.1	29.7	39.5	1.2
1960	22.7	4.6	32.1	40.2	0.4
1963	25.0	2.8	27.0	44.8	0.3
1965	24.1	—	30.0	42.3	—

Source: National Planning Institute.

Money Supply and Purchasing Power

Table 5 shows the evolution of two measures of the supply of money and two measures of the purchasing power of the sole;

"currency" includes currency in circulation and deposits in the Central Reserve Bank, and "means of payment" is defined as "currency" plus demand deposits. The "cost-of-living" figures are for blue-collar workers in Lima and Callao, since these are the only satisfactory figures available that extend back to 1950.

Table 5   **MONEY SUPPLY AND PURCHASING POWER**

YEAR	CURRENCY	MEANS OF PAYMENT	COST OF LIVING (1934/36=100)	EXCHANGE RATE (SOLES PER DOLLAR)
	(IN MILLIONS OF SOLES)			
1950	1,334	2,206	482	15
1955	2,408	4,073	683	19
1960	5,419	8,114	1,022	27.5
1965	11,370	14,231	1,541	26.8
TOTAL INCREASE	752%	546%	220%	79%

Source: Central Reserve Bank.

It should be noted that currency grew at a faster rate than the total means of payment. Although the cost of living was constantly rising, the rate was far from even. The rates of increase for the five-year periods shown in the table were 41 per cent for 1950-55, almost 50 per cent for 1955-60, and 51 per cent for 1960-65. In contrast to the cost of living, increases in the exchange rate have been interspersed with periods of relative stability, namely: 1950-53, 1955-57, and 1960-65.

Mortality Rates and Illiteracy

A nation experiencing rapid social progress will typically enjoy declining rates of mortality and illiteracy. As noted earlier, the declining mortality rate in Peru between the censuses of 1940 and 1961 combined with a constant birth rate to boost the rate of population increase from 2.1 per cent to 2.9 per cent. Over the same period, illiteracy also declined, from 57.6 per cent to 39.8 per cent of the post-school-age population (17 years old or over). Illiteracy, however, is still clearly a major problem.

2. Comparison With Growth of Other
Latin American Countries

This section will help put some of the statistics from the preceding section into perspective by comparing them with data for other large Latin American countries. Comparisons will be made of the rates of increase of population, GNP, exports, cost of living, and exchange rates.

Population

The growth of population in Latin America between 1950 and 1965 is shown in Table 6. The seven countries listed separately constituted more than 80 per cent of the total population of Latin America in 1965.

Table 6 **POPULATION OF LATIN AMERICA:**
TOTAL AND SEVEN LARGEST COUNTRIES

COUNTRY	(MILLIONS)			PER CENT GROWTH 1950-65
	1950	1960	1965	
19 Latin American Republics	149.0	196.6	226.6	52.1
Argentina	16.8	20.0	21.7	29.2
Brazil	52.0	70.5	82.2	58.1
Chile	6.0	7.6	8.5	41.2
Colombia	11.7	15.6	17.0	45.3
Mexico	25.8	34.9	40.9	58.5
Peru	8.1	10.1	11.7	44.4
Venezuela	5.0	7.4	8.8	76.0

Source: Agency for International Development.

It can be seen that population grew less rapidly in Peru (44 per cent) than in Latin America as a whole (52 per cent), due to the very high rates of Venezuela (76 per cent), Brazil (58 per cent), and Mexico (59 per cent).

Gross National Product

Table 7 gives a breakdown of GNP growth rates for Latin America and for the seven largest countries from 1950 to 1965.

Table 7   **GROWTH OF GNP IN LATIN AMERICA**
(Per cent annual average increase)

	TOTAL GNP				PER CAPITA GNP			
	1950-55	1955-60	1960-65	1950-1965	1950-55	1955-60	1960-65	1950-1965
Total Latin America (17 Republics)	5.1	4.8	4.4	4.8	2.3	2.0	1.5	1.8
Argentina	3.1	2.6	3.0	2.9	1.4	0.9	1.3	1.1
Brazil	5.7	5.8	3.3	4.9	2.6	2.7	0.2	1.8
Chile	3.0	4.2	3.9	3.7	0.7	1.9	1.6	1.3
Colombia	5.5	4.0	4.4	4.6	2.6	1.1	1.5	1.7
Mexico	6.2	6.1	5.9	6.0	3.1	3.0	2.8	2.9
Peru	6.0	4.3	6.6	5.6	3.7	2.0	3.7	3.1
Venezuela	9.0	7.1	5.2	7.1	5.1	3.2	1.6	3.1

Source: Agency for International Development.

For the entire 1950-65 period, the annual rate of growth of Peru's total GNP (5.6 per cent) was well above the Latin American average (4.8 per cent), and it was only exceeded by Venezuela (7.1 per cent) and Mexico (6.0 per cent). The growth rate of Peru's per capita GNP (3.1 per cent) was only equalled by one other country, Venezuela. In the third period, from 1960 to 1965, Peru's performance was particularly impressive, and its growth rates in both per capita and total GNP exceeded those of the other countries.

Exports

Table 8 shows the increases in the exports of the seven largest Latin American countries. During the period covered there was no change in the relative position of this group, which accounts for 85 per cent of the exports of all Latin America, excluding Cuba.

Table 8   **LATIN AMERICAN EXPORTS**

(In millions of U.S. dollars)

	1950	1960	1965	INCREASE (1950-65)
Argentina	$1,178	$1,079	$1,493	26.7%
Brazil	1,347	1,269	1,595	18.4
Chile	281	488	685	143.8
Colombia	396	466	537	35.6
Mexico	532	764	1,146	115.4
Peru	189	430	666	252.4
Venezuela	1,161	2,432	2,744	136.3
	5,084	6,928	8,866	74.4
Latin America [a]	5,955	7,950	10,370	74.1

[a] 19 countries, excluding Cuba and European Antilles.

Source: International Monetary Fund.

It is evident that Peru has had the greatest relative growth in exports among the leading countries of Latin America over the period from 1950 to 1965. Peru's 252.4 per cent increase was followed at quite a distance by Chile's 143.8 per cent (achieved primarily in 1951 and 1952), and Venezuela's 136.3 per cent.

Cost of Living

Table 9 presents the variation of the cost-of-living index over the same period for the seven countries:

The countries group naturally into three categories. At one end of the scale is Venezuela, with considerable monetary stability over the 15-year period (only a 21.1 per cent increase). At the other end, with very high inflation, are Brazil, Chile, and Argentina, where the cost of living has increased respectively by 7,823.1 per cent, 7,014.3 per cent, and 2,970.8 per cent. Colombia, Peru, and Mexico comprise a middle group with relatively moderate inflation.

Table 9   **COST OF LIVING IN LATIN AMERICA**

(Index: 1958=100)

	1950	1960	1965	INCREASE (1950-65)
Argentina	24	226	737	2,970.8%
Brazil	26	189	2,060	7,823.1
Chile	7	141	498	7,014.3
Colombia	48	112	213	343.8
Mexico	52	108	116	123.1
Peru	58	120	190	227.6
Venezuela	90	106	109	21.1

Source: International Monetary Fund.

Exchange Rates

Any meaningful comparison of exchange rate fluctuations for Latin America must be based on the free market rates, since in many of the countries the official rates have been badly distorted by controls. Table 10 shows fluctuations in the seven countries over the 1950-65 period.

Table 10   **FREE MARKET RATES OF EXCHANGE IN LATIN AMERICA**

(Units of local currency per U.S. dollar)

	1950	1960	1965	INCREASE (1950-65)
Argentina	14.00	82.70	250.00	1,685.7%
Brazil	19.66	205.10	1,850.00	9,310.0
Chile	72.50	1,050.00	4,000.00	5,417.2
Colombia	3.00	7.20	16.00	433.3
Mexico	8.64	12.50	12.50	44.7
Peru	14.95	26.76	26.82	79.4
Venezuela	3.35	3.35	4.54	35.5

Source: International Monetary Fund.

The similarities between exchange rate fluctuations and fluctuations in the cost of living are clear. Once again, Venezuela shows the most stability, while Brazil, Chile, and Argentina show the least. Peru and Mexico show moderate stability. The latter two countries have maintained stable exchange rates, Mexico since 1953 and Peru since 1960.

3. Major Factors in The Economic Development of Peru

Without any doubt, the factor that has contributed most to the economic development of Peru has been the rapid growth of its exports, presenting thus a very clear case for the decisive importance that the external sector has in underdeveloped countries. This casual relationship has been pointed out for many years, as in the case of the author's studies of Peru.[3] It has also been recognized in the studies of the Central Reserve Bank and the National Planning Institute (Instituto de Planificación Nacional). In the period of 1950-1965, the exports of Peru have grown at the extraordinarily rapid rate of 8.8 per cent annually as compared with 3.8 per cent for Latin America as a whole. Peru now contributes almost 6 per cent of the total exports of the region as against slightly less than 3 per cent at the beginning of the period under consideration. The growth rate of exports has also been much greater than the growth rate of GNP, which has averaged 5.6 per cent. This comparison reveals that the other sectors of the national economy have not been able to grow as fast as the external sector.

The visible and immediate cause of the satisfactory growth of the GNP in the country therefore has been the rapid growth of exports. The basic causes for this significant expansion of exports have been essentially the following: (1) the variety of the national resources of Peru, (2) the dynamism and entrepreneurial spirit of private enterprise, and (3) a generally sound economic policy. The interrelationship of these three factors cannot be underestimated; the absence of any one of them probably would have negated the others.

Variety of Natural Resources

Peru does not have an extensive area of cultivated land. Nor does it have great agricultural wealth comparable with that of other countries of the region, such as Argentina. Land under

---

[3] Rómulo A. Ferrero, *La Renta Nacional* (Lima, 1956).

cultivation amounts to 2.2 million hectares, amounting to only 1.7 per cent of the total land area. This averages 0.2 hectares per inhabitant, one of the lowest in the world. Argentina, by contrast, has more than one hectare of fertile land per inhabitant, and most of the Latin American counrties have a higher average than that of Peru. Mexico has only one-third of a hectare per inhabitant, and it is generally admitted that there is a land shortage in that country.

In spite of this drawback, Peru has developed a highly efficient agriculture on the coast, thanks to irrigation and use of advanced techniques. Crops such as cotton and sugar cane have yields that are among the highest in the world (575 kilograms of cotton and 17,200 kilograms of sugar per hectare). Peru can thus satisfy the demands of the internal market — which are still small — and export to world markets almost 90 per cent of its cotton and two-thirds of its sugar production.

However, the extractive industries — that is, mining and more recently fishing — are at present the foremost natural resources of Peru. Because of its geographical characteristics, particularly the Andes mountains that split the country from north to south, Peru has a great diversity of mineral wealth. The country is thus compensated in part for the obstacles to transportation and communications resulting from these mountains, the reduction in land suitable for cultivation, and the difficulty of access to the tropical regions of the east.

Similarly, while the Andes and the cold ocean current that runs along the coast (the Peruvian Current or Humboldt Current) are responsible for the aridness of the coast, the current is extremely rich in plankton, making for a plentiful supply of fish, particularly anchovies. Up until about 10 years ago the anchovies were consumed mainly by local seafowl, which produce a natural fertilizer high in chemical content (13 per cent nitrogen). During the last 20 years, however, a small-scale fishing and canning industry has been established. Starting in 1957, the production of fishmeal acquired considerable impetus, exceeding 100 thousand metric tons in that year and reaching 1,200,000 tons in 1962 and 1963 and 1,400,000 tons in 1964. Thanks to this rapid development, Peru has become the foremost producer of fishmeal in the world; fish products (fishmeal, fish oil, canned fish, etc.) have been first among Peru's exports since 1962, surpassing the traditional export products such as cotton and copper.

The other natural wealth of the country consists of minerals. Peru produces copper, lead, zinc, and silver (usually found together); iron ore and gold (usually found with copper); and a number of minerals of lesser importance, such as vanadium, bismuth, etc. Mineral exports other than petroleum, which has become an insignificant factor because of increased internal consumption, have gone up from 24 per cent of the total in 1950 to 40 per cent of the total in 1965.

Table 11 shows the growing diversification of Peruvian exports from 1950 through 1965 and the changing relative importance of different products.

Table 11   **PERU'S PRINCIPAL EXPORTS**

(Per cent of total exports figured at current values)

	SUGAR	COTTON	FISH PRODUCTS	COPPER	LEAD	ZINC	IRON	SILVER
1950	15.4	35.2	2.6	5.3	6.3	5.4	—	4.1
1955	13.7	25.3	3.9	10.9	9.7	5.1	3.0	6.0
1960	11.0	16.9	12.1	21.9	5.0	3.9	7.6	5.6
1965	5.4	12.7	27.1	17.6	6.8	5.2	6.8	5.7

Source: National Planning Institute.

Cotton, sugar, and copper have been the traditional main export products, making up usually about 50 per cent of total exports. Starting in 1960, however, the importance of cotton has diminished considerably and that of copper has gone up. Fishmeal exports started to acquire great importance in 1959 (nearly 10 per cent of total exports) and by 1963 they had risen almost to 20 per cent. With the addition of canned fish, fish oil, and other items, fish products accounted for more than a quarter of exports in 1966.

In all of Latin America, Mexico is the only country that may be compared with Peru in terms of diversification of exports. Mexico's exports, though less diversified than Peru's, are made up of similar products, particularly cotton, sugar, lead, and zinc. There is no doubt that the diversification of exports increases the possibilities for fast growth of the internal sector at the same time that it reduces vulnerability to the price fluctuations of primary products in international markets, an unstabilizing factor that retards the growth of Latin American economies. Whereas in Peru no one product by itself now accounts for 30 per cent of total exports, almost all the other Latin American countries depend on one or two products for the greater proportion of their exports. Thus, in recent years, coffee has represented 53 per cent of Brazilian exports, copper 64 per cent of Chilean exports, coffee 67 per cent of Colombian exports, petroleum 93 per cent of Venezuelan exports, tin 82 per cent of Bolivian exports, and bananas 60 per cent of Ecuadorian exports.

Dynamism of the Private Sector

The private sector in Peru has known how to take advantage of the opportunities offered by the natural resources of the country and to develop them and increase the country's exports. This fact has been recognized not only by independent private studies but also by official publications, such as those of the Central Reserve Bank and the National Institute of Planning.

In the *Análisis de la Situación Económico-Social del Perú,* published by the National Institute in July, 1963, the dynamism of the private sector is recognized in these words:

"Private initiative by itself — sometimes without any sort of support — has achieved spectacular results. It is particularly worthy of note that the drive to create new sources of wealth and new export products occurred at a time when the country was undergoing a difficult situation. The entrepreneurs along the coast have made an extraordinary contribution with the production of cotton and more recently with the development of the fishing industry and the export of fish products — an impressive attainment in a country without a maritime tradition. Future development depends on the encouragement of this extraordinary energy that renders so much good to the community."

The enterprise shown by the export sector has not characterized the industrial sector, which has developed to a much lesser degree. Several factors have contributed to this situation, mainly the smallness of the internal market, which is caused by the low purchasing power of the masses due to the insufficient development of the country, and by the unequal distribution of national income. About half of the population is engaged in agricultural pursuits, with a very low level of productivity and income, barring some exceptions in sugar, rice, cotton, and wool. The average income in the agricultural sector is only about one-fourth of the average income in other activities.

The fields in which the energy of private enterprise has shown to best advantage have been those offering the best natural conditions, that is, in those fields related to exports. For this reason, the greatest growth has occurred in agricultural crops directed mainly at foreign markets, such as cotton, sugar, and coffee, and in mining and fishing. Aside from the small internal market, industrial development has also been held back by production inefficiency due to obsolete equipment, inexperienced management, and opposition of labor unions to the adoption of modern working techniques.

In recent years, particularly since the adoption of the Law of Industrial Promotion in 1959, the industrial development of the country has acquired greater impetus, and a series of new industries have been established, such as chemical products (fertilizers, caustic soda, and sodium carbonate), plastics, and metallurgical products. Actually, Peru has entered the stage of intermediate production, having been limited until recently to light industry producing consumer goods, such as the traditional foodstuffs (wheat and rice milling, sugar refining, canning, etc.); beverages (wines, liquors, carbonated beverages, beer); textiles (cotton, wool, and artificial fabrics); clothing (shoes, ready-made clothing), etc.

A very important factor in the development both of exports — particularly in the mining sector and to a smaller degree in agriculture and fishing — and of traditional and new industries has been foreign capital investment, accompanied by technological and managerial know-how. Especially notable are the large investments that have been made in the past few years in developing the copper fields of Toquepala and the iron ore fields in Marcona; these investments have totaled several hundred millions of dollars.

Underlying the economic development of the country and the rapid growth of exports has been the government's economic policy since 1950. This has encouraged the exploitation of known resources as well as the exploitation of new resources, agricultural, fishing, and mineral, and it has also encouraged foreign investment.

This policy has been based on the freedom of internal prices and of foreign trade, international payments, and exchange rates. It has stressed internal monetary stability, as reflected in relatively stable price levels and cost-of-living indices, and external stability, as reflected in stable exchange rates. It has encouraged foreign investment through moderate and non-discriminatory taxation of foreign enterprises. And it has provided incentives both for national and foreign investment through appropriate codes and legislation for mining, electricity, and industry and through tax advantages. These policies will be treated in detail in the next chapter.

4. National Economic Policy Since 1950

In contrast with nearly all South American countries except Venezuela, Peru traditionally has followed a policy of economic freedom. Some controls have been and still are imposed on prices of certain basic foods and services, as described in Chapter 5. But the general rule of freedom has been maintained well in the highly important field of foreign trade and international payments, a policy notably different from that followed by most of Peru's neighbors. With the exception of the relatively brief period from January, 1945, through September, 1948, Peru has had no import prohibitions, quotas, exchange controls, or similar restrictions. This policy is of long-standing, not merely of the past 15 years, as is commonly asserted.

In effect, controls on exchange and foreign trade transactions were established throughout the world during the time of the crises of the 1930's. Peru was then on the gold standard. In May, 1932, it abandoned this system and adopted its now traditional policy of a free and fluctuating exchange rate, regulated by the Central Reserve Bank, but not against basic trends. With the exception of the 1945-49 period, Peru has maintained this system, stabilizing "de facto" its currency in some periods: 1934-37, 1940-45, 1950-53, 1954-57, and 1959-65. These periods have been interspersed by periods of climbing exchange rates — external devaluation of the currency — which have carried the soles-per-dollar exchange rate successively from 4 up to 6.5, 15, 19, and finally to 26.82.[4] After three and one-half years of exchange controls beginning in 1945, the system of certificates of foreign currency for exports was introduced in September, 1948, for the purpose of controlling capital outflows. These certificates were used to pay for imports and were sold freely in the local market, so that their quotation differed little if at all from exchange drafts used to pay for other foreign expenditures — profits, remittances, amortization payments, servicing of loans not authorized by the Ministry of Finance (Ministro de Hacienda y Comercio), other financial services, travel, etc.

---

[4] See Appendix, pages 255-256.

Because of this free system, the external level of the exchange rate generally has been in equilibrium with its internal level. During some periods it was maintained at a higher level through sales of the Central Reserve Bank, as happened in 1957 until the Bank had to withdraw from the market and let the rate of exchange find its own level. Conversely, it was maintained at a lower level at other times, as happened between the end of 1959 and 1964, due to the great growth of exports and inflows. When the currency was overvalued (1957), the international reserves of the Central Bank were exhausted. In reverse fashion, when the currency was undervalued (1960-63) reserves increased considerably.

This system has been a decisive factor in enabling the country to develop its natural resources and the private sector to increase exports and attract capital from abroad. These accomplishments would not have been possible if a system of exchange controls had prevailed with arbitrary overvalued parities, multiple exchange rates, and tardy and almost always insufficient adjustments, such as has been the case in other countries of South America, notably Argentina, Brazil, Chile, and Uruguay. The economy of Peru thus has been free of the obstacles and distortions that characterize the economies of those countries.

Relative Monetary Stability

Even though the country has experienced considerable monetary devaluation, it has had much less of this than most other South American countries. Over the fifteen years (from 1950 to 1965), the cost of living in Peru increased 227.6 per cent, while in Argentina it advanced 2,970.8 per cent, in Brazil 7,823.1 per cent, and in Chile 7,014.3 per cent. Once again, in 1965, there was a much greater cost of living increase in the countries mentioned than in Peru. The increase in free market exchange rates during 1950-65 has been thus: Peru, 79.4 per cent; Argentina 1,685.7 per cent; Brazil 9,310.0 per cent, and Chile 5,417.2 per cent.

The greater monetary stability — or perhaps more precisely, the lesser instability — of Peru as compared with most other South American countries, can be explained by the following factors: (1) smaller fiscal deficits, which have always been the principal cause of inflation; (2) smaller union demands, on a whole, for higher wages and salaries; (3) greater elasticity in the supply of exports, and consequently a greater capacity to import; (4) and more moderate price controls, which have meant less economic distortion and fewer obstacles to increases in production. Peru has shown a better record with respect to inflation than most other South American countries, and its inflation has been of the "open" and not of the "repressed" type.

Peru has thus been able to escape the unfavorable effects of inflation on economic development.[5] It is no mere coincidence that the Latin American countries which have achieved a greater degree of economic growth in a sustained manner have been those that presented a higher degree of stability.

A comparison of Mexico and Peru on one hand and Argentina and Chile on the other is revealing. Between 1950 and 1965 the first two grew at annual average rates of 6.0 per cent and 5.6 per cent respectively, whereas the second two grew at rates of 3.7 per cent and 2.9 per cent respectively. In the 1960-65 period, the growth of Mexico averaged 5.9 per cent annually and Peru, 6.6 per cent, while Argentina averaged 3.0 per cent and Chile 3.9 per cent.

An exception to this rule appears to be Brazil, which despite a high degree of monetary instability was able to grow at an average pace of almost 5.8 per cent between 1950 and 1960. This was no doubt due to the fact that during this period Brazil was able to count upon substantial help from abroad. Loans and grants amounting to more than $2 billion were received from the United States, as well as large loans from other countries, allow-

---

[5] These include distortion of the price structure; unjust redistribution of national income; discouragement of savings; lack of attractiveness for foreign investments; erosion of fixed assets; depression of basic goods and services through controlled prices (foodstuffs, housing, public services, exports); increase of the impact of progressive taxation; redirection of investments into speculative channels or as protection against devaluation (real estate, luxury or semi-luxury office and apartment buildings, inventories); capital flight; lack of a market for long-term securities to finance industries and public works; and, finally, establishment of exchange controls in a vain attempt to prevent prices from climbing, which inevitably ends in a delayed and a much worse readjustment, as controls discourage production and divert it toward secondary fields, and scare away investment.

ing Brazil to live beyond its own means and to withstand intense inflationary pressures. Nevertheless, this process could not continue indefinitely and since 1962 has developed into a crisis, to the extent that in 1963 and 1964 the Brazilian growth rate has declined well below the population growth rate. Moreover, the heavy load imposed by the servicing of foreign debts — which bear upon the country like a mortgage — reduces greatly the capacity to import and to receive new loans and investments from abroad. In fact, neither Brazil nor Argentina and Chile can actually service its foreign debts. Furthermore, these countries have distorted their economies and created a social problem quite difficult to solve.

Moderate, Non-discriminatory Taxation of Foreigners

During the greater part of the period under consideration, that is, up until 1958, the incidence of taxation in Peru had not been excessive, though in recent years it has increased considerably. Measured in terms of the relation between taxes and GNP, the tax burden has been relatively low; 10.3 per cent in 1950, 12.4 per cent in 1955, 14.4 per cent in 1960, 16.8 per cent in 1963, and 20 per cent in 1964. The tax burden on economic activities up until recently has not been highly excessive, as may be seen in the following summary.

Profits of industrial and commerical activities are taxed on a progressive basis, the maximum rate being 35 per cent, plus an additional 2 per cent unemployment tax. The average may be reckoned at 32 per cent for medium-sized enterprises and at 36 per cent for large enterprises. The distributed-profits tax paid by stockholders on dividends received amounts to 30 per cent, plus a 1 per cent unemployment tax, which added to the tax on profits gives a grand total of 53 per cent for medium-sized enterprises and 55.8 per cent for larger enterprises. Tax rates were much lower until 1958, as the dividend tax was only 15 per cent plus 1 per cent unemployment tax.

Foreign enterprises pay the same tax on profits, and, in addition, if they are branch offices, they pay on the remainder a complementary tax of 19 per cent plus 1 per cent unemployment tax. Consequently, they pay a grand total, if they are large enterprises, of 48.8 per cent. If they are incorporated as Peruvian subsidiaries, they pay the same rates as local enterprises.

Undistributed profits of local Peruvian enterprises are taxed at the rate of 10 per cent if they are capitalized up to six months after presentation of financial statements, and 10 per cent provisionally, as payment on account of the complementary tax if they are not distributed or capitalized within the indicated period. Therefore, this portion of profits pays a grand total, including the tax on profits, of 38.8 per cent for the medium-sized enterprises and 42.4 per cent for the larger ones.

Mining activities have been favored by a special schedule of taxes, which will be dealt with in greater detail later on. Petroleum activities are regulated by special laws. Industrial activities have also received a series of very important concessions, which will also be described later on.

The constant increase in the tax burden in recent years is to be regretted. Moreover, the Congress recently approved a new increase in the complementary tax which puts the total burden at levels even higher than those in the United States, a fact which undoubtedly will discourage enterprises from making new investments. This point will be dealt with in greater detail in Chapter 5.

Incentives for Investments

The incentives for capital investment, both national and foreign, in general are of two kinds: First, freedom of exchange, which as already described permits capital inflow without restrictions, and unrestricted outflow of amortization, profits, or interest; and second, tax incentives granted for different activities through the Mining Code, the Law of Electricity, and the Law of Industrial Promotion.

The Mining Code was established in June, 1950, and its main provisions (some of which have been modified subsequently) were the following:

• Mining activities were exempted from the tax on excess profits and from the unemployment taxes (on profits, dividends, and branch remittances abroad). Mining activities were also exempted for 25 years (until 1975) from any new taxes that might be created.

As a payment on account of the tax on profits, provision was made for payment at the moment of exporting the mineral at the rate of 4 per cent on the net value (2 per cent in the case of coal and nonmetallic minerals).

• A depletion deduction was authorized, amounting to 5 per cent of the value of production for coal and nonmetallic minerals and 15 per cent for metallic minerals. This deduction is limited to 50 per cent of net profits (i.e., profits remaining after payment of taxes but before the deduction of the depletion allowance).

• Provision also was made that the operator of a mining concession could ask the government to establish, as a substitute for the tax, a profit-sharing agreement with the government, to be negotiated at between 10 per cent and 20 per cent.

This system gave a great push forward to mining activities, and together with the freedom of trade and payments, resulted in the investment of considerable sums, both for the development of existing mines and new ones. Among the latter, the most important were the mining fields of Toquepala, with an investment of $250 million, and the iron ore fields of Marcona, both previously mentioned. Most important among the established companies was the Cerro Pasco Corporation, which invested more than $130 million, thereby increasing its production from $29 million annually prior to the Mining Code, to a 1964 level of $114 million. With all of these new investments, production and exports of minerals increased considerably, as has already been shown in Chapter 1, and mining exports, excluding petroleum, went up from $47 million in 1950 to $198 million in 1963.

The Law of Electricity (No. 12378) was enacted in June, 1955, and has contributed greatly to the development of the electrical industry, particularly with regard to the expansion of existing installations that supply electric power for Lima and Callao and for the numerous industries established in these areas. The principal measures of this law are the following:

• Electrical concessions are granted for a period of no more than 50 years or less than 15, and may be renewed for a period of no more than 50 years or less than 25 if the electric energy is of hydraulic origin, and no more than 25 years or less than 15 if it is of thermal origin.

• The National Commission on Rates was created, with delegates from the government, the University of Engineering, the National Society of Industries, the Association of Electrical Technicians, and the Association of Electrical Entrepreneurs. The Commission has power to set, review, or modify rates for electricity.

• Rates for electricity shall cover the cost of production plus a yearly dividend and the commercial profit. The yearly dividend amounts to 8.5 per cent of the equity of the operator when the production of energy is greater than 50 million kwh, with a maximum of 12 per cent for production under that figure. The commercial profit is set at 3 per cent on the owner's equity.

These standards serve as a base to set rates, taking into account the nature of the consumption, its importance for the social progress of the country, its incidence on the cost of living, and the economic capacity of the consumers.

Besides the usual charges, the cost of production recognizes the servicing of bonds and other indebtedness, losses for exchange differential in the payment of foreign currency obligations, and a yearly quota for a depreciation fund as well as a yearly quota for an expansion fund.

Two other important provisions of the Law of Electricity apply to taxation:

• The operators of electrical public services are subject only to the taxation in force at the moment the law became effective, the taxes to be calculated after deducting from profits the annual fixed dividend of 8.5 per cent.

• Machinery, spare parts, materials, and equipment necessary for operation are exempted from the payment of import duties and additional taxes.

As a result of this law, installed generating capacity in the country increased from 321 thousand kwh in 1950 to 972 thousand kwh in 1963 — a three-fold increase.

The Law of Industrial Development became effective in November, 1959.[6] The benefits it offers consist basically of the following: (a) Partial or full exemption from import duties on new machinery and equipment as well as on raw material or partially manufactured components that are not produced in the country; (b) exemption from all taxes, except the stamp tax, of basic industries established in the first 10 years, on variable terms according to the regions of the country; (c) exemption from taxes on that part of profits which are reinvested, with amounts and terms varying according to the region where the industry is established; (d) authorization to calculate depreciation charges on machinery and installations, taking into account monetary devaluation; (e) authorization to utilize accelerated depreciation rates for machinery and equipment; and (f) reduction of the tax on profits for industries established in the sierra and in the jungle, but not in the coastal region.

Expansion of the activities of the development banks has been another very important aspect of economic policy which has contributed toward increasing investment. Thus, between 1950 and 1965, loans and investments of the Agricultural Development Bank (Banco de Fomento Agropecuario) increased from 119 million to 2,643 million soles, those of the Industrial Bank (Banco Industrial) from 49 million to 2,033 million soles, and those of the Mining Bank (Banco Minero) from 54 million to 275 million soles. Altogether these three banks increased their lending activities from 222 million to 4,951 million soles, or 22.3 times. Adjusting for the decline in the purchasing power of the currency — measured by the increase of the cost of living during the period (from 481.5 to 1,634, or 3.3 times) — the real increase would be 6.7 times.

For comparison purposes, it must be added that the lending activities of the commercial banks increased during the same period (1950-63) from 1,755 million to 14,499 million soles,

---

[6] For details of this law, see Appendix page 257.

or more than seven times. Development bank credits, which in 1950 were equal to 12.6 per cent of credits granted by commercial banks, reached a level of 34.7 per cent in 1965.

Capital Inflows Accountable to Economic Policies

The favorable factors which have been listed (freedom of trade and of payments, relative monetary stability, tax incentives, etc.) have resulted in Peru's receiving an important capital contribution toward the attainment of satisfactory economic development. Thus, according to the estimates of the Central Reserve Bank in its balance-of-payments statistics, over a period of 11 years (1951 to 1961 inclusive) the inflow of private and public foreign capital reached virtually $1 billion ($991 million, to be exact), of which two-thirds ($634 million) represented private capital and the remainder official loans. To appreciate better the importance of this capital inflow, it must be added that this figure is the equivalent of 35 per cent of the value of exports during the same period ($2,830 million).

Naturally, the foregoing figures are gross inflows which must be counterbalanced by the remittances for amortization, interest, and profits. However, they do not include reinvested profits of foreign companies operating in the country, which constitute a valuable contribution to domestic production. It is well known that an evaluation of the contribution of foreign investments to the economy of a country based simply on the balance-of-payments figures is deceiving, underestimating significantly the real contribution.

5. Obstacles to Economic Development

The positive factors that have favored the economic development of the country have a reverse side in the negative factors and obstacles that have impeded development. These may be classified as:

• Natural factors, including the shortage of cultivated land;

• Human and social factors, chiefly the lack of ethnic and linguistic unity, the low level of education, the difference in socio-economic structures, and the great inequalities in regions and economic sectors;

• Factors of economic policy, including some that have been influential for about 20 or 25 years, and others that have sprung up or taken on significance in the last few years.

Natural Factors

The Andes split Peru from the extreme south to the extreme north. This has had a decisive influence on topography, climate, distribution of population, transportation, and, as a result, the economic development of the various regions of the country.

There are three well defined regions: (1) The coast, located between the sea and slopes reaching up to 1,500 meters, with an area of 144 thousand square kilometers (11.2 per cent of the total) and a third of the population of the country; (2) the sierra, with an area of 335 thousand square kilometers (26.1 per cent) and 53 per cent of the population; and finally, (3) the jungle, with an area of 806 thousand square kilometers (62.7 per cent) and only 13.5 per cent of the population.

While the climate of the coast is subtropical, it is arid because the Andes precipitate the clouds coming from the Atlantic before they reach this region, and the cold Humboldt Current running alongside the shores condenses the humidity of the winds blowing from the Pacific side. For this reason, the average temperature of Lima is about 10 degrees Fahrenheit lower than that of the city of Bahia, located in the same latitude in Brazil. The greater part of the coastal region consists of deserts, and the cultivated area (650 thousand hectares) does not embrace more than 4.5 per cent of the total land area of the region. Agriculture, mainly carried out under irrigation, has served as the basis for the development of the country's industry, commerce, and services, with the result that the coastal region produces 61.6 per cent of the national income.

The sierra has a cold climate, with rain during the summer. It has a very broken topography, with valleys, canyons, and plains at great height. The population lives at an altitude of between 1,500 and 3,500 meters. The agriculture is poor and backward, with low yields. Principal crops are foodstuffs: corn, potatoes, wheat, barley, etc. The cultivated area amounts to 1.2 million hectares (which represents only 3.6 per cent of the total land area of the region). Natural pastures account for between 12 and 15 million hectares, though most of them are of low productivity for they are located at great heights and support mostly sheep and other wool-producing animals. Mining is the most important activity in the region, and because of it, average income for the region is higher than the average income prevailing in agriculture. In spite of this, the region produces only one-third of the national income.

The jungle is located east of the Andes. Part of this region is in the mountain slopes and thus has a relatively high altitude. In this area crops such as coffee and fruit trees have been developed. However, a low part of the jungle is subject to flooding, and has a very hot and rainy climate during the whole year. The development of the region east of the Andes is only in the beginning stages, so that it produces less than 5 per cent of total national income.

Due to these topographical characteristics, the population is scattered all over the country, and transportation and communications are lengthy, difficult, and expensive. Two cross-country railroads that link the coast with the sierra, and serve as outlets for the agricultural and mining production of the sierra in the center and in the south of the country, reach the highest altitudes in the world, exceeding 4,500 meters (from Callao to Oroya and from Mollendo to Juliaca). A highway for cars and trucks goes even higher (4,900 meters).

These geographical difficulties have retarded the development as well as the unification of the various regions of the country, both in the economic and in the social fields.

For the agricultural part of the population, which constitutes half the total, the cultivated land averages only 0.4 hectares per inhabitant. As has been pointed out, this average is one of the lowest in the world, and the situation is made worse by two facts: two-thirds of cultivated land is in the low-productivity sierra, where topography, climate, soil depletion and backward techniques are retarding factors; second, the land tenure pattern is still influenced by the Spanish conquest four centuries ago, which led to the establishment of great estates, determining since then the agrarian structure.

Human and Social Factors

As a consequence of the process of conquest, Peru lacks ethnic and linguistic unity. A white race and the culture that the conquerors brought with them were superimposed on the race and culture of the indigenous people. In the four centuries that have gone by, a mixing process has occurred, encompassing more than half the population. Still there exists a large indigenous sector, greatly different from the white and "mestizo" sector not only in race and language, but also in social and economic structure, as will become evident in the succeeding paragraphs.

Three different socio-economic situations exist in Peru, presenting interactions or stages of transition:

• The capitalistic economy, more or less developed, of the coast;

• The semi-feudal economy in some parts of the sierra;

• The primitive economy, collectivist, more or less pure, of the Indian population of the sierra.

The first of these situations corresponds to a capitalistic economy, or at least pre-capitalistic. It is characterized by the development of industry and services. Agricultural activities have modern characteristics, which are maintained usually by a considerable capital investment. Compensation of workers is in monetary wages, although in a few cases they are paid partly in kind. More advanced techniques and a commercial orientation of production are salient features.

This type of organization prevails mainly on the coast. It exists in the sierra only in a limited degree, since it is confined chiefly to the large farms, mostly cattle ranches. The enterprises in which this type of organization exists are operated mainly for production of commodities and goods for export, such as cotton, sugar, and wool, and also such commodities as rice, sugar, cottonseed oil, fruits, etc., for the domestic market. Because of their greater efficiency, together with the availability of water, these enterprises have a very high production level.

The population lives under conditions far superior to those existing in the sierra. As a result, secondary and other activities, such as industry, commerce, financial organizations, and various services, have developed. The economy is fundamentally monetary, whereas this is not so to any great degree in the other two types of organizations.

The second situation prevails in the sierra, and is built around large and medium-sized estates which originated at the time of the conquest of the country by the Spaniards. The prevailing system of work has feudal and semi-feudal characteristics. Labor is paid a nominal salary, but is performed basically for the privilege of using a small lot and the right of feeding cattle on the natural pastures.

As a general rule, these operations are conducted at a very low level of technology and efficiency. The result is that their contribution to the national economy is relatively small. Due to this and to the type of labor organization prevailing, living standards are very low.

In the last situation, which is the oldest, a primitive economy exists. It represents a survival of the economic and social organization of the Aymaras of pre-Incan and Incan times, although it has been modified substantially in the course of years by the influence of the conquest and by contact with modern economic and social organizations.

As is well known, this type of social organization was characterized by collective property involving land under cultivation and natural pastures and by mutual help in economic activities. The modifications that have occurred in the system have extended to the point that today individual and family-owned cultivated land predominates, without the periodic redistribution which was conducted before, although the collective use of natural pastures continues.

The economy of this area is based generally on a self-sufficient agriculture, with some livestock, particularly of the lanate (wool-producing) varieties. Land is scarce in terms of the population occupying it. Technical levels are very backward. In consequence, the economic, cultural, and social condition is highly deficient.

As is common in underdeveloped countries, the distribution of the gross national product in Peru is not uniform, either in the different economic sectors or the various regions. Considering the population as composed of two approximately equal groups, namely, agricultural and non-agricultural, the respective shares of national income for the two groups in 1965 were 20 per cent and 80 per cent. This means that agricultural incomes were 40 per cent of the national average, while non-agricultural incomes were 160 per cent. In other words, the per capita product of the agricultural population was only one-fourth of the product of the non-agricultural population.

Passing on to the regional differences, according to data published by the Central Reserve Bank (1962), the coast in 1960 had 33.4 per cent of the population and received 61.6 per cent of national income, whereas the other two regions held two-thirds of the population (66.6 per cent) and received only 38 per cent of the income.

No great reliance can be placed on these estimates. However, what is of interest for the purpose of this study is the order of magnitude rather than the absolute figures. Thus, rough approximations of these figures may be accepted, and it may be assumed that the per capita income of the first region was three times that of the other two regions. This is due to the following factors: (a) 90 per cent of industrial and financial activities and probably more than two-thirds of commercial activities and services are concentrated on the coast; (b) the agriculture of the coast is much more productive, consisting in great part of export crops such as cotton and sugar cane. On the other hand, mining (not petroleum) is to be found almost exclusively in the sierra, without which the situation in this region would be even more unequal.

Of course, great care must be exercised in translating into real terms differences which are expressed in monetary terms, particularly when dealing with regions of different economic structures and ways of life. Nevertheless, it should be very clear that immense differences exist between the coastal region and the other two areas. These differences, which were pointed out over a quarter of a century ago by the author of this study,[7] constitute one of the most serious national problems. The author has contended that they constitute the first problem that should be attacked by a national policy of economic and social development.[8]

Factors of Economic Policy

The economic policies that have held back in some degree the development of the country, some for many years and others only recently, are the following: (a) a tendency to control the prices of basic goods and services — foodstuffs, urban transportation rates, house rentals, etc.; (b) inadequate investment in infrastructure; (c) neglect of agriculture; (d) a tendency toward exaggerated industrial protection; (e) excessive and deficit-producing fiscal expenditures with a marked increase of taxes; (f) excessive and poorly distributed social or fringe benefits. These policies have been accompanied and encouraged by the spread of erroneous economic doctrines and of misguided recommendations for economic policy. All these factors will be examined briefly in the following paragraphs.

Controls: Even though, in general, the country has followed a policy of economic freedom, particularly in the field of foreign trade and international payments, controls have been estab-

[7] *Tierras y Población en el Perú. La Escasez de Tierras Cultivadas y sus Consecuencias* (1938); *Política Agraria Nacional* (1940); and other studies of the author.

[8] *Directivas para un Programa de Desarrollo Económico Nacional* (1956); *El Desarrollo Económico y Social del Perú* (1963).

lished over the price of certain basic goods and services, such as foodstuffs (flour, bread, meat, rice, sugar) and fuel, rentals, and urban transportation rates. These controls were established, or at least were made effective, during World War II and in subsequent years, in part because of the economic difficulties resulting from the war and the inflation that produced rapid price increases during that period. To restrain the price increases, or at least to cover them up, measures were adopted, but apparently they were directed at the symptoms rather than the causes.

In some cases, these controls are exercised by the state, which sets or regulates the prices at which the producer may sell certain goods and services (flour, sugar, cement, rentals, transportation, fuel); while in other cases, the state buys the goods and sells them to intermediaries, as happens with rice and meat, sometimes, with losses that constitute a subsidy. This system has obvious disadvantages, for the tendency is to maintain prices which are lower than those prevailing in the international market (sugar, fuel), and prices are set in such a way that there is an inadequate price-cost differential (sometimes none whatever) for a profitable operation, as it happens with flour, urban transportation, and telephone services. Thus, problems are created that tend to grow worse with inflation and with population and urban growth, which increases demand. In some periods, real shortages appear and continue until prices are readjusted. The worst feature of this situation is that no stimulus is provided for the growth of the production of those goods and services that are basic for economic development, and that shortages become progressively more acute, particularly in the case of housing. Fortunately, because of the greater degree of monetary stability in Peru the situation does not reach such a grave proportion as in most other South American countries.

Inadequate investment in infrastructure: Insufficient attention has been paid to expenditures for public works aimed at providing the country with the social and economic infrastructure required for development, such as roads, housing, education, portable water, and sanitation.

While projects of this nature have been built to a certain extent, greater emphasis should be given to them. They are more urgently needed than large public buildings or works that could be financed with the help of private capital. Examples of the latter are steel plants, which are costly and inefficient and require high tariff protection, and hydroelectric works in which billions of soles must be invested.

Considering that Peru has a housing shortage (including units that need substantial renovation) of close to 1 million units, that 60 per cent of the urban population and 98 per cent of the rural population lack potable water and sewage facilities, that production of foodstuffs grows at a smaller rate than the population, that the daily average caloric intake is only 2,100, that infant mortality (under one year of age) is 10 per cent, that there is almost 40 per cent illiteracy in the population over 17 years of age and that the road network is inadequate (41,000 kilometers, of which only 10 per cent is paved) with no connection between many towns and areas, it seems beyond question that public investments should be concentrated in these types of works, which are the exclusive responsibility of the state.

Neglect of Agriculture: The agricultural production of the country has grown at a much smaller rate than the gross national product and other activities. Thus, while GNP grew between 1950 and 1965 at an annual average rate of 5.6 per cent, agricultural production only increased by 3.8 per cent; even this growth was due mainly to gains in exports, as agricultural production for domestic consumption increased by less than 3 per cent yearly. Because agriculture for domestic consumption has grown only about as rapidly as the population, the consumption of foodstuffs has not improved despite an increase in imports. The daily average caloric intake of 2,100 is about the same as it was 15 years ago. A brief mention of the yields of the main agricultural crops for human consumption should suffice to show the low level: wheat yield is 1,000 kilos per hectare; corn, 1,250 kilos; barley, 1,000 kilos; and potatoes, 5,500 kilos. These yields would be acceptable if the ratio between cultivated land and population were favorable, as is the case in the United States, Canada, and Argentina. But they are extremely unsatisfactory for a country where there is a shortage of cultivated land. There is a marked contrast between such yields and those for the export crops, cotton, and sugar. This situation is due to the natural difficulties that have been previously pointed out, to the existence of backward latifundia in the sierra, and to the lack of a program of agricultural expansion, technical assistance, and credit to small farmers, including the Indian communities (producing mainly in the sierra and in parts of the coastal region). The budget of the Agricultural Ministry is only 5 per cent of the total budget of the government, and there is no law of agricultural development as there is for mining, industry, oil, and electricity. In some cases, price ceilings have discouraged production, as for example with meat and milk. For these reasons, the necessary agrarian reform, which has been initiated, must give priority to production for domestic consumption, or the situation will grow worse.

Protectionism: Besides the neglect of agriculture, there has been a strong tendency in recent years to increase the tariff protection of domestic industries, as is shown clearly in the Budget Law of 1964 which contemplates an advance in import duties to the average levels prevailing in other member countries of the Latin American Free Trade Area (LAFTA).

The arguments in favor of reasonable protection of domestic industries are well known — "infant industries," disguised unemployment, difference between private and social costs, etc. It is also widely recognized that Latin America has gone too far in this direction, as has been pointed out not only by some highly qualified economists (Viner, Haberler, Kaldor, Tinbergen, etc.) but also by the Economic Commission for Latin America (ECLA), through its spokesman, Dr. Prebisch, on various occasions.[10] Excess protectionism raises the level of internal prices, increases input costs for export industries, and encourages the development of inefficient industries. Considering that among members of LAFTA, average protective tariffs range around 100 per cent, there is more than adequate cause for this concern.

[9] Rómulo A. Ferrero, *Comercio y Pagos Internacionales* (Lima, 1962).
[10] *Hacia una Dinámica del Desarrollo Económico Latinoamericano* (Lima, 1963).

Figures for 1964 show Peru's imports increasing by only 5 per cent and revenues from import duties rising by 40 per cent. This means that import duties in 1964 increased, as a whole, by approximately 35 per cent, rising roughly from 27 per cent to 36 per cent of the value of all imports and to a level of about 50 per cent of the value of all duty-paying imports.

Rising expenditures and taxes: In the last few years, the fiscal budget has been increasing at an extremely rapid pace. Expenditures rose from 9.8 billion soles in 1960 to close to 25 billion soles in 1964, advancing from 14 per cent of GNP to 28 per cent, and in 1965 the proportion was similar. Tax revenues rose during the same period from 8 billion to 16.7 billion soles, or from 14 per cent of GNP to 20 per cent, a rate that is extremely high for an underdeveloped country.

As a result of this growth of fiscal expenditures, taxes have had to be increased to levels that exert pressure on prices (this is true particularly of the sales tax), and in the case of direct taxes and the profits tax, rates have been raised to a point where they exceed those paid in the United States and in some European countries — a factor likely to discourage foreign investment. Taxes on distributed corporate profits, for example, add up to a total rate of 60 per cent in the case of domestic enterprises and 50 per cent in the case of branches of corporations with headquarters abroad.

It is certainly true that in underdeveloped countries there are many needs that must be satisfied, particularly in the basic social and economic fields — roads, port facilities, irrigation, schools, sanitation works, hospitals, etc. — and that for these purposes the government must enact taxes. Nevertheless, because these needs cannot be met in a few years, the following principles should be kept in mind: (a) expenses of purely administrative nature should be reduced to a minimum; (b) preference should be given to those public works that must be undertaken by the state because they do not yield the direct and immediate returns which would attract private investment, and likewise the state should withdraw from hydroelectric, steel, or similar projects that can be undertaken by the private sector; (c) large sums must not be spent on public buildings and other conspicuous projects; and (d) total expenditures must not be increased to a level that will cause inflation, as has occurred in Brazil, Argentina, Chile, and other countries.

In spite of the large tax increases, expenditures have exceeded revenues and the fiscal budget has frequently shown a high deficit which has been covered by loans from the Central Reserve Bank. This inflationary coverage of expenditures has been the principal cause of the tremendous increase in the supply of money since 1938, which has caused the increases in the cost of living and also the repeated devaluations of the currency in the international market.

Expense of social benefits: As in many other Latin American countries, laws establishing or increasing social benefits without any technical criteria are continuously being approved in Peru without calculation of real costs or forecasting of probable effects.[11]

The present system has the following main defects:

• A very high cost, which already exceeds 60 per cent of wages and salaries, without including voluntary benefits such as the frequent gifts of food and other benefits in kind which workers receive in rural areas.

This high cost inevitably reduces the direct compensation of the workers, as there is a limit imposed by the productivity of labor.

• A defective distribution of social benefits in which insufficient attention is paid to social security, while excessive importance is assigned to secondary types of benefits (vacations, compensation for length of service).

• Duplication of social benefits, as in the case of life insurance and survivors' pensions, compensation for length of service (terminal pay) and old-age pensions, pensions after 30 years of service, and old-age pensions at 60 years of age.

---

[11] *Realidad Económica de los Beneficios Sociales* (1957, 1963); *Estudio Económico de la Legislación Social Peruana y Sugerencias para su Mejoramiento* (1957); *Estudio Económico de la Legislación Social Peruana para Obreros* (1960).

• Important gaps in social benefits, such as the lack of family allowances and survivors' pensions for blue-collar workers who do not reach pension age.

• Finally, social benefits whose cost is borne exclusively by the employer and the value of which relates to the length of service and not the need, such as the compensation for length of service, the bonus of 30 per cent after 30 years of service, and full pension rights after 30 years of service.

• A system of this kind discriminates among workers, as only some of them reach the last two benefits, and the amount of the first one varies according to time. A source of friction is also created, since delays in salary increases help to reduce the higher costs of special benefits. Enterprises are also forced to maintain extremely high reserves, which sometimes reach a volume many times higher than that of the total wage bill and are occasionally even in excess of the capital of the enterprise.

Erroneous Economic Doctrines

During the last few years in Peru, there has been increased acceptance of a number of economic misconceptions which are already popular in other Latin American countries, and which have contributed to the poor situation of Argentina, Brazil, Chile, and Uruguay, among other countries. Essentially these ideas may be summarized as follows:

An underestimation of the importance of fiscal deficits as a cause of the severe inflation suffered by certain countries, with a consequent underestimation of the importance of balancing public finances and of establishing credit and monetary policies to prevent or contain inflationary pressures.

An overestimation of the so-called "structural" causes of inflation, such as unequal distribution of national income, concentration of land ownership, lagging agricultural development, and insufficient growth of exports. This approach ignores or discounts the fact that erroneous economic policies have influenced the last two factors through controls on the prices of foodstuffs and basic services, overvalued exchange rates, and exaggerated industrial protectionism, since such policies have adverse effects on other economic activities by increasing costs through a general upward pressure on internal prices.

Recommendations to increase taxes — which have already reached a very high level in most of the Latin American countries — while neglecting the essential problem of tax evasion, although it is generally accepted that evasion is quite common and causes a direct loss of tax revenue. This should not be interpreted to mean that it is not possible, or even necessary in many cases, to introduce modifications in the tax system.

Exaggerated emphasis on agrarian reform without equal insistence on the need to increase agricultural productivity.

Excessive emphasis on industrial development, neglecting the development of the agricultural sector, whose backwardness and inefficiency impedes the former both by limiting the expansion of the rural market and by reducing the over-all market through increased costs of foodstuffs.

Exaggerated emphasis on the redistribution of national income, unaccompanied by equal emphasis on the need to increase production. Even admitting that income distribution is unequal, as is true in all the underdeveloped countries and even in some developed ones, to improve the situation demands above all an increase in domestic production, correction of the abuses that exist in backward or weak sectors, higher productivity of workers, application of a progressive but moderate tax system, and optimum use of fiscal revenues. In practice, the policy of income redistribution has been manifested in many countries by excessive wage increases, salaries and social benefits, excessive tax increases, and similar measures that have not been and cannot be successful. This assertion is proved by the experience of countries that have attempted income redistribution without success, releasing instead strong inflationary processes, evidenced by higher costs and prices, excessive governmental expenditures, and discouragement of production.

Exaggeration of the imperfections of the market mechanism on the one hand and of the advantages of planning and state intervention on the other — without any attempt to improve the market mechanism by eliminating abuses and monopolies (sometimes created by protection of the state) or by giving direction to the private sector and making up for its deficiencies.

APPENDIX

The Exchange Rate in Peru

The exchange rate remained stable between 1934 and 1937 (years of national and international recovery), fluctuating around four soles per dollar; but in the two following years it weakened because of a decrease in exports, distortions in the world market caused by the world war, and the beginnings of internal inflation. In May, 1940, the exchange rate was stabilized at 6.50 soles per dollar; even though excessive, this devaluation, together with the impossibility of obtaining imports, permitted the maintenance of stability until the end of 1944. By this time, inflation had produced a disequilibrium in the exchange rate, and at the end of January, 1945, the free exchange rate was replaced for the first time by controls on imports and foreign exchange.

The controls became increasingly rigid as inflation and internal devaluation continued. With a backed-up demand for imports, there developed an increasing difference between the official rate and the real rate. Exports were caught between increasing costs and an inflexible exchange rate. This, together with distortions that the controls caused generally in production, trade, consumption, and capital flows, brought about the decision finally to eliminate the controls, which was carried out gradually so as to reduce the impact of readjustment.

In September of 1948, when the author of this study was Minister of Finance, he granted freely-negotiable foreign exchange certificates to exporters to pay for imports. These were granted for an amount equal to 35 percent of exports after deducting duties, which was equivalent to 28 per cent of the total export value. In December, the latter figure was raised to 55 per cent, and the requirement of an import license was abolished. In August, 1949, 100 per cent foreign exchange certificates were granted for mineral exports, and for exports paid for in "surplus" or soft currency (sterling or Argentine pesos). Finally, in December of the same year this percentage was extended to include all exports. A list was drawn up of merchandise which was prohibited to be imported; but the list was quickly reduced and eventually eliminated with the prosperity brought about by the Korean War. Thus, the process of eliminating import prohibitions took a little over a year; and the system of distributing foreign exchange certificates, originally created to prevent the drain of capital, was left as the only throwback to controls. This system also was eliminated in May of 1960.

Table of Franchises and Benefits of Industrial Promotion Law (No. 13270, November 30, 1959) for Peruvian and Foreign Capital

Tax exemptions and franchises	Firms producing articles classified as basic (according to a revisable list)			Firms that produce non-basic industrial articles (established or to be established).
	For established industries.	For industries to be established within ten years following approval of the Regulations (April 29, 1960), for the production of:		
		Basic articles not yet produced in the country.	Basic articles already produced in the country (as of April 26, 1960).	
I.–General permanent franchises (for the whole country)				
a) Exemption from import duties on new and essential machinery and equipment which do not compete with domestic manufactures.	100%	100%	100%	50% to 100% (according to a revisable list for each industrial group).
b) Exemption from all import duties on essential raw materials and semi-manufactured goods which are not produced domestically and which do not compete with domestic products, according to special lists.	100%	100%	100%	"
c) Right of direct purchase of government lands, including coastal and river sites.	Yes	Yes	Yes	No
d) Right of acquisition through favorable enforcement of the Law of Expropriation.	Yes	Yes	Yes	No
e) Other benefits granted before enactment of this Law for the periods conceded in previous legislation.	Yes	—	Yes	No

II.—Tax benefits dating from approval of the Regulations (April 26, 1960).

a) Exemption from all taxes except the stamp from the day the plant starts operating, for the following terms:				
Lima and Callao	No	first 3 years	No	No
Other coastal provinces	No	first 5 years	No	No
Sierra[a]	No	first 10 years	No	No
Selva[b]	No	first 15 years	No	No
b) Exemption from taxes that are directly applied to the production or trade of articles, except for stamp, income, patent, excise, and municipal taxes: (From the day the plant starts operating, for the following terms:)				
Lima and Callao	15 years	15 years	15 years	15 years
Other coastal provinces	15 years	15 years	15 years	15 years
Sierra	15 years	15 years	15 years	15 years
Selva	15 years	15 years	15 years	15 years
c) Right to invest tax free a part part of net profits:				
Lima and Callao	30% for 15 years	30% for 15 years	30% for 15 years	40% for 10 years
Other coastal provinces	50% for 20 years	50% for 20 years	50% for 20 years	60% for 15 years
Sierra	80% for 40 years	80% for 40 years	80% for 40 years	80% for 30 years
Selva	100% for 50 years	100% for 50 years	100% for 50 years	100% for 40 years
d) Right to apply depreciation costs to machinery, spare parts, and installations, taking into account depreciation of the national currency of more than 5% in relation to the U.S. dollar:				
Lima and Callao	Permanent	Permanent	Permanent	Permanent
Other coastal provinces	,,	,,	,,	,,
Sierra	,,	,,	,,	,,
Selva	,,	,,	,,	,,

a Highlands.
b Lowlands east of the Andes.

e) Right to increase the annual depreciation rate of machinery or industrial equipment:				
Lima and Callao	10 years	10 years	10 years	10 years
Other coastal provinces	15 years	15 years	15 years	15 years
Sierra	30 years	30 years	30 years	30 years
Selva	40 years	40 years	40 years	40 years
f) Reduction of the tax rate on profits:				
Lima and Callao	No	No	No	No
Other coastal provinces	No	No	No	No
Sierra	40% first 10 years / 30% next 10 years / 20% next 10 years	40% first 10 years / 30% next 10 years / 20% next 10 years	40% first 10 years / 30% next 10 years / 20% next 10 years	40% first 10 years / 30% next 10 years / 20% next 10 years
Selva	50% first 10 years / 40% next 10 years / 30% next 20 years	50% first 10 years / 40% next 10 years / 30% next 20 years	50% first 10 years / 40% next 10 years / 30% next 20 years	50% first 10 years / 40% next 10 years / 30% next 20 years

Note: Besides the general benefits appearing in the above table, granted by the Law of Industrial Promotion (No. 13270), there are special franchises designed to encourage and promote the establishment of assembly plants and related industries (Laws Nos. 13270 and 9140, and Supreme Decree No. 3 of January 27, 1961).

Exemption from import duties:

100% for 3 years
85% for the 2 subsequent years
70% for the 3 subsequent years
50% for the 9th and 10th years

Obligations of the firms:

10% of the materials must be acquired within Peru over the first 3 years
20% of the materials must be acquired within Peru over the next 2 years
40% of the materials must be acquired within Peru over the subsequent 3 years
50% to 70% for 2 more years, according to the size of the established industry.

260.

BRAZILIAN

INFLATION

Postwar Experience and

Outcome of the 1964 Reforms

Mário Henrique Simonsen

for

Instituto

de Pesquisas e Estudos Sociais

Rio de Janeiro

The Author

MARIO HENRIQUE SIMONSEN is one of the outstanding younger economists of Brazil. In 1961 he became a professor at the Graduate School of Economics of the Getúlio Vargas Foundation and four years later, at the age of 30, he became director of the school. At the same time he was also appointed to the administrative board of the National Housing Bank. Mr. Simonsen has been director of the Economic Department of the Brazilian Association of Manufacturers and an economic advisor to private enterprises. He was graduated from the University of Brazil as a civil engineer and economist.

Title of the original:

'A EXPERIENCA INFLACIONARIA NO BRASIL/

Mário Henrique Simonsen/ Estudo preparado sob o patrocínio do Instituto de Pesquisas e Estudos Sociais (IPES-GB) Brasil em cooperação com o Committee for Economic Development/ Novembro 1964.

SPECIAL STUDY **Brazilian Inflation**
Postwar Experience and Outcome
of the 1964 Reforms */ *Mário Henrique Simonsen*

*By arrangement with IPES of Brazil.

Brazilian Inflation

Tables

Introduction

The purpose of this study is to describe Brazilian inflation in the postwar period and to suggest some explanation for its arresting nature and outcome. The Brazilian experience challenges many of the traditional ideas about the consequences of a continuous and steep price rise. For some 15 years the country was able to support a high rate of growth in real product despite chronic inflationary pressures. Real wages rose, inventories were tightened, and real estate investment was discouraged — all contrary to what one usually reads in the textbooks on inflation. Nor did the Brazilian inflation, despite its accelerating pace, degenerate into hyperinflation such as that suffered by Germany in the early 1920's or by Hungary in the late 1940's. Granting that the traditional concepts are not exact scientific laws, the fact remains that they signally failed to apply in the Brazilian case.

But by no means can the findings of this paper be construed as a defense of Brazilian inflation. The evidence shows only that economic growth and violent inflation can be present at the same time — in other words, they can coexist. But this does not mean that there is any causal correlation between the two, as is sometimes assumed. Most certainly the Brazilian experience does not provide any evidence for the assumption that a continuous rise of prices is favorable to development. The chronic price rise developed a series of distortions that can hardly be regarded as healthy conditions for growth. Furthermore, the earlier pattern was broken after 1962, and since then the economic growth of the country has slowed down considerably. Throughout 1963 and 1964, we saw in Brazil a stagnant economy in the grip of a convulsive inflationary process.

The findings of this paper thus give no aid or comfort to a priori economic thinking at either end of the spectrum. The sum of the matter is that some of those things, which according to traditional thinking ought to have occurred, did not occur, with the result that the inflationary experience has been less unhappy in Brazil than in other countries.

The author assumes that the readers of this study have some elementary knowledge of the theories of inflation but do not wish to become entangled in highly sophisticated model-building. Theoretical constructions therefore have been kept to a minimum. This not only makes for easier understanding but also is suitable for the task at hand, since the Brazilian inflation does not seem to require a new abstract model. When some unscientific prejudices have been set aside, conventional theory is adequate for an analysis of the Brazilian experience.

This paper is concerned not with what could have happened but rather with what actually *did* happen. The author rejects — to borrow from legal language — the *ceteris paribus* approach. It is provocative to consider what conceivably might have occurred had all other things been equal. But what is interesting about inflation is that it changes a lot of things. Would Brazil have grown more (or less) rapidly had prices been stable? This paper will not supply an answer to the question for a very simple reason: It is naïve to look at economic development as a function of a single variable — e.g., the rate of inflation. Such a judgment implicitly assumes that the rate of inflation acts as a precise and definitive barometer for an economy.

Or take the question of "optimization," which also intrigues the theorists. It would be very difficult to believe that inflation can provide the optimal path for economic growth. This paper certainly does not assume this to be true — but cannot prove the opposite case. Such an argument could only be carried on in terms of arbitrary postulates built on statistical science fiction.

The aim of this paper is more modest. It is to examine the development of Brazilian inflation, its compatibility with rapid economic growth through 1961, and the way in which inflation has been accompanied by stagnation thereafter — a fascinating study in and of itself.

1. A Brief Historical Survey of Brazilian Inflation

There has been a long-term bias in Brazil toward inflation since the beginning of the last century. Undoubtedly because of the chronic tendency toward budgetary deficits, the country has not known price cycles similar to those of the United States — long waves of inflation followed by extended down-swings. The Brazilian history roughly divides into two distinct periods. Throughout most of the nineteenth century, under the Empire, Brazil experienced a continuous, moderate inflation — no price cycles, but rather a steady inflation rate averaging 1.5 per cent a year.[1] The creation of the Republic was accompanied by a brief burst of printing-press inflation, lasting about five years. This was followed by a period of deflation and stabilization of prices until the beginning of World War I. Thereafter, the pattern has been one of rather extended periods of inflation of varying degrees of intensity, interrupted by relatively brief periods of deflation and stabilization. (See Tables 1 and 2.)

As might be expected, Brazil suffered sharp inflation during World War II along with much of the world. South America was largely cut off from imports from the industrial nations, though it sold raw commodities to them. The double impact of shortages of supplies coupled with surpluses in the balance of payments brought about a price rise in Brazil of about 15 per cent a year between 1939 and 1948. After a brief period of restraint, prices again began to soar in 1950 at a rate of about 17 per cent annually. (See Table 3.)

It was in 1959 that Brazilian inflation really broke into a gallop, the proximate cause being the government's abandonment of a promising program for monetary stabilization. Between January and December of that year, the general index of wholesale prices spurted 36.1 per cent, while the cost of living

---

[1] Oliver Onody, A *Inflação Brasileira, 1820-1958*. The author's findings, though they give a broadly accurate picture, must be taken with some reservation. The whole subject of Brazilian inflation tends to be obscured by the lack of sound figures until the appearance in 1939 of regular indexes prepared by the Fundação Getúlio Vargas, the Servico de Estatistica da Previdência do Trabalho, and other sources.

jumped 42.7 per cent in Sao Paulo and 52 per cent in Guanabara. In 1960 the rate of inflation fell off a little; the price rise
for the year was 25 to 30 per cent. But in 1961 it shot up to 40
and 50 per cent, and in 1962 to 50 and 60 per cent.

In 1963 the process was further aggravated. The government first tried a stabilization program that was aimed at restraining demand, but which, oddly enough, neglected price controls.
The program was then dropped. Meanwhile, the deficit reached
a new high as wages climbed with government encouragement.
That year prices rose 80 per cent. (See Table 4.)

Table 1   **COST OF LIVING INDEX: 1829 TO 1912**

YEAR	INDEX	YEAR	INDEX
1829	100	1881	190
1834	104	1887	231
1844	136	1896	497
1857	153	1900	460
1860	149	1912	455
1874	177		

Source: Oliver Onody, *A Inflação Brasileira, 1820-1958* (Rio de Janeiro, 1960).

Table 2   **COST OF LIVING INDEX IN THE CITY OF**
RIO DE JANEIRO:
1912 TO 1939
(Basis: 1912 = 100)

YEAR	INDEX	YEAR	INDEX	YEAR	INDEX
1912	100	1922	188	1932	235
1913	102	1923	207	1933	233
1914	102	1924	242	1934	251
1915	111	1925	258	1935	265
1916	119	1926	266	1936	304
1917	131	1927	273	1937	327
1918	147	1928	269	1938	341
1919	152	1929	267	1939	350
1920	167	1930	243		
1921	172	1931	234		

Source: *Conjunctura Económica.*

During the first months of 1964, the final period of João Goulart's government, the price rise was no less than 25 per cent. At this rate, inflation, geometrically projected, would have come to 144 per cent per year — a calculation frequently noted by the succeeding government under Castelo Branco.

The Castelo Branco government, immediately after taking

Table 3   **COST OF LIVING INDEX**
FOR RIO DE JANEIRO: 1939 TO 1966

Annual Average and December indexes for each year
(Basis: 1953 = 100)

YEARS	ANNUAL AVERAGE		DECEMBER EACH YEAR	
	INDEX	ANNUAL CHANGE %	INDEX	ANNUAL CHANGE %
1939	21.6	—	23.1	—
1940	22.2	4.2	24.7	−6.9
1941	24.6	10.8	27.7	12.1
1942	27.4	11.4	32.4	17.0
1943	30.3	16.6	33.8	4.3
1944	34.1	12.5	38.7	14.4
1945	39.7	16.4	44.1	14.0
1946	46.3	16.6	53.5	12.1
1947	56.4	21.8	56.7	6.0
1948	58.3	3.4	58.7	3.5
1949	60.9	4.5	62.2	6.0
1950	66.5	9.2	69.1	11.1
1951	74.5	12.0	76.6	10.9
1952	87.4	17.3	92.5	20.8
1953	100.0	14.4	108.0	16.8
1954	122.4	22.4	136.3	26.2
1955	150.7	23.1	162.4	19.1
1956	182.2	20.9	197.6	21.7
1957	211.9	16.3	224.0	13.4
1958	242.9	14.6	262.7	17.3
1959	338.0	39.1	399.4	52.0
1960	437.4	29.4	494.3	23.8
1961	582.9	33.3	707.7	43.2
1962	884.0	51.7	1,099.0	55.3
1963	1,507.0	70.4	1,985.0	80.6
1964	2,889.0	91.7	3,704.0	86.6
1965	4,787.0	65.7	5,385.0	45.4
1966	6,764.0	41.3	7,600.0	41.1

Source: Fundação Getúlio Vargas.

office, put into effect a well-conceived program aimed at gradually restraining the inflationary process. The program was not fully successful, since the actual inflation rates exceeded by far the official forecasts. Nevertheless, the restraining policies of the government were able to reduce the price rises to about 40 per cent a year in 1965 and 1966. The basic lines and the execution of this program will be described in the last chapter of this study.

Table 4 **INDEX OF WHOLESALE PRICES: 1939 TO 1966**

Annual Average and the December index for each year
(Basis: 1953 = 100)

YEARS	ANNUAL AVERAGE		DECEMBER EACH YEAR	
	INDEX	ANNUAL CHANGE	INDEX	ANNUAL CHANGE
1939	17.4	—	19.0	—
1940	18.5	6.3	18.8	−1.1
1941	21.5	16.2	23.6	25.5
1942	25.4	18.1	27.7	17.4
1943	30.3	19.3	31.7	14.4
1944	34.5	13.9	36.8	16.1
1945	39.7	15.1	40.7	10.6
1946	45.8	14.5	49.6	21.9
1947	48.7	6.3	49.1	−1.0
1948	53.2	9.2	55.0	12.0
1949	58.0	9.0	64.2	16.7
1950	65.8	13.4	73.4	14.3
1951	78.8	19.8	82.5	2.4
1952	86.9	10.3	90.4	9.6
1953	100.0	15.1	113.2	25.2
1954	130.3	30.3	140.3	23.9
1955	147.4	13.1	153.5	9.4
1956	175.7	19.2	192.9	25.7
1957	197.6	12.5	199.4	3.4
1958	221.8	12.2	255.0	27.0
1959	305.5	37.7	347.1	36.1
1960	399.8	30.9	460.8	32.8
1961	552.1	38.1	691.6	50.1
1962	846.0	53.2	1,037.0	49.9
1963	1,468.0	73.5	1,886.0	81.9
1964	2,813.0	91.6	3,645.0	93.3
1965	4,254.0	51.2	4,676.0	28.3
1966	5,787.0	36.0	6,413.0	37.1

Source: Fundação Getúlio Vargas.

2. The Social and Political Roots of Inflation

Before we analyze the specific causes of Brazilian inflation, it would be well to examine the social and political pressures that underlie it. This not only gives a comprehensive view of the problem but also throws some light on the prerequisites for a successful stabilization program.

The root of Brazilian inflation lies in the government's distributive policy. Each social group is dissatisfied with its participation in the national product; in order to quiet this discontent, the government seeks to divide the product into parts the sum of which is greater than the whole.

This attitude, however naïve, has affected a great number of governments in less-developed countries — particularly those touched by the revolution of rising expectations. The reason is simple enough. A poor people whose consumption horizon increases rapidly through the operation of the so-called "demonstration effect," tends to look for a faster improvement in living standards than the increase in productivity will permit. Everybody is honestly convinced that his wage is both insufficient and unjust. Under pressure, the government tries to increase the shares of some in the national product without reducing the shares of others. However, price increases reduce the actual share of each group, so that the sum of the parts is adjusted to the dimensions of the whole. The claimants then go back to the government and ask for more. To the extent that the cycle repeats itself, inflation becomes chronic. And as the reaction time speeds up, inflation is accelerated.

But this is not all. The governments of such countries soon come to realize, quite correctly, that the acceleration of the development process requires an increase in that fraction of the national product intended for the formation of capital. But now a new conflict appears: The government seeks to increase the share saved from the national product but does not want to compress the share consumed. The result, naturally, is a monetary swelling of the cake and an adjustment of the shares through further price increases.

The operation of this mechanism requires, of course, certain cultural and political conditions. There must be a general lack of sophistication concerning the causes of inflation, a situation likely to exist in less-developed countries. In Brazil, for example, although the masses abhor continual price increases, there is no popular outcry against budgetary deficits. Politicians must be willing to go along with the popular view out of ignorance — and this cannot be discounted — or expediency. Although it is true that inflation discredits governments, it is equally true that a demagogue wins easy popularity by ordering increases in wages and public expenditures. Weighing one against the other, a politician might opt for inflation — particularly when the electorate cannot distinguish readily between causes and effects.

Once inflation gets going under these circumstances, it is difficult to contain, harder to stop. Each group, hurt by price increases, clamors for a return to its original position. The government accedes. On the face of it, this looks as though the government has some intention of redistributing the shares of national income. But actually the motive is very simple: It is a desire — impossible of attainment — to increase everyone's slice of cake. Thus, inflation becomes chronic.

An important phenomena tends to develop marginally to the chronic increase in prices; namely, fluctuations in the real income of different individuals. During an inflation of long duration, it is difficult for any individual or group to maintain purchasing power at a stable or continuously rising level. What normally occurs, in individual cases, is an oscillation of real income. In the case of wage-earners, undoubtedly the most important group, nominal wages are adjusted only intermittently while prices rise continuously. Immediately after each readjustment, wages reach a peak; from then on purchasing power begins to decline until the next readjustment, when wages reach a new peak, and so on.

From an aggregate standpoint, oscillations in the real income of different groups of individuals virtually offset one another. When some groups are at their real income peaks, others are down in the valley, while still others are half way up — readjustment dates being different for each of them. The overlapping of these de-phased cycles produces a movement that is free from oscillations, as when alternating current is converted into direct current. The appearance is that of a comfortable stability of average levels, when in fact individuals are living in purchasing power cycles.

These oscillations in the real income of individuals produce an important psychological byproduct.[2] The previous peaks of purchasing power, however transitory, become a yardstick that few individuals will relinquish. In fact, a sort of mystique gathers around these previous peaks; they represent the minimum distributive justice that each one has a right to expect.

The difficulty is, of course, that the peaks for different groups are out of phase. To stabilize all individuals at the peaks would be practicable only if the real product of the economy were to rise considerably. This necessary increase would probably be much higher than the prospects of short-term growth.

All this explains the practical political difficulties of monetary stabilization. In particular, it explains a phrase commonly used: "stabilization sacrifices." It becomes necessary to introduce a policy of promising less so that further inflation does not erode what was promised. But such a policy is hardly acceptable. Some people hope that stabilization will work a miracle and that the transitory peaks of past purchasing power will last. Others, with less confidence in price stabilization, fear that smaller promises will produce correspondingly smaller results.

This, then, is the fertile ground in which the direct causes for Brazilian inflation—uncontrolled public deficits, rapid monetary expansion, and disorderly wage adjustments — flourished. Nor is it surprising that several attempts at stabilization failed out of an inability to cope with the political problem; i.e., bringing income distribution into line.

---

[2] The idea of the influence of previous peaks, though in a somewhat different style, was broadly analyzed by Duesenberry, *Income, Saving and Theories of Consumer Behaviour* (Cambridge, Mass.: Harvard University Press, 1949).

3. Direct Causes of Inflation

Brazil's experience fits the normal pattern of the inflationary process. On the demand side, the continued rise in prices has been fostered by two factors: 1) federal government deficits financed through expanded loans from the monetary authorities to the national treasury and 2) expansion of bank credit to companies. These have been the main causes of the increase in the money supply, which in Brazil's case has been correlated closely with the increment in the total demand for goods and services. On the cost side, prices have been pushed upward by the frequent wage adjustments granted by the government and carried beyond the levels that would normally be paid by the market. In other words, institutional variables rather than market forces have pushed wages.

It is impossible to measure what share of Brazilian inflation is due to which cause — excess of demand or pressure of costs. It should be noted, for example, that wage increases have been a source not only of cost inflation but of demand inflation as well, as in the case of public servants and employees of subsidized government corporations. There are further difficulties encountered in attempting to sort out the matter. Statistics on wages are still incomplete. And beyond this, there is no safe way to answer such questions as these: What would wage increases in the private sector have been were it not for the interference of the public sector? How would the expansion of credit to companies have behaved had there not been wage increases?

Since there are no sure answers to these questions, it is impossible to calculate the effect — though clearly a considerable one — of the institutionally forced increase in costs. This has been the result of increased interference on the part of the government, the trade unions, and the labor courts in handling collective bargaining disputes. Obviously, this type of pressure on prices leaves the authorities with no satisfactory alternative. They must either expand credit, thus encouraging further inflation, or tighten monetary controls, thereby generating a crisis. In Brazil's case, the former policy prevailed. Indeed, part of the monetary expansion of recent years was brought about by the concern shown by the monetary authorities in aiding enterprises whose production costs had been increased as a result of the government's salary policy. A clear example of this is the loans the Banco do Brasil granted to private enterprises for payment of the "thirteenth-month" salary, a Christmas bonus paid at the end of the year.

The institutional pressure on salaries was not as strong in the years immediately following World War II as it later became. The turning point probably can be pinpointed as July, 1954, when the monthly minimum wage was doubled. After 1965, however, the wage pressures were considerably softened by the restraining policies of the Castelo Branco government.

What happened after 1952 is illustrated in Tables 5 and 6, showing the evolution of minimum wages in Guanabara and their relationship with cost-of-living increases. The granting of salary readjustments at a rate higher than the cost-of-living increases, through 1959, raised the real minimum wage by an annual average of 4.5 per cent — a rate clearly higher than that of the increase in real per capita income. In 1960, the minimum wage monthly average dropped by 16.5 per cent. In 1961, it was on the increase again, as a result of the readjustment which occurred in October, 1960, but it did not reach the average purchasing power of 1959. Since 1962, despite the annual revisions made over the period and the introduction of the thirteenth-month salary, the real minimum wage declined substantially.

On the whole, these and other available figures suggest that up to 1959 real urban salaries actually increased and that workers, although suffering the hardships of inflationary instability, did receive a significant share of the benefits of development. As of 1960, however, real urban salaries began to decline, at least at the minimum wage level.[3]

Unfortunately, the increase in real salaries does little to clarify the question concerning the influence of institutional pres-

---

[3] It is difficult to determine whether or not this trend continued in 1963 and 1964. Information available thus far indicates a decline in the real minimum wage. However, 1963 and 1964 were years of strong labor demands insofar as salaries are concerned. Whether or not such demands were sufficient to maintain real salaries is not as yet known. A general decrease in real wages probably occurred in 1965 and 1966 as a result of governmental restraints.

sure on costs. To say that the real salary of a certain working group increased is simply to say that the productivity of that group rose, even if at the cost of a change in relative prices and a drop in employment.[4] An increase in indirect taxes, on the other hand, could check the rise of real salaries, and there have been such tax increases in recent years.

Table 5   **MINIMUM WAGE IN THE STATE OF GUANABARA: 1952 TO 1966**

READJUSTMENT DATE	MONTHLY MINIMUM WAGE (CRUZEIROS)	INCREASE OVER PREVIOUS LEVELS (PER CENT)	COST-OF-LIVING INCREASE SINCE PREVIOUS READJUSTMENT (PER CENT)
Jan. 1952	1,200	—	—
July 1954	2,400	100.0	54.4
Aug. 1956	3,800	58.3	51.4
Jan. 1959	6,000	57.9	47.8
Oct. 1960	9,600	60.0	70.0
Oct. 1961	13,400	40.0	42.2
Jan. 1963	21,000	56.3	67.1
Feb. 1964	42,000	100.0	109.5
Mar. 1965	66,000	57.1	90.3
Mar. 1966	84,000	27.3	33.7

It is far more rewarding to study Brazilian inflation from the demand side. There are substantial data on such factors as public deficits, credit expansion, and the volume of money supply. But before turning to these aspects of Brazil's inflationary experience, a few other factors ought to be brought into perspective.

The external sector, in Brazil's case, has not always acted as an inflationary factor. It has done so when there has been a surplus in the balance of payments such as in 1965, or when a decline in the terms of trade has been accompanied by a fluctuation in the exchange rate, causing an increase in import costs through exchange devaluation. The reverse conditions — a defi-

---

[4] A satisfactory index of cost inflation could be obtained if the increase in productivity and in real salaries were associated with a drop in employment level. Unfortunately, employment statistics in Brazil are still generally unreliable.

cit in the balance of payments or an improvement in the terms
of trade — have served as an escape valve for internal inflationary pressures.

Table 6   **MONTHLY AVERAGE OF REAL MINIMUM
WAGE IN THE STATE OF GUANABARA: 1952 TO 1966**

YEAR	REAL MINIMUM WAGE–MONTHLY AVERAGE (IN CRUZEIROS OF FEBRUARY, 1964)
1952	31,800
1953	27,900
1954	35,600
1955	37,000
1956	37,600
1957	41,500
1958	36,300
1959	41,700
1960	34,800
1961	40,700
1962	38,100*
1963	35,400*
1964	33,700*
1965	32,700*
1966	30,100*

*Including the thirteenth-month salary.
Source: Fundação Getúlio Vargas.

It also should be pointed out that Brazil's handling of foreign trade has created what in effect are disguised taxes, and
like all taxes — whether so-called or not — these have had the
effect of limiting the need for monetary expansion. This was the
case when multiple exchange rates were in force, and it is still
true of the Brazilian coffee export operations.[5] To this extent,

[5] Between October, 1953 and March, 1961, a very complicated system of multiple exchange rates was in effect in Brazil. Imported and exported commodities
were classed in several groups, with a different exchange rate for each. As a rule,
the prices of foreign currency charged to importers were considerably above
those paid to exporters. A disguised tariff thus emerged through this system.

foreign trade has had a deflationary effect on the Brazilian economy.

One remaining factor also ought to be taken into account. Where there is a downward rigidity in the general price structure, it often has been observed that any change in relative prices will tend to push up the entire level of prices. This explains the increase in the general price level that has occurred during bad-crop years, regardless of monetary or wage influences. And it also suggests that Brazil's import substitution policy has been a source of inflationary pressure, the end results of such a policy being that it raises the cost of such goods either through customs protection or the higher cost of domestic production. These, however, were secondary factors in the generation of Brazilian inflation save perhaps in a few isolated years during the postwar period.

(footnote continued)

After 1961, exchange rates were unified. Importers, however, have been obliged to make time deposits in the Banco do Brasil in order to receive authorization to purchase foreign currency. (The required deposits correspond to a percentage of the value of imports, usually for a six-month term.) The increase of such deposits has served as a source of funds for the monetary authorities.

Coffee exports have been treated under a special rule. Exporters must give as a grant to the Banco do Brasil a certain amount in dollars per bag sold abroad — the so-called "retention quota." The cruzeiro counterpart (cruzeiros obtained through the sale of dollars by the Banco do Brasil) is intended to finance the government's purchase of any coffee surpluses. However, the retention quota has provided far more funds than required to purchase the existing coffee surpluses. This disguised tax has acted as a deflationary force.

4. The Relevance of the Quantity Theory

As we have already noted, there has been a close correlation in Brazil's case between the rate of inflation and the increase in the money supply. This relationship is made clear in Table 7, which shows the increases in gross domestic expenditure and the money supply over the 20 years of Brazil's worst inflation. The steadiness of the two is demonstrated by the comparatively slow rise in the income-velocity of currency, which is the ratio of gross domestic expenditure to the money supply.

Indeed, this slow rise is one of the outstanding characteristics of the Brazilian inflation. We know from experience that

Table 7   **INCOME-VELOCITY OF MONEY**

YEAR	GROSS DOMESTIC EXPENDITURE AT MARKET PRICES (BILLIONS OF CRUZEIROS) A	MONEY SUPPLY- ANNUAL AVERAGE (BILLIONS OF CRUZEIROS) B	INCOME VELOCITY OF CURRENCY $\frac{B}{A}$
1947	164.4	47.7	3.4
1948	187.0	47.7	3.9
1949	215.5	53.9	4.0
1950	253.5	66.8	3.8
1951	306.3	84.4	3.6
1952	351.1	94.9	3.7
1953	429.4	112.6	3.8
1954	552.2	136.9	4.1
1955	691.7	162.7	4.3
1956	884.4	196.6	4.5
1957	1,056.5	243.3	4.3
1958	1,310.0	338.7	3.9
1959	1,788.9	411.7	4.3
1960	2,385.6	568.7	4.2
1961	3,552.0	823.1	4.3
1962	5,586.8	1,266.1	4.4
1963	9,591.2	2,007.6	4.8
1964	18,867.3	3,742.2	5.0
1965	31,000 *	6,838.9	4.5
1966	45,000 *	9,700.0	4.6

*Preliminary estimate.
Source: Fundação Getúlio Vargas and the Central Bank.

a continuous rise in prices tends to discourage the holding of cash balances, hence to accelerate the income-velocity of currency, because a given money supply would circulate more rapidly and thus support a higher level of money income. But the Brazilian experience would roughly fit the class "quantity theory" of money, which asserts that the general price level varies directly in proportion to the amount of money in circulation, except for the growth of the real product. (The quantity theory in effect assumes that the income-velocity of money is constant, which implies that gross domestic expenditure or product rises and falls in direct relation to the rise and fall in the money supply.)

But before making any assumptions, we should first take note of some elements in the Brazilian situation that helped bring about this interesting result. There were at least four factors that prevented a further cut-back in the use of cash (i.e. the demand for money in the form of transaction balances) throughout the economy despite the existence of inflation:

1. There was not much leeway to cut down further on the amount of cash balances held for transaction purposes by individuals and business, since even before inflation these balances had always been low, with little reserve beyond immediate transaction needs.

2. The industrial spurt in the country and the considerable growth in the number of business firms should naturally increase the demand for cash balances. This provided a counteracting effect to the general tendency of cutting down transaction balances because of inflation.

3. Despite the continuous inflation, wage earners were never strong enough to impose an escalator clause and a subsequent reduction in the customary space of payroll periods, as they did in other countries.

4. Many people did not know how to protect their savings from inflation. Moreover, few assets were available as substitutes for cash balances, since the capital market of the country was rather weak. Foreign exchange purchases often attracted investors, but they were discouraged by administrative difficulties and by the risks of short-term oscillations in the exchange rate.

Apart from the over-all tendency toward a gradual increase in the income-velocity of the currency, there were short-term fluctuations during certain years covered in the table. In general, these fluctuations resulted from pressures brought about by monetary policy. Thus, in years of tight credit, as in 1956 and 1964, the income-velocity tended to increase as a result of the squeeze on companies' cash reserves. The reversal of expectations about price increases has probably been the main cause of the decline of the income-velocity in 1965 and 1966.

The seeming conformity of the Brazilian experience to the classical quantity theory of money could be misleading. It would be wrong to assume that a successful stabilization program can be achieved by depending *solely* on constricting the means of payment. This is a necessary, but not sufficient, condition. And it should always be borne in mind that in view of an increase in costs — caused by the institutional rise in wages, by the exchange rate, or by an imbalance in the relative price system — the expansion of money supply may be the sole alternative to crisis and unemployment. In order to succeed, any stabilization program requires a synchronized fight against inflation, both from the side of costs and from that of demand. The latter, however, basically depends on the control of monetary expansion.

5. The Behavior of the Federal Public Sector

One of the main causes of Brazilian inflation has been the violent pressure of the federal government's deficits on the monetary system. The lack of a market for public debt securities until 1964 caused these deficits to be covered almost completely by the expansion of Banco do Brasil's loans to the national treasury, setting in motion the familiar mechanism of multiplied expansion of the money supply. (Even had a market for public securities existed, it could hardly have reached the size required to absorb the deficits that occurred in some years.)

Table 8 shows the expenditure, revenue, and deficit of the federal government as a percentage of gross domestic product from 1947 through 1966. Until 1955, existing deficits seldom reached 1 per cent of GDP, and in three of these years there were actual surpluses. This means that until 1955 the federal government was not a main cause of inflationary pressures.

In fact, the monetary expansion before 1955 derived to a greater extent from the expansion of loans by the banking system to private enterprises, government corporations, and state and municipal governments. Starting in 1956, however, the federal government became the main force behind inflation. In 1955, the cash deficit was only 0.8 per cent of gross domestic product; it rose to 2.2 per cent in 1956 and reached 5.1 per cent in 1963.

The reason for the rapid real growth of the federal deficit is to be found in increased expenditure; it averaged 9 per cent of GDP in the ten-year period from 1945 to 1955 but rose to 14.6 per cent in 1963. Public revenues increased slightly as a percentage of GDP. But in view of the successive revisions of tax legislation, revenue in no way managed to keep up with the expenditure increases.

The accelerated increase in federal expenditure, in turn, stemmed from three main factors:

• The spoils policy in the public sector padded payrolls and forced successive increases in salaries.

• There were continuous increases in public investment due to the vicious cycle of inflation. The government in-

creasingly found it necessary to invest in certain sectors of
the economy as private capital withdrew, either exhausted
by inflation or discouraged by price controls in these areas.

• There were growing deficits in government corporations and in the so-called "mixed" companies (government
and private capital), particularly in the railways and
merchant marine.

Table 8   **EXPENDITURE, REVENUE, AND DEFICIT OF
THE FEDERAL GOVERNMENT AS A PERCENTAGE
OF GROSS DOMESTIC PRODUCT: 1947 TO 1966**

YEAR	BILLIONS OF CRUZEIROS				PER CENT OF GDP		
	EXPENDI-TURE	REVENUE	DEFICIT	GROSS DOMESTIC PRODUCT	EXPENDI-TURE	REVE-NUE	DEFICIT
1947	13.4	13.9	(0.5)	164.4	8.1	8.4	(0.3)
1948	15.7	15.7	—	187.0	8.4	8.4	—
1949	20.7	17.9	2.8	215.5	9.6	8.3	1.3
1950	23.7	19.4	4.3	253.5	9.4	7.7	1.7
1951	24.6	27.4	(2.8)	306.3	8.0	8.9	(0.9)
1952	28.5	30.8	(2.3)	351.1	8.1	8.8	(0.7)
1953	39.9	37.0	2.9	429.4	9.3	8.6	0.7
1954	50.5	46.5	4.0	552.2	9.1	8.4	0.7
1955	61.4	55.7	5.7	691.7	8.9	8.1	0.8
1956	93.4	74.1	19.3	884.4	10.6	8.4	2.2
1957	126.7	85.8	40.9	1,056.6	12.0	8.1	3.9
1958	46.2	17.8	28.4	1,310.0	11.2	9.0	2.2
1959	211.5	157.8	53.7	1,788.9	11.8	8.8	3.0
1960	297.5	219.8	77.7	2,385.6	12.5	9.2	3.3
1961	447.9	317.5	130.4	3,522.0	12.7	9.0	3.7
1962	778.7	497.8	280.9	5,586.8	13.9	8.9	5.0
1963	1,435.0	930.8	504.7	9,591.2	14.6	9.5	5.1
1964	2,770.0	2,010.0	760.0	18,867.3	14.7	10.7	4.0
1965	3,826.0	3,738.0	588.0	31,000.0*	12.3	10.4	1.9
1966	5,700.0*	5,700.0*	500.0*	45,000.0*	12.7	11.6	1.1

( ) Surplus.
* Preliminary estimate.

NOTE: The data through 1953 are on a somewhat different basis from that for
the years following. From 1954, the official figures indicate "cash expenditure"
and "cash deficit."

Source: General Accountant's Office and Fundação Getúlio Vargas.

The Castelo Branco government, which came into office in April, 1964, developed successful methods to reduce the budgetary deficit — both by cutting expenditures and by increasing the tax revenue. As can be seen from Table 8, the cash deficit, as a percentage of the gross domestic product fell from 5.1 per cent in 1963 to 1.1 per cent in 1966. Moreover, the government was able to finance the major part of such deficits through the sale of public bonds, with monetary correction for inflation, rather than by printing money as it had formerly done. Thus it can be said that since 1965 the government deficit has not been a significant cause of the continuing Brazilian inflation.

6. The Operation of the Monetary System[6]

As noted before, the money supply in Brazil has been growing in recent years more or less in proportion to the general increase in prices plus the increase in the real product. This growth has served as a monetary vehicle for the propagation of inflation.[7] Between December, 1947 and December, 1966, the money supply increased 223 times, as can be seen in Table 9. By comparison, the general wholesale price index rose 131 times, the difference being due to the growth of the real product and, to a smaller degree, to the variations in the income-velocity of money.

The most familiar ally of the money supply, the balance of paper money issued, has been growing a little less rapidly. It increased by 139 times between December, 1947, and December, 1966. (See Table 10.) This resulted from the increase in the ratio of money supply to the balance of paper money issued, which in turn was caused by the growing preference of the public for bank money. (In other words, there was a decline in the share of money supply held by the public in the form of paper money.)

In 1965, 19.4 per cent of the existing money supply corresponded to paper money held by the public, 17.3 per cent to cash deposits with the monetary authorities, and 63.3 per cent to cash deposits in commercial banks. During the period from 1950 to 1965, the composition of the money supply clearly changed with respect to the preference of the public for bank money, as can be seen in Table 11. This change in composition can be ascribed to the development of the banking system within the country.

The expansion of the money supply resulted from the traditional operating pattern of the banking system in Brazil, which

---

[6] For a fuller explanation of the monetary system, see Appendix.

[7] In fact, the money supply has grown a little more rapidly than the general price level and a little less rapidly than the gross domestic product at current prices. This latter phenomenon is due to the slow or gradual increase in the income-velocity of the currency.

has been biased toward monetary inflation. The monetary authorities have been powerless to curtail federal budgetary deficits, to control credit generally, or to function effectively as do central bankers in many other countries. Until 1964, the Banco do Brasil served in part as a central bank, with its regulatory powers over credit and commercial banks shared with the Superintendencia da Moeda do Credito (SUMOC). The Banco do Brasil has not only acted as the government's banker, but also as a commercial and rediscount bank. Furthermore, it had not had the power to reject any loan requirement made by the government. Since 1965, a more adequate control has been put into effect with the creation of a Central Bank separate from the Banco do Brasil.

In expanding loans to the government, to the private sector, and to commercial banks, the monetary authorities were forced

Table 9   **TOTAL MONEY SUPPLY**

(As of December 31)

YEAR	MONEY SUPPLY IN MILLIONS OF CRUZEIROS	PER CENT INCREASE
1947	46,538	—
1948	50,063	7.6
1949	58,265	16.4
1950	78,322	34.4
1951	90,749	15.1
1952	104,152	14.8
1953	124,069	19.1
1954	151,474	22.1
1955	177,922	17.4
1956	217,283	22.1
1957	290,938	33.9
1958	353,138	21.4
1959	500,572	41.7
1960	692,032	38.2
1961	1,041,842	50.5
1962	1,702,305	63.4
1963	2,792,183	64.0
1964	5,190,700	85.9
1965	9,074,600	74.8
1966	10,400,000*	14.6

* Preliminary estimate.
Source: Central Bank.

Table 10   **TOTAL MONEY SUPPLY**
AND PAPER MONEY ISSUED
(Balance as of December 31)

YEAR	TOTAL MONEY SUPPLY (MILLIONS OF CRUZEIROS) A	PAPER MONEY ISSUED (MILLIONS OF CRUZEIROS) B	RATIO $\frac{A}{B}$
1947	46,538	20,395	2.28
1948	50,063	21,693	2.31
1949	58,265	24,042	2.42
1950	78,322	31,202	2.51
1951	90,749	35,316	2.57
1952	104,152	39,280	2.65
1953	124,069	47,002	2.97
1954	151,474	59,039	2.57
1955	177,922	69,340	2.57
1956	217,283	80,819	2.69
1957	290,938	96,575	3.01
1958	353,138	119,814	2.95
1959	500,572	154,621	3.24
1960	692,032	206,140	3.36
1961	1,041,842	313,858	3.32
1962	1,702,305	508,780	3.35
1963	2,792,183	888,768	3.14
1964	5,190,700	1,483,700	3.50
1965	9,074,600	2,174,800	4.17
1966	10,400,000*	2,841,800	3.66

* Preliminary estimate.
Source: Central Bank.

to launch new money into circulation. This paper money later returned to the commercial banks as a result of public deposits. The banks, holding excess cash, increased their loans. The money received by the borrower ultimately returned in part to the banks in the form of new deposits, and so on ad infinitum. Additionally, some monetary expansion took place merely through a change in the public preference for bank money as opposed to currency.[8]

---

[8] It should be noted that open-market operations in government securities were virtually nonexistent in Brazil until 1964. In more recent years they became more common on the basis of the public bonds with an escalator clause (monetary correction index).

Table 11

MONEY SUPPLY

(Balances as of December 31)

YEAR	MILLIONS OF CRUZEIROS					PERCENTAGES				
	PAPER MONEY HELD BY THE PUBLIC (A)	BANK MONEY (B)			TOTAL MONEY SUPPLY (A+B)	PAPER MONEY HELD BY THE PUBLIC (A)	BANK MONEY (B)			TOTAL MONEY SUPPLY (A+B)
		MONETARY AUTHORITIES	COMMERCIAL BANKS	TOTAL			MONETARY AUTHORITIES	COMMERCIAL BANKS	TOTAL	
1950	25,116	8,289	44,917	53,206	78,322	32.1	10.6	57.3	67.9	100.0
1951	28,429	10,096	52,244	62,320	90,749	31.3	11.2	57.5	68.7	100.0
1952	31,533	12,283	60,336	72,619	104,152	30.3	11.8	57.9	69.7	100.0
1953	37,868	14,942	71,259	86,201	124,069	30.5	12.1	57.4	69.5	100.0
1954	48,957	17,624	84,893	102,517	151,474	32.3	11.6	56.1	67.7	100.0
1955	57,099	18,487	102,336	120,823	177,922	32.1	10.4	57.5	67.9	100.0
1956	67,458	23,184	126,641	149,825	217,283	31.0	10.7	58.3	69.0	100.0
1957	81,277	33,614	176,047	209,661	290,938	27.9	11.6	60.5	72.1	100.0
1958	99,731	37,275	216,132	253,407	353,138	28.2	10.6	61.2	71.8	100.0
1959	127,025	51,916	321,631	373,547	500,572	25.4	10.4	64.2	74.6	100.0
1960	169,354	84,433	438,245	522,678	692,032	24.5	12.2	63.3	75.5	100.0
1961	255,774	175,223	610,845	786,068	1,041,842	24.6	16.8	58.6	75.4	100.0
1962	396,678	267,878	1,037,749	1,305,627	1,702,305	23.3	15.7	61.0	76.7	100.0
1963	683,825	404,440	1,703,918	2,108,358	2,792,183	24.5	14.5	61.0	75.5	100.0
1964	1,155,800	965,300	3,069,600	4,034,900	5,190,700	22.3	18.6	59.1	77.7	100.0
1965	1,756,000	1,574,400	5,744,200	7,318,600	9,074,600	19.4	17.3	63.3	80.6	100.0

Source: Central Bank.

Table 12 shows how the expansion of the money supply burgeoned between 1953 and 1965. In short, the expansion of the money supply corresponded to the excess of the banking system's investments over the non-monetary resources it received. The increased investments, in turn, were concentrated on two main items: the expansion of credit to the national treasury to cover the latter's deficits and the extension of loans to companies and the public in general. There are two interesting points regarding the evolution of the monetary expansion mechanism:

1. During the 1950's, the structure of the banking system's operations was substantially altered, a larger portion of credit being assigned to the government at the expense of the private sector. This shows up clearly in Tables 13 and 14. The first table demonstrates how loans to the public as a proportion of total money supply have decreased. The second stresses that, between 1951 and 1966, the balance of banking loans to the private sector was practically unchanged in real terms, although *the real product rose by 110 per cent* during the period.

2. Until 1963, foreign commerce gave the monetary authorities the opportunity to obtain sizable resources through the so-called "agios on bonus" when multiple exchange rates were prevailing, through coffee retention quotas after 1961, and through the compulsory deposits by importers. Even if allowance is made for compulsory earmarkings (such as the purchase of coffee surpluses), these resources substantially reduced the need for expansion of the money supply by the banking system, thus acting as a kind of brake against Brazilian inflation.[9] In 1965, however, the foreign sector was responsible for a huge monetary expansion, as a counterpart of the accumulation of about 500 million dollars of foreign currency reserves.

---

[9] The coffee sector is often held responsible for an inflationary impact that actually did not exist except in one or two isolated years. For some years (1957 to 1961) the government had to purchase approximately half the crop, which corresponded to the production surplus. Coffee exporters, in turn, only received half the exchange value of their sales either because of the low value of the coffee dollar until March, 1961, or as the result of retention quotas from then on. Since the latter condition prevailed almost constantly, the government obtained more resources from the coffee sector than it provided.

Table 12

CONSOLIDATED BALANCE OF THE BANKING SYSTEM, COMMERCIAL BANKS, AND MONETARY AUTHORITIES

Annual changes in millions of cruzeiros

ITEM	1953	1954	1955	1956	1957	1958	1959	1960	1961	1962	1964	1963	1965
ASSETS													
Loans to the national treasury financial operations*	5,577	3,154	8,893	24,761	39,413	26,201	40,718	77,805	128,605	242,326	437,517	679,800	297,000
Loans to state and municipal governments, government corporations and other public entities	3,105	7,545	2,017	473	259	560	2,851	8,338	7,535	5,860	39,405	77,700	337,700
Loans to the private sector	18,081	31,834	19,211	34,044	49,060	57,068	89,282	164,185	216,378	473,050	691,376	1,560,500	2,041,200
TOTAL	26,763	42,533	30,121	59,278	83,732	83,829	132,851	250,328	352,878	721,236	1,168,298	2,318,000	2,675,900
RESOURCES													
Total money supply	19,917	27,405	26,448	39,361	73,655	62,200	147,434	191,460	349,810	660,463	1,089,878	2,398,500	3,883,900
Resources associated with exchange control (net balance) and import deposits	(602)	9,327	2,224	15,839	5,061	11,394	13,816	23,789	57,059	149,073	84,895	(148,100)	(1,327,000)
Time deposits	1,240	2,391	901	1,420	3,836	3,118	5,215	16,406	9,497	(429)	32,202	58,900	56,000
Other accounts (net balance)	6,208	3,410	2,350	2,658	6,180	7,117	5,982	18,673	(63,488)	(87,871)	(38,677)	8,700	63,000
TOTAL	26,763	42,533	30,121	59,278	88,732	83,829	132,851	250,328	352,878	721,236	1,168,298	2,318,000	2,675,900

( ) Indicates minus.
* Including national treasury bonds for paper money issued.
Source: Central Bank.

The shift in investment in favor of the government and away from the private sector was achieved mainly through the increased compulsory deposits of commercial banks at the order of SUMOC. A certain conservatism in rediscount limits (which expanded less rapidly than the general price level) also contributed to the same result. The fear that inflation might escape control, together with a lack of courage in cutting public expenditure or in raising taxes, seems to have been the main motivation behind this monetary policy. No doubt, a relative reduction in the real value of loans to the private sector has been one way to check inflation. However, better and more equitable results could have been attained through an adequate fiscal policy.

Table 13 **LOANS TO THE PUBLIC VERSUS MONEY SUPPLY**

(Balances as of December 31)

YEAR	LOANS TO THE PUBLIC (A) (MILLIONS OF CRUZEIROS)	BALANCE OF MONEY SUPPLY (B) (MILLIONS OF CRUZEIROS)	RATIO $\frac{A}{B}$
1951	85,647	90,749	0.944
1952	102,279	104,152	0.982
1953	120,360	124,069	0.970
1954	152,194	151,474	1.005
1955	171,405	177,922	0.963
1956	205,449	217,283	0.946
1957	254,509	290,938	0.875
1958	311,577	353,138	0.882
1959	400,859	500,572	0.801
1960	565,044	692,032	0.816
1961	781,422	1,041,842	0.750
1962	1,254,472	1,702,305	0.737
1963	1,945,848	2,792,183	0.697
1964	3,506,300	5,190,700	0.675
1965	5,547,500	9,074,600	0.611
1966	6,657,300*	10,400,000*	0.640

* Preliminary estimate.
Source: SUMOC

Table 14   **REAL BALANCE OF LOANS TO THE PUBLIC**

(Balances as of December 31)

YEAR	LOANS TO THE PUBLIC (MLILIONS OF CURRENT CRUZEIROS)	GENERAL WHOLESALE PRICE INDEX (BASIS: AVFRAGE 1953 = 100)	REAL LOANS TO THE PUBLIC (IN MILLIONS OF 1953 CRUZEIROS)
1951	85,647	82.5	103,815
1952	102,279	90.4	104,898
1953	120,360	113.2	106,325
1954	152,194	140.3	108,478
1955	171,405	153.5	111,664
1956	205,449	192.9	106,505
1957	254,509	199.4	127,637
1958	311,577	255.0	122,187
1959	400,859	347.1	115,488
1960	565,044	460.8	122,622
1961	781,422	691.6	112,988
1962	1,254,472	1,037.0	120,971
1963	1,945,848	1,855.0	104,897
1964	3,506,300	3,645.0	96,104
1965	5,547,500	4,638.0	119,610
1966	6,657,300	6,413.0	103,810

Source: SUMOC and Fundação Getúlio Vargas.

7. Inflationary Distortions

A violent inflationary process obviously brings about profound economic and social changes in any nation. Brazil is no exception. Perhaps Brazil's experience has not been so unfortunate as that of other countries, in the sense that the inflationary distortions have not reached the point of blocking development. Even so, these distortions have left deep marks on the country's economy in terms of the misuse of resources and of sacrifice on the part of the people.

Some of the most flagrant distortions produced by inflation in Brazil since the end of World War II are described in the following pages.

Instability and Salary Disorder

There is no empirical evidence that over any prolonged period Brazil's inflation has depressed the average real earnings of the working class.[10] In fact, real salaries have revealed a rising tendency since the end of World War II, and there is no reason to believe that any mechanism to systematically delay salary readjustments has been associated with inflation. It is unquestionable, however, that inflation has caused real salaries to be unstable, making them oscillate through the combination of continuously rising prices with intermittent revisions. Such violent fluctuations no doubt impose heavy burdens on wage-earners, especially those at low-income levels.

Aside from the over-all instability, the wage and salary structure has been considerably distorted by the inflationary process. Chronic price increases served as an excuse for disorderly salary readjustments, without reference to productivity or to other factors.

---

[10] According to the estimates made by the Fundação Getúlio Vargas, the participation of wage-earners in the gross domestic income rose from 56.1 per cent in 1947 to 64.9 per cent in 1960 (figures refer to the urban sector only). In relation to the GDP at market prices, the increase was considerably smaller, on account of the growing pressure of indirect taxes. But an increase did occur, nonetheless.

Public Utility Rate Controls

As has happened in other countries, the Brazilian government was unable to resist the temptation of fighting the symptoms rather than the causes of inflation. Such a policy — supported by the people's misconception of the real causes — was naturally based on price controls.

The traditional victims of this kind of policy have been public utilities, whose rates are regulated by government because of their natural monopolistic characteristics. The typical case was that of electric power rates, which were supposed to cover production costs and provide the company with a 10 per cent remuneration on the historical value of its investment. The historical value was interpreted in a purely nominal sense, without any. monetary correction. Under such conditions, the real remuneration of capital invested in electric power became absurdly small. Furthermore, depreciation of equipment was also computed on the basis of historical cost, which reduced even further the profitability of utility companies.[11]

It is curious why this clearly unfair criterion has persisted for so long. In open discussion, the government has always agreed that basing rates on nominal historical cost was indeed irrational under inflationary conditions. Despite this, however, the desire to stop prices has prevailed. The sizable foreign investment in public utilities has influenced this policy of resisting rate influences.

Under these circumstances, there obviously was no incentive for private capital to enter the public utilities field. As a consequence, some crisis always developed. In order to keep essential services going, and to prevent bottlenecks in the economy, the government was forced to supply capital to the public utilities — the first step toward socializing a strategic sector. This completed a cycle begun by price controls and fostered by an illusion: What people did not pay in the form of higher rates, they now paid through inflation or tax increases.

---

[11] Such interpretation prevailed until 1964, when the Castelo Branco government officially recognized the monetary correction of the investment of. the concessionaires. In more recent years public utility rates have been raised to quite realistic levels.

But this was not all. The government did not enter the field as an investor at the precise moment when private capital withdrew. There was an interim period, sometimes prolonged, during which demands could not be met and service deteriorated; e.g., the Brazilian telephone services, which are still unable to take on new subscribers and which give deplorable service. Private capital was then represented to the public as unable to supply these services and the transfer to government control was completed after a demoralizing campaign against free enterprise.

Exchange Control

The attempt to restrain inflation has often been extended to the exchange market. As part of the price control policy, it is usual to maintain overvalued exchange rates at the cost of a certain quantitative control on imports. Obviously, a fixed exchange rate cannot be indefinitely sustained during chronic inflation. But it is always possible to let the rate lag behind price increases and then to readjust the rate periodically if foreign currency expenditure is repressed.

In Brazil's experience with exchange control, the period that caused the greatest distortions — in the price system, in the guidance of economic activities, and in the structure of the balance of payments — was that from June, 1947 to January, 1953. Its basic characteristic was the freezing of the exchange rate at around 18.50 cruzeiros to the dollar at the same time that the internal price level was continuously inflated. (During that period, the cost of living in Guanabara rose by 67 per cent.)

The results of this policy of immobilizing the exchange rate during the inflation were what might be expected. Exports and foreign capital inflow were discouraged, while imports and remittances of capital and profits were stimulated to such a point that it became necessary to restrain them by means of quantitative restrictions. Finally, through stimulation of the black market, foreign currencies were naturally valued well above the fixed rate. In fact, exchange-rate freezing could only be sustained by the extraordinary rise in the external prices of coffee; this brought many dollars into Brazil at the time, but was responsible for the subsequent world overproduction of coffee.

After 1953, the government pursued a more realistic policy vis-a-vis exchange rates, but it, too, was frequently full of distortions. In January of that year, a free exchange market was established for financial transfers. In October, a system of multiple exchange rates was adopted for imports and exports. The exchange system became increasingly complex. There was a time when some dozens of exchange rates prevailed in Brazil. These included the official rate; the official rate plus minimum surtaxes; rates for five import categories that varied according to type of commodity and to the convertibility area of the foreign currency; rates for four export categories that also varied according to whether or not exports were made to convertible currency countries; specific auction rates; the free market rate; and so forth. Finally, in August, 1957, with enactment of Law No. 3244 (Law of Customs Tariffs), the exchange system was somewhat simplified by the reduction of the import categories from five to two. (However, imports favored by the so-called "exchange cost" persisted.) And a considerable degree of complication continued to exist until March, 1961.

It is not possible to analyze thoroughly in this study the effects of the exchange policy over the entire period from 1953 to 1966. The policy had many motivations besides that of price control; e.g., protectionism for domestic industry, defense of external coffee prices. Suffice it to say that the spirit of the price control system was kept alive in at least two ways:

• The maintenance of especially favored exchange rates for certain imports — wheat, petroleum and its by-products, printing paper, etc. — at the cost of heavy subsidies;

• The systematic lagging of export taxes behind internal price rises.

In March, 1961, with the enactment of Instruction 204 of SUMOC, subsequently reinforced by Instruction 208, the exchange system moved toward realism. Rates were unified, except for special treatment for coffee and for imports considered superfluous, though the rates for these two categories were made flexible. The Goulart administration, however, re-established the practice of letting the exchange rate lag behind inflation.

This immediately brought into being a parallel black market for financial operations, and eventually the country made a partial return to the multiple system. The current policy of unification and exchange freedom was finally established by the Castelo Branco administration in May of 1964.

Financial Unpredictability

One of the traditional effects of inflation consists in destroying the possibilities of financial forecasts. The cost estimates of any project are repeatedly shattered by cost increases. Even if allowances are made in financial calculations for the inflationary effect, the inflation rate still moves beyond expectations. The cost of any undertaking extending over three or four years becomes almost completely unpredictable.

Without any doubt, this has been one of the most upsetting consequences of the Brazilian inflation for entrepreneurs. Financing plans rapidly become obsolete, and many undertakings must be stopped periodically until new resources are found. Inflation dramatically prolongs investment schedules. As a result, private capital shies away from those basic sectors of the economy requiring long maturation terms for investment. And governmental projects are hindered as well by the continuous shattering of forecasts and by the need for supplemental funds.

Illusions about Profits

Inflation is the eternal source of illusions about profits. The real profit earned by companies is almost always far below that appearing on the published balance sheets. Indeed, part of the nominal profits appearing in the accounts are in reality merely reserves for depreciation, since the reserves set aside explicitly for this purpose are utterly inadequate for replacement of fixed assets. This again goes back to the legal requirement that depreciation must be calculated on historical cost.[12] At the same time,

---

[12] This has been changed. Law No. 4,357, passed on July 17, 1964, allows the deduction of depreciation for income-tax purposes on the basis of reappraised assets. The Decree Law No. 62, passed in November, 1966, went one step further, creating the full monetary correction of the balance sheets. According to the new accounting procedures, illusory gains will be treated as expenditures and not as profits.

a part of the retained profits represents no more than a reserve for the replacement of working capital. (This is due, among other things, to the need for replacing inventories that have become more costly because of inflation and for maintaining the real value of cash reserves.) Such items are nothing but illusory balance sheet profits since their reinvestment adds nothing to the real assets of the business.

The exact amount of these illusory profits cannot be calculated, though some idea of their magnitude can be arrived at from an analysis of their relation to working capital. According to data published by *Conjuctura Econômica,* illusory profits in the replacement of working capital between 1958 and 1964 absorbed from one-half to three-fourths of the stated profits of stock corporations, as shown in Table 15.

On top of all this, one must take into account still a further and even more basic distortion. It is impossible to state a realistic ratio of profits to capital, since total capital is grossly understated by calculating it on the value of past cruzeiros without adjustment for inflation.

All of this results in a very distorted picture, not only for entrepreneurs but likewise for the government and the public. Unable to rely on accounting as a true reflection of their situation, entrepreneurs often make poor decisions; not a few companies have decapitalized themselves through distribution of dividends. The government has taxed illusory profits as though they were real, frequently as excess profits. The result has been a strong incentive for evasion. The public, lacking the sophistication to see what was really happening, views the seemingly high profits of business as an abuse of economic power. This has strengthened the popular belief that the increased cost of living has been caused by the greed of businessmen, and this in turn has worsened the climate for private enterprise.

Loss of Merits of the Price System

Most of the merits of the price system as a guide to production and investment have been invalidated by Brazilian inflation. Rational entrepreneurial decision-making has been made difficult by the uncertainties and risks inherent in inflation, by the

Table 15   **ILLUSORY PROFITS IN THE REPLACEMENT OF WORKING CAPITAL OF STOCK CORPORATIONS**

YEAR	1958	1959	1960	1961	1962	1963	1964
A. Number of Companies	6,818	7,104	5,587	6,441	6,822	6,998	7,915
B. Working capital at the beginning of the fiscal year (millions of cruzeiros)	112,876	156,437	163,873	201,279	298,284	404,639	712,357
C. Inflation rate (per cent)	27.9	36.1	32.8	50.1	50.3	81.9	93.3
D. Illusory profits in replacement of working capital (BxC) (millions of cruzeiros)	31,943	56,474	53,750	100,838	150,037	331,399	664,629
E. Total balance of profits (millions of cruzeiros)	58,399	84,936	102,849	168,287	288,193	447,975	1,140,187
F. Percentage (D/E), per cent	53.9	66.5	52.3	59.9	52.1	74.0	58.3

Source: Calculated from data appearing in *Conjuntura Econômica.*

unfairness of taxation, by price controls, and by similar distortions. Basic and long-term investment has been discouraged while speculation has been stimulated. All of this has blurred the idea that social benefit arises from private profit and that production effort yields personal reward. A substantial number of Brazilians were persuaded that it is better to be clever than to work.

In addition to these distortions, inflation created great problems in two other areas. The credit market has been highly distorted, as we shall see in the next chapter. And there has been damage to social investment, reflected in the discouragement of investment in housing; this will be treated in Chapter 9.

8. The Credit Market and Inflation

In examining the credit market, we touch on a very interesting phenomenon — the way in which Brazilian institutions have adapted themselves to inflation. The credit market has developed very complicated devices to circumvent legal restrictions that were put into effect during a period of stability and remain in force because of popular prejudice. These evasions have exerted a certain stabilizing effect on the credit market, reducing to some extent the gap between demand and supply, though it is true that shortages have persisted, particularly in the area of long-term credit.

A chronic and violent inflation obviously produces deep distortions in the credit market of a country. At the outset, it is the borrowers who first profit, since they pay back their borrowings in devalued currency. However, this so-called "debtor's profit" is eventually frustrated by the lenders, who begin to include inflation in their forecasts. They raise their interest rates in anticipation of further inflationary pressures. But since there often are legal ceilings on these rates, inflation drives the real and the nominal interest rates far apart.

In Brazil's case, a 1933 "Usury Law" prohibits loan contracts with interest rates of more than 12 per cent a year. Though this is certainly a very high rate during periods of monetary stability, it obviously becomes ridiculously inadequate when the inflation rate reaches 50 per cent or more. However, various devices have been used to get around the Usury Law. Lawyers and finance experts always find legal formulas to replace the words "loan" and "interest." They respect the form of the law, but disobey the content.

Aside from the legal problems involved, however, another problem arises with interest rates when a country goes into such a steep inflation as that experienced by Brazil. Forecasting the rate of inflation — and hence the interest rates that should be charged — becomes very difficult, particularly over fairly long periods of time. This naturally makes long-term lending extremely unattractive and cuts down the supply of money available for such loans.

One way to adjust to the problem would be to introduce an escalator clause in loan contracts, in accordance with some agreed-upon price index. But the Brazilian gold clause law of 1933 specially forbids this, and up to now no one has found a legal loophole.[13] Yet even were escalator clauses allowed, they would not constitute a wholly satisfactory solution to the problem. For prices and wages during inflation do not move up evenly, and the borrower would always run the risk of having his income lag behind the index chosen for the escalator clause.

Let us now examine the distortions experienced by commercial banks.

The interest on bank deposits, both demand and time deposits, is controlled by the monetary authorities and cannot exceed a very small limiting rate. Some banks used to pay additional interest rates to some long-term depositors, but this is an irregular operation which now tends to disappear. The natural consequence has been the almost complete disappearance of time deposits. These deposits, which in 1950 represented about one-fourth of total banking deposits, are reduced today to an extremely small fraction — less than 5 per cent — of the total.

In making loans, the commercial banks until fairly recently, did obey the limits of the Usury Law, even though inflation already had reached 20 per cent a year. Obviously, the banks could do this because they paid even smaller interest rates to their depositors. Lately, however, the barriers of the Usury Law have been wholly surmounted. This has been achieved by three main devices, sometimes in combination:

Under-the-table interest. This is the crudest device; it consists of charging extra interest without any accounting entries either in the bank's or the borrower's books.

Overcharge of banking fees. This is the most common device. Besides the interest rate, the bank charges the borrower several fees — for opening the account, for collection of bills, etc. Such fees (duly inflated) raise the actual interest rate far above the limits of the Usury Law.

---

[13] The capital market law passed in July, 1965, now permits the escalator clause in loan contracts. Borrowers, however, seem to resist such a clause. This appears to be the main difficulty to the development of private investment banks.

Linked accounts. This device — the most sophisticated of the three — consists of tying a loan to a time deposit until the debt is paid off. The borrower takes out a loan much larger than he needs and deposits part of this money in the bank. Since the interest rate paid on such deposits is far less than the rate charged for the loan, the effective interest rate is far above that appearing in the contract.[14] For the banks, this type of loan has the inconvenience of causing an increase in compulsory deposits, at the order of the Central Bank. Since the account of the bank deposits increases artificially, bankers naturally prefer to use the other devices.

The fact that banks charge effective interest rates far above the Usury Law is a question of supply and demand. It would be impossible to keep supply and demand in equilibrium if the interest rates, under inflationary conditions, were limited to the legal 12 per cent. It must be said that the effective rates presently charged are still below the pace of inflation, which means that the real interest is negative. Also, the present rates are not sufficiently high to balance the supply and the demand for loans. Because credit is rationed, a certain margin of demand remains unsatisfied. It is obvious, however, that the situation would have been more unbalanced if the Usury Law had been effective.

Let us now examine the medium-term credit market. The demand for this type of credit has increased extraordinarily in recent years with the development of the consumer durable-goods and capital-goods industries, especially with the development of the automobile industry. These industries, in order to broaden their markets, had to turn to installment selling on terms up to 18 or 24 months. But commercial banks, because they were unable to attract time deposits, were not in a position to grant medium-term loans. After a certain period of difficulties, the problem was solved by the so-called "credit and finance companies," through the use of some perfectly legal devices to get

---

[14] Here is a simple illustration: Let us suppose that an individual wishes to obtain a loan of 1000 cruzeiros. The bank lends 2000 cruzeiros at 20 per cent a year and requires that the borrower deposit half the amount in a time account yielding 2 per cent a year. The effective interest rate in this instance will come to 38 per cent a year.

around the Usury Law. These were successful in attracting medium term funds equivalent to time deposits.

The finance companies have developed two main methods of operation — participation accounts and bills of exchange (Letras de Cambio).

The first method consists of substituting participation-account partnership contracts for deposits and loans. Under the Brazilian Commercial Code, partnerships can be set up without the formalities required for other types of firms, which exempts these from the usual bureaucratic red tape. Above all, they are very flexible. In the formation of a participation fund, the finance company itself is the open partner and time depositors are the hidden ones. The resources of the fund are then used in new participation-account partnerships, in which the borrowers of the company are the open partners and the fund is the hidden one. In reality, there is only a change of label. Deposits and loans take the name of participation-account partnerships and the interest rates take the name of profits. This change of words, however, allows escape from the Usury Law regulations, because the earnings of participation-account partnerships are considered profit, not interest. Thus, finance companies are able to pay their depositors (officially known as "participants") interest rates around 40 per cent a year. The borrower pays this rate, plus an extra amount to cover the expenses and a margin of profit for the finance company.

The second system, employing bills of exchange, is even more ingenious. The borrower exchanges promissory notes for bills of exchange drawn by him and accepted by the finance company.[15] The due dates of the bills of exchange are scheduled in such a way that before the due date of each an equivalent amount of promissory notes brought in by the borrower become due. Thus the finance company assures the payment of the bills it has accepted through the previous falling due of bills received by it. The company charges no interest for this operation — which would make no sense in this case — but merely an acceptance fee. Up to then, the borrower simply exchanged

---

[15] Instead of promissory notes Brazilian firms often use the "duplicatas," a special bill tied to commodity sales, created by Brazilian commercial laws.

promissory notes for bills of exchange. However, since the bills of exchange are considered as securities it is possible to sell them at a discount in the capital market. Thus, the borrower keeps the money he requires. (In practice, a company that resells the securities buys them from the borrower and resells them to the public.)

For the purchaser of the security, interest is replaced by the discount thereof and, once again, this substitution allows escape from the Usury Law regulations. In this way, a one-year security that is resold for 74 per cent of its nominal value (that is, with a 26 per cent discount) assures the purchaser an implicit interest of 26/74, or 35.1 per cent per year. The borrower, who exchanged his promissory notes for bills of exchange, indirectly pays this implicit interest rate, plus a series of taxes and commissions. Recently, the discount system has been replaced by the bonus device. Securities yield a bonus, called "fixed monetary correction," which is tax exempt.

Loans from finance companies can legally extend up to 24 months, though in practice they rarely exceed 18 months. While this solves in part the problem of medium-term credit, it does not touch the problem of long-term credit. With the exception of certain governmental institutions, such as the National Bank for Economic Development (BNDE), there is no available supply in Brazil of long-term loans.

In this case, the main problem is no longer the legal ceiling on the interest rate — which could always be by-passed by discounts or some other device. The main obstacle is the uncertainty regarding the pace of inflation. And in an inflationary situation such as Brazil's, the most important determinant of a free-market interest rate is precisely this unpredictable factor.

A characteristic symptom of the long-term credit difficulty is the thinness of the Brazilian bond market. Although the Corporation Law (Lei das Sociedades Anônimas) allows companies to issue bonds up to an amount equivalent to their capital, few enterprises have succeeded in launching fixed-interest securities. Suffice it to say that in 1962, while Brazilian corporations issued a total of 341 billion cruzeiros in stock, the total issuance of bonds was only 2.4 billion — less than 1 per cent of the total float of new stock. And it should be added that a large part of these issues were short term, generally less than one year.

Thus, the supply of long-term credit in cruzeiros is very tight. The main sources, as previously noted, are governmental — first, BNDE, which is the largest source of long-term financing for the basic sectors of the economy, and, next, the Banco do Brasil and regional or state-owned agencies. Some international agencies, such as the Inter-American Development Bank and the Agency for International Development occasionally lend cruzeiros on a long-term basis. For certain specific purposes, such as the purchase of houses, there is a supply of funds from the *caixas economicas* (private savings banks), from some of the social security institutions, and from the National Housing Bank.

The cost of the money loaned by these agencies is extremely low,[16] in view of the present inflationary rate. (BNDE frequently prefers to purchase stock rather than grant loans.) Interest, fees, and surtaxes together usually do not exceed 30 per cent a year, which is far below the effective rates for short- and medium-term loans. Obviously, for the borrowers, financing under these conditions constitutes a gift from the government. But, as with all gifts, they are very scarce.

---

[16] Except in the case of mortgage financing, which now includes an escalator clause.

9. The Coexistence of Inflation and Development

For an orthodox observer, the most surprising thing about Brazilian inflation has been its coexistence, at least until 1961, with a high rate of economic growth. Indeed, between 1947 and 1961, notwithstanding the chronic increase in prices, the country's real product rose at an average rate of 5.8 per cent per year — one of the highest rates in the world during the postwar era. Per capita real product expanded at an average of 3.0 per cent per year — a highly satisfactory pace of economic development. (See Table 16.)

Table 16   **REAL GROSS DOMESTIC PRODUCT**

YEAR	TOTAL REAL GROSS DOMESTIC PRODUCT			PER CAPITA REAL GROSS DOMESTIC PRODUCT		
	AT 1949 PRICES (BILLIONS OF CRUZEIROS)	INDEX (1949 = 100)	ANNUAL VARIATION PER CENT	AT 1949 PRICES (THOU-SANDS OF CRU-ZEIROS)	INDEX (1949 = 100)	ANNUAL VARIATION PER CENT
1947	186.1	86.5	1.8	3.8	89.8	—
1948	203.8	94.5	9.5	4.2	97.5	8.5
1949	215.2	100.0	5.6	4.3	100.0	2.5
1950	226.0	105.0	5.0	4.3	101.9	1.9
1951	237.6	110.4	5.1	4.4	104.1	2.1
1952	250.9	116.6	5.6	4.6	106.7	2.5
1953	258.9	120.3	3.2	4.6	106.9	0.2
1954	278.9	129.6	7.7	4.8	111.8	4.6
1955	297.8	138.4	6.8	4.9	115.9	3.6
1956	303.4	141.0	1.9	4.9	114.6	− 1.1
1957	324.3	150.7	6.9	5.1	118.9	3.8
1958	345.8	160.7	6.6	5.3	123.1	3.5
1959	371.2	172.5	7.3	5.5	128.3	4.2
1960	396.0	184.0	6.7	5.6	132.8	3.5
1961	424.8	197.4	7.3	5.8	138.2	4.1
1962	447.6	208.0	5.4	5.9	141.2	2.2
1963	454.7	211.3	1.6	5.8	138.9	− 1.6
1964	468.3	217.6	3.0	5.8	138.9	0
1965	489.4	227.4	4.5	5.9	141.0	1.5

Source: Brazilian Institute of Economy and Fundação Getúlio Vargas.

More surprisingly, there was no slowdown in development rate even when inflation was accelerated from 20 per cent to 40 per cent a year. On the contrary, between 1957 and 1961, total real product managed to grow at a rate of 6.9 per cent per annum. Although this high rate was influenced somewhat by the overproduction of coffee (accounting for approximately 0.5 per cent), this is a highly aberrant result from an orthodox standpoint.

Of equal interest is the excellent capital output ratio during the inflationary period. According to the estimates of Fundação Getúlio Vargas (see Table 17), the average rate of gross capital formation from 1947 to 1960 equalled 16.6 per cent of gross domestic product. Correcting this to account for fixed capital depreciation, estimated at 5 per cent of GDP, we would have a net investment of 11.6 per cent. Comparing that rate with the 5.8 per cent, the yearly average growth of the real product, we

Table 17   **GROSS CAPITAL FORMATION AS A PERCENTAGE OF GROSS DOMESTIC PRODUCT**

YEAR	GROSS PRIVATE SAVINGS	GOVERNMENT SAVINGS	FOREIGN SAVINGS	INVESTMENT RATIO
1947	9.6	4.1	1.9	15.6
1948	11.2	4.0	0.4	15.6
1949	8.0	4.1	1.0	13.1
1950	9.4	2.7	− 0.7	11.4
1951	11.4	4.7	2.8	18.9
1952	11.4	3.6	3.7	18.7
1953	12.7	1.0	− 0.1	13.6
1954	15.0	3.6	1.2	19.8
1955	13.5	1.9	0.1	15.5
1956	14.0	0.8	− 0.1	14.7
1957	12.3	1.5	1.3	15.1
1958	8.0	4.4	1.4	13.8
1959	10.4	4.6	1.8	16.8
1960	9.7	5.2	2.4	17.3
1961	15.5	1.7	1.3	18.5
1962	14.9	0.2	3.1	18.2
1963	15.5	0.6	1.3	17.5
1964	16.5	0.5	− 0.6	16.4

Source: Fundação Getúlio Vargas.

may conclude that the incremental capital/output ratio would have been equal to 2.0 on the average — a high index of investment productivity.

One may go even further. Statistics show that in the last years of the 1947-61 period, while the investment rate declined the growth rate of the real product increased. (See Table 18.) This would correspond to an improvement of the capital/product ratio, precisely during the most intense period of the inflation.[17] It is true that estimates of capital formation in Brazil are not entirely reliable.[18] Nevertheless it seems irrefutable that Brazil managed, until 1961, to reconcile a high inflation rate with an excellent capital/output ratio — something that many orthodox thinkers would not have predicted.

The breaking of the pattern in 1962 and the recession of 1963 and 1964 — when the inflation rate hit 80 per cent a year — may restore some confidence in the traditional ideas. However, one may doubt whether the recession was the result only of the increase in prices. The drop in per capita real product in 1963 and 1964 was due largely to purely seasonal factors. Drought in some areas and frost in others hurt crops, though the decline in coffee production should not be exaggerated as a factor since coffee is in surplus. Seasonal factors also forced the rationing of electric power, which cut back industrial production. Furthermore, until March, 1964, strikes and social agitation, openly encouraged by the government of the period, undoubtedly discouraged investment and impaired the country's production.

In view of all this, it would be too simple a solution to pin the main blame for the economic recession of those two years on the inflationary rate — even if we start from the sensible assumption that an 80 per cent annual price increase is not a good

---

[17] An interesting analysis along these lines was prepared by Werner Baer, "Brazil: Inflation and Economic Efficiency," in *Economic Development and Cultural Change*, July, 1963, pp. 395-406.

[18] The first direct capital formation estimates were for the years 1949 and 1958 and were derived from data obtained in the 1950 census and the industrial production survey. For other years, estimates were made indirectly by extrapolating these basic data, using an index combining apparent raw material consumption with the imports of capital goods.

prescription for development. Rather, it would be more reasonable to view the 1963 inflation and recession as having a common political origin. Nevertheless, even if we assume rather arbitrarily that the possibilities of coexistence of inflation and development had been exhausted, the question still remains how coexistence managed to persist *until* 1961.

Table 18 **INVESTMENT RATIO IN 1953 CRUZEIROS**

(as a percentage of gross domestic product)

YEAR	INVESTMENT RATIO
1947	10.1
1948	10.6
1949	9.7
1950	10.9
1951	19.1
1952	19.8
1953	13.6
1954	16.0
1955	13.6
1956	14.7
1957	15.9
1958	13.6
1959	15.1
1960	15.2
1961	16.0
1962	15.6
1963	14.7
1964	13.8

Source: Fundação Getúlio Vargas.

In order to answer this question, it would be useful to review some traditional arguments about the negative effects of inflation on growth. From these, many have concluded that chronic price rises make development impossible.[19] It is argued that inflation:

[19] A detailed statement of this anti-inflationary argument may be found in G. Dorrance, "The Effect of Inflation on Economic Development," in *Inflation and Growth in Latin America*, edited by Werner Baer and Isaac Kerstenetsky (Homewood, Ill.; Irwin, 1964).

- Discourages voluntary private savings;
- Encourages investment with an unfavorable capital/output ratio and with low social productivity; e.g., real estate and inventories;
- Encourages the flow of internal savings toward the purchase of foreign currency;
- Discourages the inflow of foreign capital;
- Discourages the flow of private capital in long-term investment as a result of the unpredictability of costs;
- Generates the most varied bottlenecks through discouragement of investment in basic sectors;
- Upsets credit and the capital market;
- Subverts the social order.

It should be pointed out that even if all these points are valid, the most that can be inferred from them is that inflation is bad for development. However, one cannot infer that *inflation is incompatible with development* — an erroneous conclusion that led many observers to regard the Brazilian experience as paradoxical. Yet at the same time it is fair to question whether some of the conventional arguments summarized above are of great importance, inasmuch as they take into account merely some of the factors involved. They are only partial explanations. In the aggregate they do not comprise a complete analysis of the determinants of growth.

Let us take one of the most touted of the conventional tenets; i.e., that inflation discourages voluntary private savings. It would be more correct to say that inflation discourages the retention of private savings in the form of cash holdings, which is another way of saying that inflation accelerates the velocity of money. Even admitting that in fact this does inhibit voluntary private savings, it should not be forgotten that inflation forces savings through the expansion of the money supply.

Apart from these general considerations, it is important to note that many of the traditional assumptions regarding the unfavorable impact of inflation on growth simply failed to operate in the Brazilian case. Perhaps the most curious aspect of the country's experience has been a sort of sectoral sum of distortions, with strongly negative results from the social standpoint but with substantially milder effects from the standpoint of the development rate:

• Contrary to the traditional assumption, Brazilian inflation discouraged rather than encouraged the purchase of real estate, a point made earlier in this study. (Exception must be made of the large real estate boom of the first years following the close of World War II.) This was basically due to two factors: First, the continuance of a lease law that half-froze nominal rents and made investment in rental housing extremely unattractive; second, the atrophy of mortgage credit money as a result of the Usury Law, which obviously greatly restricted home-building. (The number of licenses for residential building in major cities has declined sharply — about 40 per cent in 1961 — from the 1953 postwar peak.[20])

What exists now in Brazil is an enormous housing crisis, accompanied by a growing proliferation of slums and unhygienic housing. This socially painful situation was, however, associated with a lowering of the capital/output ratio for the economy as a whole since a high ratio item was compressed in the investment list. (This is so since the output of houses, e.g., rents, is small compared to their capital value.) Thus an overlapping of distortions in the housing sector aggravated the social effects of inflation, but neutralized some of its negative impact on growth by altering the investment pattern in such a way as to lower the marginal capital/output ratio for the economy as a whole.[21]

• One may also doubt the effect in Brazil, on a significant scale, of the traditional hypothesis that inflation encourages over-accumulation of inventories. This hypothesis is founded on the common observation that when prices rise, it is good business to borrow money from banks at low interest rates and invest it in inventory, whose value follows inflation. But, as previously noted, the banking system's loans to the private sector have declined in relation to the real product. This alters a basic condition underlying the conventional theory about inventory

[20] In 1964 escalator clauses were introduced in mortgage contracts and also in rent contracts by Laws 4380 and 4494.

[21] Obviously, the stockpiling of coffee, arising from reasons other than inflation, does not enter into this discussion.

accumulation. Of course, the phenomenon can take place where companies have easy access to credit, but there is no evidence that this has occurred in any widespread fashion. Of course, companies can finance inventories with their own money. But outweighing this is the effect of taxation, which makes the profits from this kind of investment illusory since the revalued income that a business may earn by selling inventories at a higher price later on in time is taxed as profits instead of accepted as an example of reappraised assets in the face of inflation.

While there is no sure evidence that can be brought to bear on this whole subject, it is worth noting that in recent years the value of corporations' inventories in Brazil has been growing less rapidly than the general wholesale price index. (See Table 19.) This represents something very different from the traditional theory about the effects of inflation.

Table 19   **INVENTORIES OF BRAZILIAN CORPORATIONS**

(1958 = 100)

YEAR	INDEX OF INVENTORY VALUE	INDEX OF WHOLESALE PRICES
	(AS OF DECEMBER)	
1957	100	100
1958	120	128
1959	159	174
1960	205	231
1961	316	347
1962	462	521
1963	874	946
1964	1,675	1,828

Source: Wholesale index from *Conjunctura Economico*. Inventory index estimated by analyzing consolidated balance sheets of corporations.

• Price controls that might have distorted production and investment simply failed to work.

If food price control by Comissão Federal de Abastecimento a Preços (COFAP) and more recently by Superintendência Nacional de Abastecimento (SUNAB) had been carried out too strictly, it would seriously have discouraged agricultural production with grave economic and social results, as occurred in Chile. However, these controls were no more than a mere tactic, the chief effect of which was to check a continuous price rise in stages. From the standpoint of economic growth, this was certainly much better than a determined effort at price control.

Along the same lines, the economy greatly benefited by the evasion of the Usury Law through overcharges, participation partnerships, and so forth. Although distorted, the credit market showed resistance that it could not have shown if the legal 12 per cent limit had been clamped down on all credit transactions.

• The government started to cover those sectors of the economy that ceased to attract private capital because of inflation; as these areas were continually expanding, governmental investments began to dominate an increasingly larger portion of the country's capital formation.

No doubt inflation, in association with certain price controls, drew private investments away from some areas of investment. The criterion of historical cost, for instance, caused the private sector to lose almost complete interest in electric power investments. Likewise, the unpredictability of costs prevented several private entrepreneurs from placing long-term investments in basic industries. This could have caused serious bottlenecks capable of blocking the economy's growth. Nevertheless, a countervailing distortion again appeared; i.e., the gradual socialization of capital formation.

Although somewhat incomplete, statistical data on the growing governmental participation in investment are very suggestive. According to Fundação Getúlio Vargas estimates, this participation, *not taking into account mixed corporations,* rose from 25.9 per cent in the four-year period 1947-1950 to 37.1 per cent in the four-year period 1957-1960.

This underestimates the role of the government in capital formation, however, since it does not include the investment by the so-called mixed companies, which are in fact government owned. No consolidated data on the investment by these companies are available before 1956, but there is no doubt they grew substantially from the end of the war up to this point. In the four-year period from 1957 to 1960 these companies were responsible for no less than an average of 10.8 per cent of the gross fixed capital formation in the country. If these companies are included, the governmental sector accounts for 47.9 per cent of fixed investments in Brazil in that period.

There are strong indications that from 1960 onward government's domination of investment has increased considerably. In 1964, the Ministry of Planning prepared a consolidated budget of all federal bodies, including autonomous entities (autarquias) and mixed corporations. Total investment in this budget accounted for approximately 60 per cent of the total estimated capital formation in the country. Part of these investments (about a fifth) was postponed because of the government's program for reducing expenditure. It should be remembered, however, that this budget did not include state and municipal public investments. It is likely that the various sectors of the government and their companies now account *for almost two-thirds of the country's capital formation.*

From the standpoint of long-term development, one may ask if this socialization of investment will not be harmful, because of the government's inefficiency. In the short run, however, this increase in the government's share of investment surely avoided the bottlenecks that inflation would have created.

These are some of the factors that explain why Brazilian inflation, until 1961, proved capable of coexisting with a high rate of economic development. It should also be remembered that this coexistence was considerably facilitated by the growing foreign debt of the country during the period.

By no means should these observations be construed as enthusiasm for the country's inflationary experience. All that has been proved is that development may be consistent with prolonged inflation — but not that there is any positive correlation between the two phenomena. In fact, Brazil offered an interesting example of how inflationary distortions can be counterbalanced, though at the cost of a regrettable sacrifice. It is probable that the same results, with less sacrifice, could have been reached through an orderly policy of economic development.

10. What Held Inflation in Check

It is often asked how Brazilian inflation could have lasted so long without turning into hyperinflation. In short, why did Brazil not suffer the experience of Germany in 1923, Hungary in 1946, or China in 1947-1948? The question may not be a very logical one, since there is no a priori reason why inflation in any given period becomes hyperinflation. But in any event, the point is worth some comment.

It is worth noting that the Brazilian experience is not unique. Other countries, such as Argentina and Chile, have also experienced strong and lasting price rises that did not develop into hyperinflationary chaos. However, it is quite possible that with prices increasing at a rate of 25 per cent a quarter in 1964, the Brazilian inflation would have entered a galloping stage had the Goulart administration continued in office.

There are some factors that explain why Brazilian inflation could persist for several years at an approximately steady rate (1950 to 1958), and why, notwithstanding its later acceleration, it did not break into hyperinflation. The main factor is political in nature. The government's inflationary behavior resulted from weakness rather than lack of understanding. No administration, even though it lacked courage to follow the way of austerity, totally abandoned all restraint in issuing paper money. There were always finance ministers concerned with fighting inflation in the right ways; they may not have stayed long in office, but they certainly succeeded in calling attenton to the problem. Several monetary stabilization programs, prior to that of the recent administration, were announced and started. One of them, prepared in late 1958, was even made public in a voluminous report. Results were short-lived or nonexistent, since none of the past governments showed the necessary courage to establish a consistent income-distribution policy. But it is likely that Brazil would have experienced much worse price increases if such attempts at stabilization were not put into effect from time to time.

Another brake on the inflationary pace was the relative political weakness of the various income groups in the economy. Though the government was always promising to divide the national product into parts greater than the whole, the various social groups did not have the necessary political strength to force the government to fulfill the promise. Minimum wage workers, for instance, were not able to check declines on the order of 40 per cent in their real income between readjustments, and this is likely to have occurred with most wage-earners. Although readjustments came more frequently as inflation worsened, no escalator clause for wages was adopted. At the same time, entrepreneurs could not avoid the very harsh tightening of credit or the growing taxation of their profits.

All these seem to have stemmed from a certain lack of social cohesion. Brazilian trade unions were mainly developed in recent years, and furthermore they were imposed from the top down. In view of the abundant supply, unskilled labor really had little power in the marketplace. And employers' associations, unfavorably regarded by populist politicians, were on the defensive. However, it is true that in 1963 and in the first quarter of 1964 the government seemed not only to accept incompatible claims but also to be doing its best to foster them. If such a process had gone on, it is very likely that Brazil would have bordered on hyperinflation. This tendency, however, was clearly interrupted by the revolution of March 31, 1964.

Along with these factors were the others that have already been mentioned — the lack of sophistication generally about how one could protect one's self against inflation; the lack of any reserve or margin to cut down further on the use of cash, which helped hold down the velocity of currency; the underdeveloped capital market, and so forth. All of these help to explain why Brazilian inflation never really cut loose.

11. The Thesis in Favor of Inflation[23]

The fact that a violent inflation and an accelerated rate of growth existed side by side in Brazil has convinced many economists that a continuous price rise may be helpful or even essential to economic growth, at least under certain conditions. This is the opposite position to that taken by the orthodox thinker, who looks with increasing perplexity on the so-called Brazilian miracle. The discussion is quantitatively vague, and loses much of its force since "good" and "bad" inflation rates are not properly distinguished. It seems, however, that some heterodox thinkers would accept a price rise of as much as 20 or 30 per cent a year as favorable to economic development.

It is useful to summarize the principal ideas behind this point of view. One of the most popular arguments in favor of inflation is the forced-savings thesis. Those who accept this theory argue that during inflation wage adjustments lag behind the rise in the general price level. As a result, real income is transferred from wage earners to entrepreneurs. Since the latter group shows a much higher marginal propensity to save, capital formation is thus accelerated by inflation.

Orthodox economists actively refute this thesis as applied to a chronic inflation. Forced savings, they say, occur only in the beginning of an inflationary process, when the price rises are still unexpected. With continuing inflation, however, price rises will be anticipated by everybody, and the forced-savings mechanism will cease to work. Wage adjustments may continue to be periodic, but they will take into account the expected future rate of inflation — thus ceasing to lag behind the general price level.

The orthodox economist also argues that inflation undermines many of the vital sources of economic development. Personal savings are discouraged. Investment is shifted from basic industries to speculation in such things as inventories, real

---

[23] This chapter has been extracted from a paper prepared by the author for "Consultec" (Sociedade Civil de Planejamento e Consulta Técnica Ltda.) under the auspices of Harvard University.

estate, and even foreign currency. The result is that the productivity of investment is lowered, while the average propensity to save declines.

Forced-saving supporters reply that structural unemployment (which they assume to exist in Brazil) substantially reduces the bargaining power of wage earners, preventing wages from rising at the same rate as inflation. This, it is argued, is the key to the validity of the forced-savings thesis in Brazil. Moreover, there is no serious reason why inflation should impair the productivity of investment. The latter would certainly tend to be true in a "laissez-faire" economy. But government may act as a supplementary investor, covering the sectors neglected by private savings, such as basic industries. Private investments may also be oriented in a healthy direction by adequate fiscal, credit, and foreign-exchange policies, which can be adapted easily to inflation. Orthodox economists, of course, do not accept the validity of these arguments, and the interesting aspects of the discussion stop at this point.

Another important group in the debate is the structuralist school, under the leadership of the Economic Commission for Latin America (ECLA). The exact limits of the structural thought are not quite clear. Some structuralists, for instance, put special emphasis on budgetary deficits among the "structural" causes of inflation. Except perhaps for the word "structural," no orthodox economist would disagree, and the debate becomes a simple game of words.[24] In the same way, structuralists often diverge as to the forced saving thesis: Some accept it, others do not (or, at least, put no emphasis on the problem). Still, many structuralists insist on the inflationary role of institutionally forced wage increases. Once again, this is nothing but the familiar orthodox conception of cost inflation.

There seems, however, to exist a central point in the structuralist thought. Economic growth is said to force relative price changes because of the required structural transformation of the economic system. Since sectoral prices almost always show a

---

[24] Structuralists usually stress that it is not enough to note that budgetary deficits cause inflation; one should also investigate the causes of the deficits. No orthodox economist would disagree on this point.

downward rigidity, relative price changes can only come about if the general price level is allowed to rise. A blind monetary policy, with no regard to these peculiar features, could stop the price rises only by hindering the process of structural change and therefore by slowing down the rate of economic growth.

Relative price changes may be imposed for a number of reasons. For example, let us assume a closed economy with two sectors, agriculture and industry. Let us assume also that the agricultural output is perfectly rigid, the possibilities of growth being limited to the industrial sector. If the demand for food products has a positive income elasticity and if industrial output increases, market equilibrium will require a change in the relative prices in favor of agriculture.

The above example is obviously naïve. Some sophisticated cases, however, may be developed by following this general analysis. The growth of exports of less-developed countries is often hampered by the low elasticity of the external demand. Since the demand for imported goods is income elastic, economic growth tends to alter the balance of payments, forcing exchange devaluation. (Exchange devaluation could also come about as a natural result of a decline in the terms of trade of the less-developed country.) The inevitable consequence of devaluation will be a rise in the price of imports relative to the price of exports. Import substitution may offset partially the need for devaluation. Upward price pressures, however, will not be avoided completely; at the prevailing exchange rates, the price of the import substitutes will certainly be higher than the price of their foreign counterparts.

This seems to be the core of the structuralist thought. One may object to the practical relevance of the above arguments, but their skillful arrangement should be recognized. Structuralists still have the merit of thinking in sectoral terms, pointing out the defects of purely aggregative analysis.

These are the basic ideas of the contending groups. Let us try to detect their weak and strong points.

The obvious defect of the structuralist thesis lies in the total absence of quantitative reasoning. The qualitative constructions are quite interesting but do not answer the basic question of what inflation rate can be considered as the inevitable result of the structural economic changes. Structuralists seem to forget that inflation is a poor word in itself, and what is really meaningful is the inflation *rate*. This makes their thesis doubly vulnerable. First, from a purely theoretical point of view, sectoral prices are somewhat, but not absolutely, rigid downward. (They could be reduced, for instance, by an increase in productivity.) If the required relative price changes over a unit of time are small, structural transformation may come about without any increase in the general price level, some prices going up, others going down (within the margins of downward price flexibility). This, however, is not the main objection to the structural thought. The central point is that the pure structuralist thesis is probably unable to justify the very high upward price pressures in a country like Brazil.

A few examples may illustrate this point. Let us assume a country, more or less similar to Brazil, where imports correspond to 10 per cent of the GNP. Let us also assume that exports are completely stationary, that the internal real output is growing at 6 per cent a year, that the income elasticity of demand for imports is equal to 2 (meaning that demand for these products will increase at 12 per cent a year), and finally, that import substitution can only be carried on with a tariff protection of 100 per cent. All these hypotheses, extremely favorable to the structuralist thesis, can justify only a 1.2 per cent a year inflation.

In the same way, let us assume that the external terms of trade are falling 10 per cent a year (which, of course, cannot last for long), bringing on foreign exchange devaluation. If imports correspond to 10 per cent of GNP, the terms of trade effect could be responsible for inflation at the annual rate of 1 per cent.

Similar arguments could be repeated for the change in the relative prices of agricultural products, etc. The final conclusion is that, in a country like Brazil, at most a very mild inflation could be interpreted as the inevitable result of the structural transformations involved in the process of economic development. This makes the structural thesis virtually meaningless in the Brazilian case.

Let us now analyze the forced-savings controversy. The central point of the discussion is to know whether, during a chronic inflation, wage adjustments do or do not lag behind the rises in the general price level. In other words, whether the wage earners' share in the gross national product will or will not be reduced by a chronic inflation.

To provide an answer one must first ask how wages are determined. Theoretical discussions often seem to be based on the hypothesis that wages in Brazil are freely determined by labor supply and demand. This, however, is a quite unrealistic assumption, which can lead to several distorted conclusions. A more realistic analysis of the wage mechanism seems to be an essential conditon for an accurate appraisal of the forced-savings thesis.

As often remarked, Brazil seems to present a dual economic system. The most striking symptom of such a dualism is the wide gap between urban and rural wages — exceeding anything that could be blamed on the imperfect mobility of labor.

The basic reason for these wage inequalities is the institutional support to urban wages; the price of labor, although almost freely determined in agriculture, is strongly protected in the cities by the government and by labor unions. Minimum wages are fixed for urban workers according to more or less vague concepts of "minimum decent standards of living" under the active influence of the demonstration effect. Indirect benefits are also assured to trade and industry employees through social security and labor laws. Most of these advantages have not been shared by rural workers.[26] Their almost freely determined wages stand considerably below the protected ones which prevail in the urban areas. As a result, disordered migratory movements take place from the fields to the cities, exceding the new job opportunities created by urban activities. A peripheral population, not absorbed by business firms, emerges in the cities as the consequence of the excess rural-urban emigration.

---

[26] Some protection to rural wages has been recently imposed by the "Estatuto do Trabalhador Rural." The degree of protection, in any case, is much lower than that prevailing in urban areas, especially as regards its effectiveness.

But let us resume our discussion of the forced-savings thesis. Since urban wages are institutionally protected and since, within a certain range, they can be manipulated by the government, there seems to be no sense in constructing a purely endogenous theory of wage behavior in a country like Brazil. Political factors — which are far from being absolutely exogenous, but which cannot at our present stage of knowledge be explained by simple deterministic laws — may deeply affect the share of wage-earners in the gross national product. In a word, the personal gifts of the President of the Republic and of the Minister of Labor seem to play an important role in the question along with the usual economic variables. Under such conditions, the debate on forced savings, because of the endogenous character of the usually involved explanations, loses a great part of its substance. Nor has the basic question — what will be the wage-earners' share in the GNP if price stabilization is encouraged? — a determinate answer. It will depend on *how* price stability is achieved.

Another question, of course, could be formulated: Is it possible to stabilize prices without increasing the wage earners' share in the gross national product? The purely technical answer will be a positive one, since real urban wages can fall without creating excess demand for labor.[27]

A political problem is involved, however. The average real income of a worker during inflation is substantially below the maximum real wage, which is only attained immediately after wage adjustments. Previous real peaks, nevertheless, exert a strong influence in the formation of the wage earners' aspirations. Workers expect a stabilization policy to sustain their real wages at the previous peaks (at least), not at the past averages. How far would these aspirations impede the achievement of a growth-conscious stabilization policy? This is not a problem of market forces, since the supply and the demand curves for labor are far from being favorable to most urban employees, but rather a question of political influence. It is certainly quite an unpleasant task for a politician to convince workers that they should give up the idea of permanently earning their previous

---

[27] Real wages obviously could be reduced by a last price rise before stabilization, with no adjustment in money wages.

income peaks. Unpleasant tasks, however, are not necessarily impossible ones, even in underdeveloped democratic countries. Unless we are extremely pessimistic, we can hope that there is the possibility of enough moral authority so as to promote price stabilization with no damages to the propensity to save. In fact, the Castelo Branco anti-inflation policies, even if they were not fully successful, proved that such a protection of the savings ratio is perfectly feasible.

12. The Strategy of Stabilization

Brazilian inflation reached its peak in the first three months of 1964, the final period of João Goulart's government. After deposing the Goulart government, the new administration under President Castelo Branco launched a serious anti-inflationary effort. A well-conceived Plan of Monetary Stabilization was incorporated in the government's Program of Economic Action; most of the proposed measures were put into effect within the two and a half years of the new administration. The purpose of this chapter is to describe the essential features of such a program.

The central concern of the Castelo Branco government program was to impose a gradual restraint on the inflationary process and at the same time to restore the pace of economic development. To reconcile these two objectives requires considerable political courage — much more than has been shown by past governments.

In the first place, it is necessary to prevent any time lag between the imposing of restraints on demand inflation, on the one hand, and on cost inflation, on the other, so that the savings capacity of the country is not impaired. Past governments tended to be tougher, and to move faster, in restricting credit than in controlling wages — hence the failure of many stabilization plans. The Castelo Branco government intended to avoid this and to synchronize the fight against inflation on its several fronts, adjusting the timing of the wage policy to that of the monetary policy.

A second requirement is the avoidance of a one-sided tight-money policy at the expense of the private sector. Previous stabilization plans were flawed by their toughness regarding loans to the private sector and their strange tolerance of public deficits. Once again, the Castelo Branco government proposed to carry out a policy of equitable treatment for both sectors, private and public.

A shock treatment of inflation, the government believed, would be undesirable from both an economic and a social point of view. It has therefore chosen the alternative strategy of a gradual restraint of price rises. The reasoning has been set forth explicitly in the program:[28]

a) The success of a shock treatment would basically depend on a general wage freeze. However, at the moment [1964], this general freeze should be considered as socially undesirable, since the real wage structure is extremely distorted.... As a reduction in the nominal wages of the more-favored groups is not feasible under existing laws, the only suitable solution for eliminating the existing distortions is the increase in the wages of the classes lagging behind inflation — and this will inevitably cause a rise of residual prices.

b) It is convenient, from the point of view of the country's saving capacity, to reduce the percentage of the government's consumption expenses in the gross national product. This reduction beyond the limits of the nominal compression politically feasible and already executed, can be done only through a certain residual rise of the general price levels.

c) The success of a shock treatment would largely depend on the immediate elimination (or virtual elimination) of public "deficits." For institutional reasons, it would be virtually impossible to reach this objective without a sizable cut in public investment.

d) Any shock treatment has a tendency to provoke abrupt changes in the sectoral composition of the demand for goods and services. As the price system usually has little flexibility downward, the immediate result of such abrupt changes is the rise of some prices and unemployment in some sectors. Because of the explosive growth of the Brazilian population, this formula of adaptation via unemployment is socially undesirable, particularly in view of the unemployment that already exists as a result of the economic stagnation of the past two years.

---

[28] Quoted from the government's *Program for Economic Action, 1964/1966,* Chapter IV.

e) The correction of inflationary distortions involves the elimination of certain price controls, as in the case of the tariffs of public utility services, etc. This will tend to provoke an inflation of residual nature, in the absence of a downward flexibility of the remaining prices.

f) The behavior of some productive sectors has been distorted by such things as the habit of borrowing money at interest rates below the inflation rate. Instead of plunging these sectors into insolvency through a shock treatment, it would seem preferable to let them return to normal behavior patterns during a period of adaptation.

g) An uncoordinated effort to curtail the issue of money, as has happened in several cases of shock treatment, may be offset partially if the velocity of money increases.

h) The international experiences described as "shock treatment" have failed to restrain inflation any faster than is foreseen in the present government program. Or they have been conducted in a context completely different from that prevailing in Brazil; as for example: 1) complete dissolution of the monetary system as a result of hyperinflation, 2) disruption of the social structure and of group resistances after the end of war or of internal upheavals, 3) solid injections of external aid, 4) absence of a chronic inflationary tradition, 5) abandonment of the democratic process of wage bargaining.

Having set forth the reasons for a gradual approach, the program went on to outline the strategy to be employed in the fight against inflation:

a) The anti-inflationary policy must start with the progressive restraint of governmental deficits. The government must lead by putting its finances in order by cutting low-priority expenditures; by eliminating the deficits of the autarchies (agencies with administrative autonomy) and of the mixed companies in order to free resources for basic investment; by improving the tax laws and tax collection; and by restoring confidence in the public debt.

b) The wage policy must adapt itself to the pace of the monetary policy, so that costs will not increase out of proportion to demand. The principle to be adopted is that price stabilization in itself can eliminate salary instability but not raise real wages. The latter can be increased, without unemployment, only through economic development. With this principle as a guide, wage increases should be calculated so as to restore, during the period in which this will be in force, the same average purchasing power they had during the previous two years, plus a small amount corresponding to the increase in productivity. When a decrease of the inflationary rate is anticipated, such a system will be consistent with the dampening of wage-price spiral. At the same time, this system assures the maintenance of the wage-earners' share in the GNP, preventing sacrifice by less-favored groups during the stabilization period.

c) Credit extension to private concerns will be sufficiently controlled in order to avoid excess demand, but the policy will realistically take into account the irreversibility of inflated costs. Within this principle, the total limits of credit to private firms should be adjusted proportionally to the growth of the national product at current prices, or because it is easier from a planning standpoint, to the growth in total money supply.

Two of the more original points of this strategy were those dealing with the credit policy and the wage policy. The first assured credit expansion to the private sector in the same proportion as the increase in money supply. This meant that the real value of loans granted to the private sector should develop at the same rate as the growth of the real product (provided the income velocity of money did not change).

It might be worthwhile to make some comments on this criterion, which is viewed with approval by business circles. At first sight, one may suspect that to expand credit to the private sector proportionally to the money supply would create a vicious circle — since the increase of financing to the private sector creates new means of payment. This vicious circle, however,

does not exist if the relation between loans to the private sector
and the money supply is below unity.[29] The loans to the private
sector simply are treated as an induced variable of the stabilization process.

As the government succeeds in reducing its deficits, the
monetary expansion will be smaller — likewise the expansion of
credit to private firms. This makes good sense from a practical
point of view. The need for credit expansion that is felt by private
firms results principally from price rises. The smaller the expansion of the money supply, the smaller the price rises, and consequently the smaller the expansion of loans required by
enterprises.

One might think that these criteria implied the weakening
of the monetary restraint policy, since a kind of multiplier of the
government credit expansion has been created. This problem
did indeed exist, and the program was aimed at resolving it
through an adequate restraint of the multiplicand — the public
deficit — even when such a restraint had to be made by increasing
the taxes imposed on the private sector. Here the program
brought about a kind of implied option between credit and fiscal
policies. From the point of view not only of money expansion

---

[29] A simplified monetary budget could be represented by the following accounting scheme:

ASSETS			LIABILITIES	
1) Loan to the government:	A	3) Money supply:	M
2) Loan to the private sector:	B	4) Non-monetary resources:	R
Total: A + B		Total: M + R = A + B	

Over a given period if there is an expansion of $\triangle$ A in government loans
and an expansion of $\triangle$ R in non-monetary resources and an expansion $\triangle$ B in
loans to the private sector, then the required monetary expansion $\triangle$ M will be:
$$\triangle M = \triangle A + \triangle B - \triangle R \, (\wedge)$$
The condition that the loans in the private sector grow in the same proportion as the money supply is equivalent to establishing $\triangle B = \dfrac{B}{M} \triangle M$
(2) from which would result:
$$\triangle M = \frac{\triangle A - \triangle R}{1 - B/M}$$
(3) Provided that $\dfrac{B}{M} = 1$. $\triangle$ M will be stably
determined in the sense that the smaller $\triangle$ A, the smaller will be $\triangle$ M.

but also from that of the aggregate expenditure capacity of the private sector, it is an indifferent matter whether taxes are increased or credit is contracted. However, in view of the imperfection of capital markets, it would seem healthier to restrict real expenditure by the private sector through increasing taxes rather than through reducing the real value of the loans. That was the core of the philosophy underlying the government's program.

The second very interesting point concerns the wage policy. The program recognized that in a chronic inflation real wages oscillate sharply between peaks and valleys, and that the proper goal is stabilizing real wages according to their average levels — not by the peaks. This implies the abandonment of the traditional criteria of adjusting wages proportionally to the increase in the cost of living since the last revision, because this simply restores the previous peak of purchasing power. Instead, the program proposed a formula which calculates the wage increases so that for a period of 12 months, during which the new nominal wages will be in force, the *real* average wage will be equal to that during the previous 24 months, plus a small percentage corresponding to the increase in productivity. The formula anticipates future inflation. Since this forecast is made at a rate below that of the price rise in the recent past (in accordance with the idea of gradually restraining the inflationary process), the resulting increases usually lag behind the cost of living increase that took place after the last revision.

The program did not establish precise targets for the restraint of price increases. Nevertheless, one could form an idea of what was intended by looking at the monetary targets, which were explicitly stated. During 1964, an expansion of 70 per cent in the money supply was anticipated. This was still a high rate, but one should take into account the inflationary inheritance left by the Goulart government. In 1965, however, this rate would fall to 30 per cent and in 1966 to only 15 per cent according to the government's estimates.

Such was the basic strategy of the stabilization program of the Castelo Branco government. The actual results of its implementation will be examined in the next chapter.

13. The Results of the Stabilization Program

It is difficult to present a comprehensive analysis of the results of the Castelo Branco stabilization program, since in many respects it is an unfinished work. After two and half years of implementation, it appears to have been a partial but not a full success. The rate of inflation was reduced from 80 or 90 per cent a year in 1963 and 1964 to about 40 per cent a year in 1965 and 1966. Such a result, however, was considerably less favorable than official forecasts announced in 1964 — according to which almost complete price stability would have been achieved in 1966. Moreover, the country did not resume its rapid economic growth as was expected (perhaps with excessive optimism) by the government.

It is interesting to compare the official forecasts made in 1964 with the actual results achieved in 1965 and 1966. As mentioned earlier, the economic program of the Castelo Branco government published in November, 1964, did not explicitly state how soon the rate of inflation would be reduced, nor by how much. However, the monetary budgets presented in the program forecast a 70 per cent expansion of the money supply in 1964, a 30 per cent expansion in 1965 and a 15 per cent expansion in 1966. Using the quantity theory of money and allowing for some growth in the real product during 1965 and 1966, this would lead to a price rise of 70 per cent in 1964, 25 per cent in 1965 and 10 per cent in 1966. The latter forecasts were understood, correctly or not, to be firm commitments of the government's economic policy.

Let us now review the actual results. During 1964 the cost of living index in Guanabara increased by 86.6 per cent and the general wholesale price index by 93.3 per cent. These were considered acceptable results, even when compared to the 70 per cent forecast, since everyone recognized the burden of the inflationary legacy left by the Goulart government. As a matter of fact, the high rate of inflation for the year was largely due to the 25 per cent price rise in the first quarter during the Goulart period. The Castelo Branco government was at least able to reduce the monthly rate of inflation to about half its former rate. Such an achievement was regarded as indeed promising.

In 1965, the actual price increases almost matched the forecasts. The general wholesale price index rose by 28.3 per cent, only slightly greater than the 25 per cent forecast. The cost of living in Guanabara increased by 45.4 per cent, but the discrepancy could be explained by the upward adjustment of rents which had been frozen for several years.

In 1966, however, the results were rather disappointing. Instead of the almost complete stability foreseen by the economic program, the cost of living in Guanabara rose by 41.1 per cent and the general wholesale price index by 37.1 per cent. It is true that never before were government policies on credit and salary demands so restrictive as in 1966. But some laxness of the 1965 controls, especially with respect to excess money supply, left its inflationary effect until 1966.

It is important to analyze how the stabilization program was managed. In 1964 the government virtually limited itself to the objectives of avoiding hyperinflation and correcting a number of price distortions left by the Goulart administration. The latter objective was to cause some unavoidable price increases which were understood as a sort of "corrective inflation": exchange subsidies were cut off, public utility rates were increased, the exchange rate was raised to a realistic level, and a new rent law (passed in November, 1964) set the rules for the gradual relaxation of rent controls with an additional provision for future escalator clauses. In order to counterbalance the inflationary effect of these corrective measures, the government made serious efforts to reduce its budgetary deficit, both by cutting public investments and by raising taxes. The final result was a deficit of 760 billion cruzeiros; i.e., 4.0 per cent of the gross domestic product. Under absolute standards, this might appear a poor result, but it certainly represented a satisfactory achievement under the conditions left by the Goulart administration. At the same time the government was to restore the confidence in public bonds by creating new securities with an escalator clause. These were to have an important effect as a source of noninflationary deficit financing in 1965 and 1966.

The credit policy in 1964 was basically managed in accordance with the rules of the economic program. Loans to the private sector were increased in the same proportion to the increasing total money supply. During the year total monetary expansion amounted to 85.9 per cent, somewhat exceeding the official forecasts. The discrepancies, however, appeared to be quite tolerable.

The weak point of the 1964 stabilization effort was to be found in the wage policy. Just after coming into office, the government authorized a very generous salary increase to public servants, about 110 per cent for civil servants and 180 per cent for military personnel. Such an increase unfortunately was to serve as a standard for wage bargaining, and by the end of 1964 the country clearly suffered from cost inflation. It is true that the government tried to enforce the official wage policy of its program through a decree by President Castelo Branco. But the labor courts, which were the final arbiters on wage agreements, did not acknowledge it.

Restraining policies became much more effective in 1965. First, the government was definitely able to put its finances in order: the budgetary deficit was limited to 588 billion cruzeiros; i.e., to 1.9 per cent of gross domestic product, more than half of it being financed through the sale of public bonds. Second, the official wage policy of adjusting real salaries by the past average level instead of the previous peak was truly implemented by Law 4725, passed in July. At the same time the government refused to concede any increase in the salaries of civil servants during 1965, and authorized a general minimum wage increase of a rather modest amount. Third, a well-oriented psychological campaign was able to promote the reversal of expectations about future price rises. Everybody became convinced that inflation was being eliminated, and a number of firms agreed to a voluntary price control program — managed by the Comissão Nacional de Estímulo à Estabilização de Preços (CONEP) in exchange for some fiscal and credit benefits. The reversal of expectations was further stimulated by a serious industrial recession in the second quarter, though this was followed by a recovery during the second half of the year. Business firms began to feel that price reduction could be an adequate policy for increasing their profits.[30] Moreover, 1965 was a year of very good harvests, which were to make the stabilization effort easier. All this explains why wholesale prices which had increased by 93.3 per cent in 1964 merely rose by 28.3 per cent in 1966.

Unfortunately, monetary policy did not succeed as well in 1965 as did the other policy measures. Although the government did not deliberately press for monetary expansion, the favorable balance of foreign trade considerably increased the domestic supply of money.

The industrial recession, import substitution policies, and new exchange rates stimulated exports and discouraged imports. Moreover, a number of foreign firms brought in funds from abroad in order to reinforce their working capital. The final result was a considerable surplus in the balance of payments, with the accumulation of about 500 million dollars of foreign reserves by the Central Bank. This was no doubt a very successful achievement from the point of view of increasing international reserves, but it had a very unfortunate monetary effect, since the Central Bank had to print money in order to purchase the exchange reserves. (It should be said that the sums involved were too big to be offset by simple open-market operations.) To gain an idea of how this effect disturbed monetary policy in 1965, one need only note that the guidelines of the economic program had forecast a net deflationary contribution of about 168 billion cruzeiros from foreign trade operations in 1965. But instead of a net deflationary impact, such operations were responsible for 1,327 billion cruzeiros of additional money supply. At the same time the preferences of the public were moving toward the substitution of bank money for legal tender, and the Central Bank had no powerful instruments to control the secondary expansion of credit by the commercial banks. As a final result, the money supply increased by 74.8 per cent during 1965, considerably beyond the official limit of 30 per cent.

It might appear surprising that such a violent monetary expansion was associated with a rise of only 28.3 per cent in wholesale prices. The obvious explanation is that the income

---

[30] As an important psychological move, the government announced in November, 1965, the creation of a new monetary unit, the "cruzeiro novo." As of January, 1967, it had not yet been put into circulation, since prices continued to rise.

velocity of money decreased by a substantial amount, probably because of the previously mentioned reversal of expectations and because of certain price controls continued in force by the government. Nevertheless an excess of liquidity clearly existed by the end of 1965; this was to be responsible for a substantial price rise at the beginning of 1966.

In 1966, all the basic measures of the anti-inflationary policy were conducted within the official forecasts. The budgetary deficit was limited to 500 billion cruzeiros — 1.1 per cent of the gross domestic product — and was almost entirely financed through the sale of public securities. The monetary expansion was held down to very conservative limits, not exceeding 15 per cent for the year, according to available estimates. The salary formula was fully obeyed and even produced lower real wages than the past averages, since the calculations were based on an underestimated forecast of future price rises. In fact, the restraining policies of the government were pushed to the point of creating a recession in the second half of the year.

Despite all these efforts, prices rose 40 per cent during 1966. Four main causes led to this result — the excessive monetary expansion at the end of 1965, the bad harvests during the year, the removal of price controls that were still in effect during 1965, and the operation of escalator clauses introduced by the government in a number of administered prices (rents, public utility rates, etc.). The 1966 experience clearly shows the difficulties inherent in any rapid stabilization program that includes escalator clauses effective throughout a substantial part of the price system. Whatever use escalator clauses may have from the point of view of avoiding long-run distortions, they always create an automatic mechanism of inflationary feedback.

Summing up, the Castelo Branco stabilization policies have achieved a partial success, but essentially they are still incomplete. The present situation, however, is a vast improvement over the general economic disorder which spread throughout the country in 1963 and in the first quarter of 1964. Brazil is now moving in the direction of price stability and economic development. But still many problems remain to be solved by the next government.

APPENDIX

The Monetary System in Brazil

The money supply in an economic system consists of the total assets held by the non-banking sector that may be utilized at any moment in the settlement of debts. In present economic systems, the money supply is broken down into two basic components: legal tender and bank money. Legal tender (or currency) is equivalent to the paper money balance held by the public; i.e., the paper money issued less cash deposits with commercial banks and monetary authorities. Bank money covers sight and short-term deposits with commercial banks and monetary authorities.

In modern economic systems, the money supply is created basically through the monetization, by banks, of non-monetary assets held by the public. More explicitly, the supply of money is created when the banking system acquires non-monetary assets held by the public or by the government, paying for them either in currency or in bank money. Thus, banks create money when they grant loans, through the discount of bills, to consumers, businesses, or government; when they acquire any goods or services from the public and pay for them in money; when they purchase bills of exchange from exporters, etc.

Conversely, banks destroy money when they sell to the public or to the government any non-monetary assets in exchange for money. In this way, there is money destruction when the public or the government redeems a loan that was previously contracted with the banking system; when the public makes time deposits in banks; when banks sell to the public, in exchange for payment in currency, any bills, goods, or services; when the banks sell bills of exchange to importers, etc.

The banking system's capacity to expand the supply of money — that is, to create money without a previous destruction of a like amount — results from an association of three factors: the issuance by the monetary authorities of paper money, the public's preference for turning its monetary assets into currency or bank money, and the banks' practice of maintaining current money reserves substantially below the level of sight deposits. The first of these factors gives the monetary authorities absolute elasticity in their capacity to expand the supply of money, save when a legal ceiling to the amount of paper money issued interferes with the system. The other two factors give the banking system the power to multiply, within limits, any expansion of the supply of money started by the monetary authorities.

This mechanism of monetary multiplication may begin by the utilization of excess reserves of commercial banks, by a change in the public preference for bank money, or more often by an expansion of the operations of the monetary authorities, as a result of which more paper money is thrown into circulation. Part of this paper money flows back to commercial banks in the form of new sight deposits according to the public's habits regarding its personal means of payment. As commercial banks only hold as reserves a fraction of their sight deposits, they actually increase the total means of payment when, as a result of additional sight deposits, they increase their loans. (The effect is as though the same money belonged simultaneously to depositor and borrower.) New deposits in turn originate new loans and so on.

The process of multiplying any increase in the supply of money (i.e., money multiplier) can be easily quantified in terms of parameters that are characteristic of the monetary system's behavior. Basically, if the monetary authorities expand by $\triangle A$ their loans to the public, the government or the rediscount banks, the resulting increase in the money supply will be expressed by:

$$\triangle M = \frac{1}{1 - d_1 (1\text{-}r)} \triangle A \qquad (1)$$

whence:

d_1 = marginal ratio of sight deposits with commercial banks to the total money supply:

r = marginal ratio of bank reserves (in legal currency and on deposit with the monetary authorities) to sight and short-term deposits with commercial banks.

In order to expand by $\triangle A$ their loans to the public, to the government, or the rediscount banks, the monetary authorities will have to put into circulation an additional amount of paper money $\triangle E$, expressed by:

$$\triangle E = \frac{c + r_1 d_1}{1 - d_1 (1\text{-}r)} \triangle A \qquad (2)$$

where d_1 and r represent the indicated parameters, and

$c =$ marginal ratio of paper money held by the public to the total money supply.

$r_1 =$ marginal ratio of legal currency reserves to sight and short-term deposits with commercial banks.

In general, the ratio between the paper money launched into circulation $\triangle E$ and the corresponding expansion $\triangle A$ of loans by the monetary authorities is less than one. This is due to the fact that the expansion of the monetary authorities' assets, in causing an increase in the supply of money, causes an increase in deposits of commercial banks and of the private sector with the monetary authorities.

The combination of the foregoing two formulas originates a third one, expressing the ratio of the increase in the supply of money to the increment of paper money in circulation. It is the well-known expression of the money multiplier, as indicated by:

$$\frac{\triangle M}{\triangle E} = \frac{1}{c + r_1 d_1}$$

The formula in question, as also the previous one, refers to paper money in circulation, that is, to paper money issued less cash reserves held by monetary authorities. Reference to paper money in circulation (and not to that issued) has the advantage of avoiding the introduction, in the formulas, of a reserve/deposits ratio for the monetary authorities, which has been quite unstable.

It is interesting to note how the above parameters and co-efficients have been evolving since the early 1950's. Appendix

Table 1 shows for the period 1950/1963, the behavior of para-meters c,r,r_1, d_1 and that of ratios $\dfrac{\triangle M}{\triangle A}$, $\dfrac{\triangle E}{\triangle A}$ and $\dfrac{\triangle M}{\triangle E}$ corresponding to those values. Although year variations have been somewhat irregular, there is an indication of a decreasing trend in the marginal percentage of the supply of money held by the public in the form of paper money and an increase in the marginal reserve ratio of commercial banks except in 1965 and 1966. This latter increase — caused by the growing compulsory deposits ordered by the monetary authorities — has made it possible to reduce to some extent the multiplier effect of the monetary authorities' original loans.

Appendix
Table 1 **CHARACTERISTIC COEFFICIENTS OF MONETARY EXPANSION***

YEAR	c	d_1	r	r_1	$\dfrac{\Delta M}{\Delta A}$	$\dfrac{\Delta E}{\Delta A}$	$\dfrac{\Delta M}{\Delta E}$
1952	0.232	0.605	0.387	0.039	1.59	0.407	3.91
1953	0.318	0.548	0.107	0.083	1.96	0.713	2.75
1954	0.405	0.498	0.270	0.049	1.57	0.674	2.33
1955	0.308	0.660	0.246	0.065	1.99	0.698	2.85
1956	0.263	0.617	0.237	0.081	1.88	0.589	3.19
1957	0.188	0.671	0.418	0.034	1.64	0.346	4.74
1958	0.297	0.644	0.302	0.091	1.82	0.648	2.81
1959	0.185	0.716	0.361	0.056	1.84	0.414	4.44
1960	0.221	0.609	0.347	0.058	1.66	0.426	3.90
1961	0.247	0.493	0.321	0.067	1.50	0.420	3.57
1962	0.213	0.646	0.411	0.097	1.61	0.444	3.63
1963	0.263	0.611	0.427	0.085	1.57	0.494	3.18
1964	0.197	0.569	0.186	0.070	1.86	0.441	4.22
1965	0.154	0.689	0.148	0.032	2.09	0.368	5.68

* The values appearing in this table are marginal ratios.

c = ratio of the increase in paper money held by the public to the increase in the money supply.

d_1 = ratio of the increase in sight and short-term deposits with commercial banks and the increase in the supply of money.

r = ratio of the increase in total reserves (currency money plus deposits with monetary authorities) to the total sight deposits with commercial banks.

r_1 = ratio of the increase in currency reserves to the increase in sight deposits with commercial banks.

$$\frac{\Delta M}{\Delta A} = \frac{1}{1-d_1 (1-r)}$$ Increase in money supply as a result of a unitary expansion in monetary authorities' assets.

$$\frac{\Delta E}{\Delta A} = \frac{c + r_1 d_1}{1-d_1 (1-r)}$$ Increment in paper money in circulation as a result of a unitary expansion in monetary authorities' assets.

$$\frac{\Delta M}{\Delta E} = \frac{1}{c + r_1 d_1}$$ Ratio of the increment in money supply to paper money in circulation.

RESEARCH
ADVISORY BOARD